Imperial Decline

Edited by

STEPHEN J. BLANK

AND ALVIN Z. RUBINSTEIN

IMPERIAL DECLINE

Russia's Changing Role in Asia

DUKE UNIVERSITY PRESS

Durham & London

1997

Printed in the United States of America on acid-free paper ∞
Typeset in Galliard by Keystone Typesetting, Inc.
Library of Congress Cataloging-in-Publication Data
appear on the last printed page of this book.

Contents

Preface

In the late nineteenth century, Russia was a rising power in Asia. Its optimism was embodied in Dostoyevsky's paean to the triumph of Russian troops over a larger but less well-armed Turkoman army at Geok-Tepe in December 1880, when he hailed Russia's civilizing mission in Asia: "Let it be only slightly fathomed (but fathomed) that Asia is our future outlet, that our riches are there, that there is our ocean; that when in Europe, because of the overcrowded condition alone, inevitable and humiliating communism is established, communism which Europe herself will loathe," then will Asia hold out to us "many a promise, many an opportunity, the full scale of which we cannot imagine."[1] But then a series of historic upheavals diverted attention away from the development of Russia's Far East region — the Bolshevik Revolution, a traumatizing socioeconomic transformation, two world wars, and a cold war. During the century after Dostoyevsky, Asia only intermittently ranked high on the Kremlin's priorities, generally only when Russia's European ambitions were checked.

Not until Mikhail Gorbachev's rise to power in 1985 did the Asia-Pacific region in general, and Siberia in particular, rank high on the Kremlin's agenda. It was then that the Soviet government began to pay attention to the incredible economic dynamism of the Asia-Pacific region and even more to the international isolation that Moscow had created for itself by its previously misguided policies. In his marathon speech to the Twenty-seventh Congress of the Communist party of the Soviet Union on 25 February 1986, Gorbachev called attention to the growing importance of the Asian and Pacific sectors of Soviet foreign policy: "In that vast region there are many tangled knots and contradictions; the political situation in some places is unstable. Here it is necessary without postponement to find the relevant solutions and paths."[2] There were no details provided, but it was a start.

As matters turned out, Gorbachev's focus was on security issues, not the development of Siberia and economic ties with nations in Asia. And, as his New Thinking evolved, it stressed interdependence. On 28 July 1986, in Vladivostok, where he presented the Order of Lenin to the city, Gorbachev spoke of "the need for an urgent, radical break with many of the conventional approaches to foreign policy"[3] and warned of the danger to the Pacific region as a whole of militarization on a scale that had occurred in the European region. It was on this occasion that he held out three conciliatory olive branches to China: for the first time, he addressed directly "the three obstacles" that China had earlier raised as preconditions for improved Sino-Soviet relations: Mongolia, Afghanistan, and Cambodia. But he also used the occasion to stress the importance of *uskoreniye* (acceleration) for the development of economic and social conditions in the Soviet Far East. Gorbachev made a number of promising moves toward improving relations with China, Japan, and South Korea, but his time ran out abruptly.

With the demise of the Soviet Union in December 1991 and the secession of the fourteen non-Russian constituent republics, the Russian Federation emerged as an independent heir to an imperial history, although having lost about a quarter of the territory of the former Soviet Union and almost 40 percent of its population. Moreover, as a result of the fallout from the rush of the non-Russian republics to independence, Russia found itself squeezed out of Europe, and its European perimeter moved significantly eastward, both territorially and strategically. One Russian scholar observed, "Never since the Middle Ages has Russia's political space been so distant from Atlantic Europe, and never were Russian national interests so strongly tied with the challenging East."[4]

But the East is no longer the spatially open or vulnerable hinterland it once was. No longer can Russia contemplate a thrust in Asia when checked in Europe. Asia has changed, as has the strategic environment within which Russia operates. Indeed, the strategic environment in East Asia differs markedly from any that was known to Russian leaders during the past two centuries. Russia and the other key regional actors — China, Japan, North Korea, and South Korea — have all undergone momentous transformations in recent decades, but only Russia is at ebb tide in an area of rising powers.

As it prepares for the twenty-first century, Russia finds itself "the sick man of Asia." A status quo power, it is no longer a threat to its neighbors. Its parlous foreign and domestic situation mandates a low-cost strategy and a policy of accommodation. Lacking are the capabilities that facilitated its imperial advances in Asia in the eighteenth and nineteenth centuries: the power to impose political domination on weak, backward, feudal kingdoms; the economic wherewithal and motivation to maintain a network of patron-client relationships; the military capability to thwart competitors and absorb the weak; an attractive ideological and cultural model; and demographic resources. Accordingly, past foreign policy behavior determinants may be irrelevant or of greatly diminished salience in assessing and anticipating Moscow's future approach to the region.

According to Charles Ziegler, "Russia's position in the Asian-Pacific economic order is limited by geography, weak infrastructure, a sparse population, and past Soviet neglect. The possibility of expanding Russian economic influence in the near future is constrained by incoherent taxation and investment, uncoordinated and frequently contradictory economic policies followed by Moscow and the regional governments, runaway inflation and currency instability, problems of defense conversion and privatization, and massive foreign debt."[5] That the obstacles facing Russian leaders are formidable is readily acknowledged by Russian analysts. Writing in *Segodnya*, the scholar Yevgeny Bazhanov noted that not only is Russia paying much more attention to the Asia-Pacific region but it is also more open to learning from the Asian experience than was heretofore the case. Moreover, Moscow recognizes that, like it or not, the Asian countries are neighbors and that, "at a time when the central government has tried without any special success to penetrate Western markets with Russian goods, the Siberians and the Easterners have been able to arrange for mutually beneficial trade with contiguous countries" and even to obtain credits, technologies, and skilled manpower.[6] Thus, a key to Russia's revived great power status is effective interaction with the Asia-Pacific region.

Although politically, militarily, and economically diminished, Russia continues to cast a long shadow. A nuclear superpower, its cooperation is essential for the creation of any system of security and stability in East Asia. The essays included in this volume examine the major changes that have occurred under Boris Yeltsin in Russia's relations with China, Japan, and the two Koreas and speculate about their consequences for

Russia's future in the region and with the United States. To enhance the book's cohesiveness, each of the essays treats the following core questions: (*a*) How has the Soviet Union's demise and Russia's emergence affected the country under consideration? (*b*) How has Russia's emergence affected its options? In what ways does its approach differ from that of the former Soviet Union? What accounts for the differences? (*c*) What are the key issues in the relations analyzed? How have they been affected by domestic considerations? (*d*) Finally, what are the implications of Russia's relations with these countries for its relations with the United States? The United States is the only "physical" outsider, but its strategic interests—of a direct nature and by proxy for local allies to whom commitments have been made—make inevitable its inclusion in any endeavor that grapples with fundamental issues of security and regional stability.

Research for the contribution of Professor Henry Trofimenko was supported by a grant from the International Research and Exchanges Board, with funds provided by the U.S. Department of State (Title VIII) and the National Endowment for the Humanities. None of these organizations is responsible for the views expressed.

We would also like to express our appreciation to the Department of Political Science, University of Pennsylvania, for its assistance in helping prepare the manuscript for publication.

Notes

1 F. M. Dostoyevsky, "Geok-Tepe: Chto takoe aziya dlia nas?" *Polnoe sobranie sochineniy* (St. Petersburg) 21 (1896): 513–23.

2 Darshan Singh, ed., *Soviet Foreign Policy Documents—1986* (Bangalore: Sterling, 1986), 69.

3 "Gorbachev Speech in Vladivostok," *Current Digest of the Soviet Press,* 27 August 1986, 1–8, 32.

4 Alexei D. Bogaturov, "Russia in Northeast Asia," *Korea and World Affairs* 17, no. 2 (Summer 1993): 298–99.

5 Charles E. Ziegler, "Russia in the Asia-Pacific: A Major Power or Minor Participant?" *Asian Survey* 34, no. 6 (June 1994): 536.

6 Yevgeny Bazhanov in *Segodnya* (Moscow), 21 July 1995, translated in *Foreign Broadcast Information Service, Central Eurasia,* 10 August 1995, 14.

What Is Asia to Russia?

OLES M. SMOLANSKY

Russia and the Asia-Pacific Region: Policies and Polemics

At present, *Atlanticism* (or *Westernism*) and *Eurasianism* denote two different trends in the foreign policy of the Russian Federation. In their latest reincarnation, these terms surfaced soon after the collapse of the Soviet Union and addressed the questions of Russia's national interests and the orientation of its foreign policy. The Atlanticists were led by Foreign Minister Andrei Kozyrev and embraced many former adherents of Mikhail Gorbachev's New Thinking, which, among other things, advocated the incorporation of the Soviet Union in a "common European home." The Atlanticists believed that the Russian Federation should at long last become an "integral part" of the West and Western civilization. Moscow could do so by renouncing the ideologically inspired Soviet foreign policy objectives of the cold war era, by abandoning reliance on military power as a method of promoting Russia's national interests, and by improving relations with the industrially developed, democratic governments of the Western world. Domestically, the Atlanticists, who, for the most part, enjoyed the support of President Boris Yeltsin, favored the conversion of Russia's command economy to a free market and upheld the principle of "democratization" of the country's institutions and political structure. They were convinced that close cooperation with the industrial giants of the West would help Moscow attain two related objectives: freeing additional resources for the development of the Russian economy and securing "large-scale [Western] support for market-oriented reforms in Russia." As Yeltsin stated in his December 1991 message to NATO, relations between Russia and the West would henceforth be founded on "recognition of common values and a single view of the ways of ensuring international security."[1]

The Atlanticists were opposed by the Eurasianists, who rejected what they described as uncritical acceptance of Western political and economic ideas. They argued that Russia's geographic position—covering as it did vast expanses of both Europe and Asia — left Moscow no choice but to develop extensive participation in the affairs of both continents. In fact, some Eurasianists suggested that Russia assume the role of a bridge connecting Europe and Asia, and many insisted that the Kremlin concentrate its attention on the East, not the West. Not surprisingly, many adherents of this school of thought were connected with the old Soviet institutes and think tanks devoted to the study of Asian affairs.

Russian Foreign Policy: The First Stage

In examining Russian diplomacy of the post-Soviet period, Sergei Rogov of the Institute of the USA and Canada distinguished between three distinct stages. During the first, which lasted from December 1991 to September 1992, the Kremlin conducted an openly pro-Western policy and uncritically accepted Western positions on such major international issues of the day as Yugoslavia, Iraq, and Afghanistan. Moscow regarded itself as part of the Western world, claimed that its interests were identical to those of Western countries, and was prepared to make concessions to its erstwhile rivals even without being asked to do so. It was during this period that Russia pulled out of Eastern Europe, paid little attention to the Commonwealth of Independent States (CIS), and, in the process, lost the cold war. At the same time, as Rogov notes, having abandoned Communist dogma, Russia espoused a different type of ideology: "With the enthusiasm of converts we went from exporting the idea of 'world revolution' to exporting 'Western values.'" Rogov found Moscow's policy during this period to be extremely shortsighted. The concessions that it made were unnecessary, and the West never reciprocated. Nor did the Kremlin ask for or receive any guarantees that the vacuums that it had created by withdrawing Russian troops would not be filled by the Western powers. In any event, the first stage drew to a close in September 1992, when Yeltsin bowed to determined pressure by the opposition and canceled his planned visit to Japan. As Rogov put it, "This was the first wave of nationalist reaction against excessive expectations. . . . And this was the first evidence that foreign policy was being turned into one of the key issues in the growing domestic policy fight."[2]

Among the initial indications of the existence of Eurasianist thinking was an article written by Sergei Goncharov, head of the Sino-Soviet section at the Institute of the Far East of the Russian Academy of Sciences (RAS). In it, Goncharov objected to Moscow's preoccupation with the West "as a development model and a business partner" and warned the Kremlin not to neglect other regions, such as "China and the Islamic world," that were of great importance to Russia.[3]

Another early exponent of Eurasianist thinking was a well-known politician, State Counselor Sergei Stankevich. Writing in March 1992, he described Atlanticism as a foreign policy line that favored Russia's rapid integration with Europe and the general world economy. More specifically, its adherents wanted Russia to join the Group of Seven (G-7), an organization of the most developed industrial nations, and to establish particularly close ties with the United States and Germany—the "dominant members of the Atlantic alliance." It is noteworthy that Stankevich and other Eurasianists did not reject Atlanticism out of hand; after all, it was the industrially advanced nations that could deliver what Russia needed most: credits, economic assistance, and advanced technology. What Stankevich and others objected to was the Kremlin's tilt toward the West at the expense of other parts of the world, most notably Asia. They argued that the dissolution of the Soviet Union confronted Moscow with a new geopolitical reality—Russia was "separated from Europe by a whole chain of independent states." This, in Stankevich's opinion, required a redistribution of "our resources, our possibilities, [our] ties, and our interests in favor of Asia." In addition to geopolitics, Russia's economic weakness made competition with the West impossible, leaving Moscow no choice but to look for trade opportunities elsewhere. In this sense, too, Asia definitely merited the Kremlin's attention. In short, Stankevich believed that Eurasianism was bound to emerge as a legitimate and important factor in the foreign policy decision-making process because Moscow "will have to look for a new balance of Western and Eastern orientations that is distinctive to today's Russia."[4]

At this juncture, it might be appropriate to note that the notion of Eurasianism was not a new phenomenon on Russia's political and philosophical scenes. It first appeared in the mid-nineteenth century as a reaction to the strong Slavophile tendencies of that period and counted among its adherents many of the empire's intellectuals, writers, and administrators. It reemerged in Russian émigré circles during the 1920s and 1930s and, in its latest version, after the collapse of the Soviet Union.[5] As exemplified by the views of Stankevich, moderate contemporary Eurasianism was neither antidemocratic nor really anti-Western. Instead, its adherents were arguing that Russia had major interests in regions other than Europe and the Atlantic and that Moscow should advance these interests independent of its relations with the Western powers.

It is noteworthy that Kozyrev addressed some of these issues only three days after the publication of Stankevich's article. Writing in *Izvestia,* the minister said that Russia's foreign policy must be based on "common sense." This meant the rejection of "messianic ideas" and their replacement by "practical concerns about the spiritual and material revival of Russia as a democratic state." Although the term *messianism* was generally understood to mean "Communist ideology," in this particular instance Kozyrev may be assumed to have attacked the adherents of Eurasianism as well. Be that as it may, he went on to say that Russia's national interests should be defined not in terms of "geopolitical alignment" but in terms of the "establishment of a high standard of living for its population and the preservation of human rights."[6] It is equally noteworthy, however, that Kozyrev did not advocate neglect of the non-Western world. In this sense, there was some overlap between the basic premises of Stankevich's Eurasianism and Kozyrev's Atlanticism.[7]

The Ministry of Foreign Affairs (MFA) position was supported by a group of scholars, associated with the Center for International Studies at the Moscow State Institute for International Relations. In an article devoted to Russian foreign policy, Andrei Zagorski, Anatolii Zlobin, Sergei Solodovnik, and Mark Khrustalev presented an image of the world economy in the shape of overlapping or concentric circles.[8] At the center were situated the G-7 states, followed by circles representing the developed and developing countries of Europe, Asia, and the rest of the world. Since the collapse of the Soviet Union and its economy left Russia on the outskirts of the world system, Moscow's main "foreign policy objective . . . should be preparing the ground for rising from the periphery to the core of the world economy and joining the Group of Seven." The scholars also argued that "another basic interest of Russia . . . [was] to retain her role as a European nation." It was not necessary for Moscow to "join every major multilateral European structure," but the Kremlin should "strengthen . . . the political dialogue and cooperation with these structures, particularly with the European Community."

Turning to Asia, Zagorski et al. attacked the Eurasianists for creating "a great illusion to reincarnate the myth of Russian 'special destiny' as a cultural and economic 'bridge' between Europe and Asia." In doing so, the Eurasianists neglected the fact that "a genuine synthesis of European and Asian cultures" had been going on since 1945, as evidenced by a "growing number of Asian states joining or approaching the core of the world economy." Therefore, Russia's task was not to serve as some mythical "bridge" but "to join in the process of synthesis [between Europe and Asia] that was already going on." Specifically, Moscow was urged to gain "access to mechanisms of regional cooperation and development" in the Asia-Pacific region (APR), a task that, as will be shown below, Kozyrev had already begun to tackle. In any event, during the first stage of Russia's foreign policy, the Atlanticists, led by Kozyrev and backed by Yeltsin, clearly had the upper hand.

Russian Foreign Policy: The Second Stage

The second stage (September 1992–December 1993) produced some early indications that the Kremlin was now ready openly to contradict the West. For one thing, the two began to differ over trade in weapons and missile technology. Moscow also modified its anti-Serbian policy in the Yugoslav conflict and began to shift its stand on Iraq. Nevertheless, the basic pro-Western thrust of Russia's foreign policy remained intact, as evidenced by Yeltsin's initial consent to letting Poland and other East European states join NATO. In another new development, as Rogov reports, "Russian diplomacy came to be openly party-oriented and became a tool for mobilization of foreign policy support for . . . forces competing in the Russian political arena." Reference was made here to Kozyrev's call for Western backing in Yeltsin's struggle against the "reds and browns," which led to a conflict between the Ministry of Foreign Affairs and the Supreme Soviet and eventually culminated in an open confrontation between the government and the parliament in October 1993.[9]

In the meantime, in his 22 October 1992 speech before the Supreme Soviet, Kozyrev made a bow to the Eurasianists, saying that Russia should not limit its opportunities in the international arena to any one region. Rather than choosing between the West and the East, Moscow should seek a "maximum of possible interactions" in Europe, Asia, and elsewhere. Some observers were not sure whether this display of evenhandedness signified a change of heart on the part of Russia's leading Atlanticist or whether Kozyrev, the consummate diplomat, was simply mindful of his audience. (It will be recalled that the conservative legislature and its speaker, Ruslan Khasbulatov, were often critical of the pro-Western slant to Moscow's foreign policy.) In retrospect, it would appear that the second explanation was closer to the mark. Nevertheless, in November and December 1992, respectively, Yeltsin traveled to South Korea and China. Both visits were intended to promote trade and improve economic cooperation between the Russian Federation and the two important East Asian states—an indication that, rhetoric aside, Yeltsin's Kremlin was aware of Asia's importance to Russia.[10]

Still, in terms of the public debates of the second stage, the deck remained stacked in favor of the Atlanticists. An interesting analysis of Russian foreign policy appeared in late 1992.[11] Written by Aleksei Arbatov (Center for Geopolitical and Military Prognosis), it endorsed many of Kozyrev's pet positions and initiatives, including the notion of close cooperation between Russia and the United States. This course of action was all the more desirable because Washington no longer harbored expansionist, "hegemonic" ideas. Rather, as its power declined, and as it "reduce[d] its military presence . . . in Europe and the Far East, the United States . . . [was] not interested in disturbing the regional and subregional balance of forces." Since Arbatov saw "a strong democratic Russia . . . [as] a most important element in this balance," he concluded that Moscow's "constructive role correspond[ed] to American interests of maintaining regional stability." All this seemed to pave the way for close cooperation or what will later be described as a "strategic partnership" between the former cold war rivals.

To help maintain stability, Arbatov suggested that Moscow adopt "various methods in various regions." In Europe, Russian interests were best served by continued "American military presence and leadership in [NATO's] command structures." In the Middle East and South Asia, Russia should be concerned about threats to the security of the new Transcaucasian and Central Asian republics. To help protect them, the

Kremlin should not shy away from the use of force, a course of action to which Washington, presumably, would not object. (Arbatov did not elaborate.) In the Far East, as in Europe, "Russian interests (as distinct from those of the USSR) are met by retaining the American military presence in Japan." Arbatov arrived at this conclusion in the following manner: U.S. withdrawal was bound to lead to the remilitarization of Japan and, in due course, to a confrontation between Tokyo and Beijing. Such a turn of events would not serve Moscow's interests: "A sharp change in the balance of power in favor of either China or Japan, and the appearance of hegemonistic aspirations in one of these powers, could create a direct threat to the Russian Far East." Elsewhere, Moscow should seek Washington's consent for "joint measures . . . for maintaining stability in the western part of the Pacific Ocean."

In early 1993, Kozyrev circulated in the Supreme Soviet the draft of a document entitled "The Concept of Russian Federation Foreign Policy."[12] According to the foreign minister, it was being used by the MFA as "the basis for its own political activities." It was noted at the time that this draft "Concept" rested on three "fundamental postulates":

1. The ideologically motivated struggle between the "two systems" was over, rendering a "large proportion of arms accumulated in the era of confrontation unnecessary." (V. Isakov, an opposition member of the Supreme Soviet who publicly commented on the draft "Concept," attacked this proposition on the ground that the world was still a dangerous place, that some of the old contradictions remained, and that the collapse of the Soviet Union made "the situation even more unpredictable." For these reasons, Russia should not engage in unilateral disarmament.)

2. "The chief threat to world stability today comes from the countries of the 'third world.'" This made it necessary for Moscow and Washington to cooperate in efforts to maintain international security. "For these purposes," the draft "Concept" noted, "we should reorient our military potential toward ensuring global stability and creating in conjunction with the United States reliable guarantees of our common safety." (To Isakov, the casting of Russia in the role of an international policeman—even on equal terms with the United States—made no sense: "Don't we look rather ridiculous in this cowboy get-up?")

3. "Russia is a democratic rule-of-law state sharing 'a general understanding of the fundamental values of world civilization.'" (Isakov

found this pronouncement hypocritical. Since when had this been the case? he asked. "Since Yeltsin read his manifesto on a tank?")

In any event, the draft "Concept" made clear that the MFA regarded Washington as Moscow's most important partner in international affairs: "For the foreseeable future, relations with the United States of America will remain one of Russia's top foreign policy priorities. . . . Russia will strive for a steady development of relations with . . . [the United States] with the aim of strategic partnership and in the future—alliance." Turning to Asia, the draft "Concept" was less than kind to a former Soviet ally, the People's Republic of China (PRC): "A realistic transformation in the nature of our relations with China must take into account the differences in ideology and sociopolitical systems of the two countries as well as Russia's lack of alternative to intensive and saturated neighborly ties with it." At the same time, Moscow had to make sure that "third countries" did not use the "China card" in their relations with Russia, while also guarding against the use of the "Russia card" in Beijing. This curious formulation—highlighting the ideological differences between the two states but emphasizing the overriding need to cooperate—came back to haunt the MFA later. Otherwise, the draft "Concept" advocated the establishment of close relations with Japan and the Republic of Korea without explaining how this worthy goal was to be attained. As attested to by Isakov's comments, the parliamentary opposition had little use for Kozyrev's document.

Criticism of the draft "Concept" came from other sources as well. Some analysts, who objected to its overriding "Westernism" and were sympathetic to the Eurasianist point of view, noted that the document failed to take into account the "salient features of Russia and its people." A major omission, this jeopardized the "effective implementation" of the "Concept." Iakov Pliais explained that the document disregarded the "unique geopolitical and geocultural position" of the Russian Federation. Situated in Europe and in Asia, Russia could "successfully perform the role of a connecting link . . . between the developed West and the rapidly developing East." For this reason, Pliais argued that one of the "most important tasks of Russian diplomacy" should be assistance in constructing a "bridge between the West and the East." Otherwise, he believed, Moscow should exert its influence to "lower the level of military confrontations" in Europe as well as in Asia and to serve as a "mediator" in efforts to solve the "problems arising in the Eurasian space."[13]

In addition, as noted, attacks on the Kremlin's pro-Western orientation or, more specifically, on the perceived neglect of the Asia-Pacific region in general and of Siberia and the Russian Far East in particular were also made by scholars specializing in Asian affairs. Thus, in an article written in late 1992–early 1993,[14] Aleksei Bogaturov of the Institute of the Far East argued that, no matter how much Kozyrev and his associates might be drawn to the West, they would not be able to get around "two hard facts: . . . never, since the Middle Ages, has Russia's political sphere been more distant from Atlantic Europe, and never were Russian national interests so strongly tied to the challenging East."

Turning to the Asia-Pacific region, Bogaturov insisted that the policy of relative retreat, initiated by Gorbachev and adhered to by Yeltsin in spite of some statements to the contrary, would have to be revised for the following reasons: (1) The Russian Federation was facing "possible economic isolation from what may become a Japan-China-Kazakhstan 'business belt,'" likely to be established "along newly built railroads south of the Trans-Siberian line." (2) Russia was beginning to confront new political realities in relations with such former allies as Mongolia, Vietnam, and North Korea, where Soviet influence had once prevailed. All three, as well as Laos, had been abandoned by Russia and were trying to establish trade relations with and secure economic assistance from the West (or China).

To deal with some of these problems, the Kremlin would have to initiate a vigorous program of economic development in Siberia and the Far East. It would also have to play a "positive strategic role" in the Pacific region. As Bogaturov explained it, although Russia "retreated from forward boundaries to its national territory, . . . she remains a Pacific nation whose principal objective is to be engaged in a constructive way in the U.S.-based regional system." This formulation is noteworthy because it shed some light on the thinking of at least some Eurasianists during the early post-Soviet period: they objected not to Moscow's cooperation with Washington but to Kozyrev's European orientation. In fact, recognizing America's military and economic superiority, they urged Russia to form a "strategic partnership" with the

United States in the APR. They considered the Russian Federation to be "militarily strong enough to defend [its] national interests" but argued that these "interests would be protected more safely by . . . [means of] political understanding with the United States." As Bogaturov saw it, such an accord would provide for "shared responsibilities and cooperative practices" and would enhance "peace and stability in the Pacific" region.

It might be noted in passing that the view advanced by Bogaturov foreshadowed the position that the MFA adopted in late 1993. In a new document entitled "Concepts of the Foreign Policy of the Russian Federation," which superseded the earlier draft "Concept," the ministry argued that Russian interests would be best served by sharing with the United States the responsibility for maintaining security in the Asia-Pacific region. This meant, in part, that the "military potential" of the Russian Federation would be "reoriented" without negatively affecting regional stability and that Russia and the United States would jointly establish "reliable guarantees of general security."[15] In short, during the second stage of Russia's foreign policy, occasional criticism did not significantly affect Kozyrev's determination to pursue his Atlanticist policies. Even those of his critics who openly objected to the MFA's European orientation expressed themselves in favor of a "strategic partnership" with the United States in the Asia-Pacific region. A major shift occurred only in 1994, following the parliamentary elections of December 1993 and the stunning victory of the Communists and, above all, of Vladimir Zhirinovsky's right-wing Liberal-Democratic party.

Russian Foreign Policy: The Third Stage

The third stage was ushered in by the December 1993 elections. Surprised and shocked by the success of the extremist groups, "many recent liberal Westernizers found themselves caught up in efforts to 'out-Zhirinovsky' Zhirinovsky." In the realm of foreign policy, top priority was now assigned to the "defense of national interests," while the Commonwealth of Independent States was declared a Russian sphere of influence. The Kremlin also went on record admitting that some Russian interests did indeed diverge from those of the Western powers. Bosnia and Iraq were cited as illustrations of this contention, but "the most striking change" occurred with respect to NATO. Brushing aside its earlier complacency, the Kremlin "became sharply critical of any expansion of the North Atlantic alliance through inclusion of the Soviet Union's Warsaw Pact allies." However, even at this juncture, Moscow could not completely shake its "pro-Western inertia." The Kremlin announced that it had entered into a "mature strategic partnership" with Washington, agreed to join NATO's "Partnership for Peace" program, and signed an accord with the European Union.[16] But, in reality, these declarative intentions amounted to little or nothing.

The December 1993 victory of the extremists resulted in extensive soul-searching on the part of Russia's political and intellectual elites. One of the more impressive efforts flowed from the pen of Professor Viacheslav Dashichev of the Institute of Economic and Social Research (RAS), who listed several factors that accounted for the negativism displayed by the Russian electorate. In addition to wounded national pride—yesterday's superpower had become today's developing nation ("an Upper Volta with nuclear weapons," as one Russian joke described the Russian Federation)—the Russian economy and statehood (*gosudarstvennost'*) had also collapsed. The country's political elite and, for that matter, the society as a whole were in a state of "moral decay," crime was rampant, and the masses were impoverished and therefore disdainful of the efforts of the liberal reformers, like Yeltsin and former Premier Yegor Gaidar. In contrast, small groups of entrepreneurs and corrupt officials enjoyed unprecedented but, in most instances, ill-gotten wealth. Since many Russians associated the worsening economic situation with the Western-inspired efforts at rapid economic reform, their attitude gradually turned anti-Western and particularly anti-American. As both the left and right wings of Russia's political spectrum were peddling anti-Westernism, an electoral shift in their favor should not have come as a major shock. These developments left Yeltsin and his associates no choice but to engage in a verbal *perestroika* of their own. They did so, in early 1994, by emphasizing "nationalist accents" and by "demonstrating their adherence to the traditional 'special' nationalist interests of Russia as a great power in the European space." A complementary, and no less important, task was to dispel the impression that the Kremlin was "submissive[ly] following the Western, and particularly American, foreign policy course."[17]

Indeed, the change in tone of the Russian leaders' public pronouncements was remarkable. In an article published in February 1994,[18] Kozyrev continued to favor a "consistent . . . promotion of [Russia's] national interests through openness and cooperation with the outside world." Adherence to these principles improved "Russia's positions in the international arena and creat[ed] a favorable climate for international development." At the same time, echoing some of the sentiments expressed by his left- and right-wing critics, Kozyrev admitted that the end of the cold war did not usher in an "idyllic" stage in international relations. Instead, "new threats to our interests" were on the rise, requiring the Kremlin to promote and defend these interests "energetically and, where necessary, uncompromisingly."

In revising the former set of priorities, Kozyrev was now arguing that precedence should be given to Russian interests in the Commonwealth of Independent States as well as in the West. ("In the European sphere our central task is to participate in building a peaceful, democratic, united Europe," he wrote, indicating continued adherence to Gorbachev's notion of a "common European home.") At the same time, in another concession to the Eurasianists, Kozyrev allowed that "an important foreign policy task is to use in Russia's interests its unique position as a Eurasian power." He went on to say that, "in recent years," Moscow succeeded in "paving the way to large-scale cooperation with leading Asian states — India, China, Japan — and also . . . in developing relations with our new partners (South Korea, the countries of ASEAN and the Persian Gulf)." The time had now come to exploit "these new opportunities in the sphere of economic, . . . scientific, and technical cooperation." Another important task was the "effective incorporation of the regions of Siberia and the Far East in international cooperation in the Asia-Pacific region." Conspicuously absent from Kozyrev's discussion of Moscow's policy in Asia were references to the United States and the former allies of the Soviet Union. These omissions tended to reinforce the widely held suspicion that the Kremlin had found it difficult to explain its attitude toward these issues to the increasingly skeptical and vocal opposition.

Additional light on the subjects of Russo-American relations and of Russian interests in the APR was shed in April 1994, when the state Duma's Committee on International Affairs organized a conference attended by representatives of the Ministry of Foreign Affairs as well as numerous academic specialists on Asia and the Pacific. The discussants covered a variety of topics, including the general political situation in the APR, Moscow's bilateral relations with the states of that region, and the specific problems of the Russian Far East.[19]

Discussing the general political situation, A. Muradian (Institute of International Economics and Political Research) argued that the events unfolding in the Asia-Pacific region were heavily influenced by the political situation in the "strategic quadrangle" that included Russia, the United States, China, and Japan. In describing the "optimal strategic line" that Moscow should follow, Muradian disagreed with the thrust of the policy advocated by some of his pro-Atlanticist colleagues and also, in the past, by the MFA. While seeking to establish mutually profitable relations with the other powers, Russia should maintain a "correct distance from all of the 'corners' of the quadrangle" and should not enter into strategic partnerships with any of them, including the United States. Muradian explained his position in terms of Russia's current military and economic weakness, which precluded Moscow from dealing with Washington on even terms. This meant that Russia could not, for the time being, become a viable strategic partner of the United States, reducing Moscow to the role of Washington's "junior partner." Turning to the MFA, Muradian described its ambitions as an outgrowth of the "previous ideological globalist approach, when the Soviet Union had certain grounds to claim the status of a 'superpower.' "

According to Muradian, "historical experience and political theory" demonstrated conclusively that the state of imbalance of power, characteristic of current U.S.-Russian relations, usually results either in the balancer (the United States) supporting the weakest link in the "strategic quadrangle" (the Russian Federation) or in a collusion between the balancer and one or two of the stronger partners at the expense of the weakest. These issues, Muradian concluded, must be studied thoroughly before the decision to enter into a "strategic relationship" is made. A similar argument, emphasizing Russia's weakness ("Russia's weight in the APR corresponds roughly to that of . . . Indonesia") and urging the maintenance of the regional military and political status quo, was also advanced by N. Maletin and S. Solodovnik of the Institute of International Relations. They decried the continuing adherence to Soviet-style "gigantism" in Russian foreign policy and warned against excessive determination to achieve a "breakthrough" in Moscow-Washington relations. Accordingly, they opposed the notion of a "strategic partnership" with the United States and advocated Russian participation in the affairs of the APR on a "realistic" and limited basis.

Others, in contrast, continued to favor close cooperation between Russia and the United States. Among them, A. Boliatko (Institute of the Far East) argued that two of the regional great powers—China and Japan—were working to undermine Moscow's influence in the APR. Their task was made easier because Russia's military and economic potential was on the decline and because the Russian Federation was contributing less than 1 percent of the region's economic activity. At the same time, the United States was engaged in serious economic competition with Japan, China, and other APR countries. Washington was also vitally interested in cooperating with Moscow in an effort to reduce their respective nuclear arsenals. These considerations created favorable conditions for close cooperation between the two states. At the same time, Boliatko objected to the gradual unilateral disarmament program, which he felt Russia had engaged in without regard for the policies and actions of the other Asian states. Many of them, he pointed out, were increasing their military budgets and stepping up their military preparations.

Muradian also summarized other participants' remarks. According to V. Urliapov (Institute of Oriental Studies, RAS), the Kremlin had to resolve one "cardinal issue": "Will Russia recognize the leading role of the United States in guaranteeing the insecurity of the APR or will it choose a different strategy and tactics. [And, if so,] which?" He went on to note that South Korea was advocating the creation in the APR and, above all, in Northeast Asia of a political system resembling the Organization for Security and Cooperation in Europe (OSCE). Issues of regional security were also being discussed at the meetings of ASEAN. Urliapov believed that two subregional security organizations would emerge as a result of these deliberations, one in Northeast Asia, the other in Southeast Asia. In due course, they might join to form one broad organization. Other experts agreed—it was important for Russia to participate in the processes aiming at regional integration and security. In the meantime, however, the Kremlin should also endeavor to improve bilateral relations with the states of the Asia-Pacific region.[20]

Turning to the problems of the Russian Far East, many participants in the Duma conference expressed alarm at the state of regional affairs and agreed that Moscow's current main task was to preserve control over (*sokhranit' za soboi*) that remote area. It was also felt that, in order to foster development, the Russian Far East had to be integrated economically into the APR and, even more important, into Northeast Asia. Among other things, international investment had to be encouraged and exports increased.[21]

In summing up the discussions, Muradian closed on an upbeat note: in spite of a "certain inconsistency" in Russian diplomacy, important changes had been introduced, and the MFA had begun to implement a "realistic, deideologized foreign policy . . . in the APR." In the process, Moscow distanced itself from the "previous globalist approach," basing this move on a desire to achieve a "unified all-Asian policy and a regional security system." Instead, the Russian diplomats now accepted the view that Moscow's political and economic relations with the countries of the APR must be "diversified" and that it was more useful to pursue one's objectives in "small but concrete steps" rather than issuing "global . . . declarations" that were impossible to implement. Equally important was the growing realization that economic interests were closely tied to political interests. Some conferees even spoke of the wisdom of subordinating Russia's foreign policy to its economic interests.

The next step in the enunciation of Russia's changing attitude toward the Asia-Pacific region was taken in November 1994, during a meeting of the MFA's Foreign Policy Council.[22] Presided over by Deputy Foreign Ministers A. Panov and A. Chernyshev, the meeting was devoted to the subject of "Problems of Security, Stability, and Integration in the APR and the Interests of Russia." As reported by *Diplomaticheskii vestnik,* the discussions demonstrated that rapid economic growth as well as political and economic interaction among the states situated in it had now rendered the APR one of the priority regions for the Russian Federation. With this in mind, the speakers urged Moscow to persevere in its efforts to establish new "regulatory mechanisms" and to strengthen regional security. The participants also agreed that Russia had to try to join the region's "integrationist processes." This meant that Moscow should attempt to increase bilateral economic relations with the APR states and, in addition to participation in the work of the Pacific Economic Council (PEC) and the Council on Pacific Economic Cooperation (CPEC), continue its efforts to gain admission to the more exclusive Organization for Asian-Pacific Economic Cooperation (APEC).

The highlight of the meeting was a speech by Deputy Foreign Minister Panov. Because of its importance, his presentation deserves to be considered in some detail. Panov began by accepting the Eurasianist position that Russia could not secure its national interests without an "active and full-scale policy in the East." In this sense, Russian policy in the East had to be placed on an equal footing with Russian policy in the West. In fact, he went on to say, "the stronger [Russia's] positions are in the East, the more confidently and decisively we can act in the West." It was with this in mind that the MFA had designated 1994 as the "year of Asia."

Panov noted that Moscow's policy in Asia was now based on the pursuit of the following objectives: (1) developing "normal, good-neighborly, [and] mutually beneficial . . . relations with all countries" of the APR; (2) "securing Russia's participation in the region's political and economic processes"; and (3) securing "assistance . . . for the economic transformations" in Russia and the "inclusion of Siberia and the Far East in the international cooperation of the APR."

In pursuing this policy, Panov continued, the MFA had to take into account Russia's weak economic base in eastern Siberia and the Far East. It also had to overcome "certain shortcomings . . . in our Eastern diplomacy" of the early post-Soviet period. Although the MFA had disassociated itself from the Communist approach to the countries of the APR, "we adopted another ideologized approach" and virtually abandoned the Soviet Union's Asian allies, among them North Korea, Vietnam, Laos, and Mongolia. "Given the amount of resources [that the Soviet Union had] invested in their economic development," Panov admitted, this was an "irrational approach." To rectify these mistakes, in 1994 Russia set out to restore economic cooperation with these states. Elsewhere in Asia, however, Moscow was able to achieve some successes: "Trade with the countries of the APR is growing faster than with Europe and now constitutes more than 40 percent of Russia's total commodity exchange."

Nevertheless, serious problems remained. For one thing, various government agencies had yet to discard their "one-sided" pro-Western orientation and their acceptance of the "syndrome of remoteness" of the Asia-Pacific region. It was also necessary to pursue more actively new forms of trade and economic cooperation with various Asian states, including China, Vietnam, North Korea, and Mongolia. But, above all, Moscow had "to devote radically more attention to the socioeconomic development of our Far East, to attracting the population, including migrants from the Near Abroad, [and] to granting the inhabitants of the Far East more independence in the sphere of economic activity." Shifting the focus, Panov also referred to "individual problems of bilateral relations" between Russia and some APR states that the opposition was using for its own political purposes. Among such issues were the "so-called 'threat of Chinese expansion in the Russian Far East' as well as the projected territorial concessions to China and Japan." The minister found the use of these issues by the opposition reprehensible — it unnecessarily complicated problems with which the MFA was trying to deal.

Although Russia was seeking to establish "equal and mutually beneficial" relations with all the states of the APR, it was not interested in entering into any bilateral or multilateral alliances. Not only would such arrangements create suspicions about Moscow's motives, but they were also bound to lead to countermeasures. This would be all the more regrettable, Panov argued, because Russia was no longer regarded by the Asian-Pacific countries as a threat to their security. On the contrary, many of the region's "middle-level" states favored Russian military presence in the APR, regarding it as essential for the maintenance of a "stable balance of power." For this reason, as well as to protect its own security and to deny unnamed others the opportunity to play a "special role" in the APR, Panov believed that Russia should maintain its military potential in the Far East "at an appropriate level."[23] In implicitly criticizing Washington's aspirations to a "special role" in the Asia-Pacific region, and in agreeing that Russia should maintain a military presence in the Far East, Panov demonstrated how far the MFA had come in accepting some of the major planks of the Eurasianist position. It is equally noteworthy, however, that, in emphasizing the "appropriate level" of military strength, the Kremlin remained far apart from the opposition's demands for a significant increase in Russia's military forces in the Far East (see below).

In any event, Panov believed that the best way to ensure the safety and security of the APR was to develop a "mechanism which would be acceptable to all" the region's states. It was not an impossible task, a view that was shared by most of the APR governments. As for Moscow, it no longer favored "global, broad-based ideas and concepts" but preferred "scrupulous, step-by-step" negotiations, designed to lead to "concrete agreements." Panov explained that Russian policy was now based on the assumption that the projected "regional security mechanism" would consist of several stages and would come in "many variants," which would reflect the "actual willingness of individual states to participate in specific security structures." The "mechanism" would also take into consideration the "specifics of bilateral relations and alliances." And, finally, such a "mechanism" would evolve from "local agreements to a far-flung network of general regional structures" and would move from "simple forms of cooperation . . . to more complex forms of regional interaction." Panov concluded by noting that Russia's policy in the APR would be guided not so much by military as by economic considerations. As he put it, the MFA continued to emphasize "securing Russia's worthy participation in the regional economic structures."

Additional light on the official position was shed by Valerii Denisov, deputy director of the First Asian Department at the MFA.[24] He reiterated that "Russia, as a major Eurasian power," was determined to participate fully in the affairs of the Asia-Pacific region and listed the "elimination of the sources of tension" as one of Moscow's main regional tasks. Denisov then proceeded to spell out what Panov, and Kozyrev before him, had merely implied: that the end of the cold war did not terminate the "struggle for military and political leadership in the Asia-Pacific region." Instead, it had become evident that Washington remained determined "not only to maintain but actually to reinforce its position" and that the "military factor . . . [was] the most important element in American strategy in the Asia-Pacific region."

In contrast with the United States, "Russia favors an active and constructive dialogue on issues of security" in the APR. With this in mind, Moscow was taking part in "informal meetings on security and cooperation between the Northeast Asian countries (the Russian Federation, the United States, the PRC, the Republic of Korea, and the Korean People's Democratic Republic)." Russia also participated in a "trilateral dialogue

(Russian Federation–United States–Japan) on security in the northern part of the Pacific Ocean" and in the deliberations of the Asia-Pacific Council on Security Issues. A major "breakthrough" was achieved when Moscow became a participant in the ASEAN Regional Forum. During its July 1994 session in Thailand, Kozyrev made several suggestions, designed to stimulate regional cooperation in dealing with some of the area's most pressing problems. Among them were "reinforcement of the nuclear non-proliferation regime (development of an arms trade code and register), and greater efforts in the fight against organized crime, maritime piracy, and drug smuggling." Moscow was also interested in promoting "confidence-building measures . . . in the military realm." Among them were exposition of "military doctrines (publication of 'White Books' on defense), increased contacts between military agencies, notification of military maneuvers, invitation of foreign observers to attend maneuvers, and restrictions on the length of maneuvers."

Shifting to individual countries, Denisov, not surprisingly, painted a rosy picture. Having "markedly stepped up its efforts aimed at strengthening . . . [ties] with the Asian and Pacific states," Moscow was pursuing a policy of "constructive partnership, genuinely equal cooperation, and good-neighborliness with China." Denisov emphasized that the Kremlin was determined to "comply with the 1991 border regulation agreement [between the two states], despite demands by the governor of Maritime Krai that the document be revised."[25]

Turning to Japan, Denisov explained that it was Moscow's intention "to develop its relations with Japan in strict accordance with international standards and without any linkage whatsoever to the so-called 'territorial issue.'" A dialogue between the two governments was continuing, as both sides strove "to accumulate positive potential on a basis of pragmatic interests." Thus, they agreed "to begin negotiations on fishing issues in the South Kuril Islands region." Relations with South Korea were "based on principles of constructive and mutually complementary partnership," while efforts were continuing to move relations with North Korea out of their "stage of decline." Otherwise, progress was also being achieved in fostering cooperation between the Russian Federation on the one hand and Mongolia and the countries of Indochina and ASEAN on the other.[26] Summing up, Denisov concluded elsewhere that, of late, "Russia's policy in the APR has been acquiring a measure of dynamism." In the process, the Kremlin was said to have "stead[ied] its foreign policy, gearing it more to defending national interests and expanding both multilateral and bilateral cooperation."[27]

The Ministry of Foreign Affairs — as well as the entire Yeltsin administration — did indeed come a long way in publicly embracing some of the Eurasianist-inspired criticism and in distancing the Kremlin from earlier attempts to join the U.S.-dominated regional security system. But how serious and how successful had they been in pursuing Russian interests in the APR? On this question, the opinions of the bureaucrats and of their critics differed widely, and it is to this issue that I now turn.

The Critics

Whatever one may think of Yeltsin's style of leadership or of the content of his policies, he does deserve recognition for letting his opponents speak their mind. Freedom of expression and of the press is a fact of life in the Russian Federation, as evidenced, in part, by the criticism leveled at the MFA's policies in the Asia-Pacific region. Thus, at the very MFA Foreign Policy Council meeting of November 1994 where Panov presented a flattering account of Moscow's relations with the states of the APR, Georgii Arbatov (Institute of the USA and Canada) expressed disappointment that "complications" in relations with the Western powers were not translated into "successes" in the East. Partly to blame was the Yeltsin administration's failure to devise a coherent strategy for the Asia-Pacific region. "Our steps . . . [toward China] are not entirely well planned." "Confusion" reigned in Russo-Japanese relations, while relations with the two Koreas and Mongolia were stagnant. Arbatov was also most unhappy about the situation that had developed in the Russian Far East, which he described as the country's "Achilles' heel." He believed that "everything is being done to tear" this territory away from Russia. If this trend continued, "trade and any forms of relations of our Far East with the APR states will be more intensive than they are with the European part of Russia."[28]

Sergei Rogov was another noted critic of the Kremlin's policy in the Asia-Pacific region.[29] In his already-quoted article, he observed that it had recently become fashionable among government officials to pay lip service to the Eurasian concept. Its adherents were arguing that, since "Russia cannot become a part of the West," it should search for "an alternative to its pro-Western orientation on the Asian continent." Words aside, however, in the overall context of Moscow's foreign policy, Rogov argued, Asia continued to "play a secondary role." While the Soviet Union had sought to establish a continent-wide "system of collective security in Asia," the Russian Federation had no such ambitions. Instead, Rogov thought it "more accurate to speak of separate, poorly coordinated and often mutually contradictory attempts by Russian diplomacy to revive individual sections of its Asian policy, mainly through concessions on our part." Little wonder, therefore, that "Russia's positions in the Asia-Pacific region have begun to weaken markedly."

Rogov provided the following illustrations in support of his contention. The economic gap between eastern Siberia and the Russian Far East, on the one hand, and European Russia, on the other, was widening, prompting large numbers of Russians to migrate west. Paralleling this trend was the increase in economic cooperation between the eastern provinces and the Asia-Pacific states. These developments did not bode well for the long-term security of the Russian Federation. To make matters worse, in November 1994, Moscow had not been "invited to join the newly formed Asia-Pacific Economic Community," thus calling into question "Russia's very presence in the region." These considerations led Rogov to conclude that "Russia is threatened with isolation not only in the West, but in the East as well."

Turning to individual countries, Rogov noted that "Russia's coolest relations" were with Japan. Moscow was responsible for this deplorable state of affairs because it separated "the territorial issue . . . from issues of greater security and development of economic cooperation in the Far East." The Kremlin's stance led the Russian public to see the Kuril problem as a Japanese "demand for unilateral concessions." To make matters worse, the Russian government then "succeeded" in convincing Tokyo that Moscow was prepared to hand over the southern Kurils to Japan. When the Kremlin changed its mind, Tokyo stiffened its position, and relations between the two states remained "frozen." Given Japan's intention to assume a more assertive role in world politics, Rogov was "very alarmed" at the prospects of its future interaction with Moscow. The Kremlin misplayed its hand in the Korean peninsula as well. Hasty efforts to improve relations with Seoul produced no tangible results but antagonized Pyongyang, thus "basically undermin[ing] Russia's diplomatic role" in that area.

Nor could Moscow expect anything but trouble in its relations with China. Initially, in its early Atlanticist stage, the Kremlin "even attempted to lecture Beijing about human rights." Mercifully, this phase did not last long — "economic considerations and trade won out," and normalcy returned to Russo-Chinese relations. But surface calm was misleading, as the limits of possible rapprochement between the two countries soon became evident. For one thing, "Russia today has turned into a market for Chinese consumer goods . . . [of] much poorer quality" than those exported to the West. In return, Moscow was shipping to Beijing some of its best military equipment. Equally worrisome to Rogov was the fact that the People's Republic was "clearly winning by default the competition with Russia in the area of economic reform." Beijing was also narrowing the technology gap, "thanks in part to Russian arms shipments," and would soon "surpass Russia in terms of GDP." Finally, China's population was "eight times larger than Russia's." All these considerations and the uncertainty about the impending change in China's leadership convinced Rogov that the future of Moscow-Beijing relations is likely to be rocky at best.[30]

Another well-reasoned critique of the government's policy was produced by Professor A. Iakovlev of the Institute of the Far East.[31] Focusing on Northeast Asia (NEA), Iakovlev argued that the political situation in this part of the world, where Russia now found itself virtually without allies, would be greatly influenced by the development of relations between China, on the one hand, and the United States and Japan, on the other. If these relations were strained, Beijing would attempt to build up Russia as a counterweight to the United States and Japan. But, if China established close working relations with Washington and Tokyo, Moscow would have to rely on itself to protect its interests, including "sovereignty, territorial integrity, and security." How well Russia would react to these challenges depended on the inclinations of its ruling elite.

Iakovlev argued that, under Yeltsin, Russia underwent "unprecedented weakening . . . in all the key parameters [of national power] — military, economic, [and] sociopolitical." Nor were matters helped by the rise of what Iakovlev termed *new federalism,* driven by the outlying regions' determination to conduct their affairs without regard for the central government. In view of this deplorable situation, it was "unwise" to take seriously the Kremlin's claims of diplomatic successes, allegedly achieved in both Europe and Asia. It was true that no one threatened Russia militarily. However, it was clear to Iakovlev that the current state of its security in the West and the East had been achieved by means of Moscow's willingness to make concessions and to "engage in self-destruction." Since Gorbachev's Soviet Union and its successor, the Russian Federation, had built their foreign policy on concessions, the Kremlin was now expected to continue compromising Russia's "sovereignty, territorial integrity, defense, [and] economic interests" across the geographic board. Not only were Moscow's "partners" pursuing their own interests, but they were now demanding that the Kremlin should not act in accordance with its status as a great power. And, if it did, Russia would be immediately accused of "neo-imperial ambitions."

Iakovlev was particularly upset about unilateral disarmament, implemented in Northeast Asia and elsewhere by the practitioners of "new political thinking." The reduction of forces in Siberia and the Far East had not been emulated by anyone else in the region, leaving Russia more vulnerable to outside pressures. Indeed, while other countries were increasing their military power, Russia was losing the "only tangible source of its authority and influence in the region." (It had previously discarded its "only official military ally," North Korea.) This approach, Iakovlev continued, was justified in terms of the need to reduce defense-related expenditures and of the alleged vast improvement of relations with the United States, China, South Korea, and, to a lesser extent, Japan. However, Iakovlev argued, this line of reasoning disregarded the following problems: security based on military might was different from security that rested on "good will, peaceful and goodneighborly assurances of partners" who were openly increasing their own military might; and the political climate in Northeast Asia was highly unstable and could lead to "major complications" affecting Russia's national interests.

Therefore, in order to secure respect for its national interests, Moscow needed to restore its military potential in the Far East, even at the risk of being accused of initiating a new regional arms race. This was all the more necessary, Iakovlev argued, because the current balance of power in Northeast Asia did not favor either Russia's near- or its long-term interests. For example, the decline in Russia's military power in the Far East has led to the following important consequences. The regional economy, which, during the Soviet period, depended heavily on the presence and activities of the armed forces, has been deprived of their contribution to the area's general well-being. The resulting economic decline has discouraged new Russian settlers (former inhabitants of the "Near Abroad") from moving to the Far East, where they are desperately needed in order, in part, to offset the influx of Chinese nationals, now freely crossing the border in large numbers.

Nor did Iakovlev approve of the economic policies conducted by regional authorities in eastern Siberia and the Far East. In "opening the doors" to foreign economic exploitation, local officials sanctioned what he described as the "plundering of the [Siberian] natural resources." These consequences of Moscow's shortsighted policies could be eliminated only by the federal government itself—the Kremlin alone could prevent the "disintegration of Russia," a goal that was also being pursued by unidentified "powerful global forces."

Getting back to Northeast Asia, Iakovlev supported some of the MFA's initiatives. Specifically, he agreed that, given Russia's weakness, Moscow should do its utmost to help create "collective mechanisms for prevention and settlement of possible international conflicts." This task should be facilitated by the fact that other Northeast Asian governments were paying lip service to these notions. Equally important, in Iakovlev's opinion, should be the constant search for improvement in bilateral relations with Japan and North Korea as well as the region's other powers. Otherwise, he called for an early reestablishment of the "governance of Siberia and the Far East from the federal center." This did not mean re-creating the old system but was intended to turn "new federalism" in Russia into a unifying rather than a divisive force.

In concluding, Iakovlev urged the Kremlin to introduce changes in its current policy on Northeast Asia. Decisive action was needed, in part, to offset what he described as "unfavorable tendencies in the Russia-policy of our partners in NEA." Among such tendencies, Iakovlev listed the following: (1) the partners' "inadequate response" to Moscow's unilateral disarmament initiatives, particularly those affecting the Pacific Fleet; and the open display of anti-Russian tendencies on the part of Moscow's "most preferred partners in NEA," the United States and

Japan, as evidenced by their stand on Tokyo's territorial claim in the Kurils; a "sufficiently real danger of an informal collusion on the part of the U.S.A., Japan, China, [and] South Korea for the purpose of weakening and undermining Russia's sovereignty over the regions of Siberia and the Far East"; and, last but not least, "perfectly obvious, powerful . . . egotism of our Western partners which makes it absolutely essential for Moscow to execute a cardinal shift from a pro-Western to a pro-Russian orientation." It was the latter that should underlie and "determine the essence of strategic and tactical actions of the Russian diplomacy on both the global and local levels."[32]

The polemics continued in mid-1995, with the former premier, Yegor Gaidar, mounting a spirited defense of the "Atlanticist" approach to Russian foreign policy.[33] Its basic aims remained the "preservation of democratic freedoms [in Russia] and the increase in the population's standard of living." To achieve these goals, Moscow had no choice but to seek Western cooperation.

At the same time, it had to be recognized that the West was afraid of Russia, partly because of "tradition" and partly because democracy was "not yet firmly established in our country." Russia, in contrast, had "no reason to fear the West—at least in the military aspect." Economic competition was another matter, but that was the way of life in the Western world. Moreover, the Russians had to recognize that they were losing economic competition with the West in part because the Kremlin continued to carry a heavy—but largely useless—military burden that the country could not afford. Gaidar admitted that it was "necessary to 'defend ourselves' . . . [in] the economic sphere" but insisted that it was "absurd" to spend the proceeds from the sale of natural resources "on the arms race on the pretext . . . of protecting ourselves from the destructive influence of Western monopolies." Instead, money should be spent on "developing an infrastructure which can ensure the country's rapid economic growth and give it the opportunity to compete successfully with Western countries in the only real, economic . . . field."

In terms of the Eurasianist challenge, Gaidar argued that the Russian Federation had lost the Soviet Union's former status as one of the world's two superpowers. But it was, and would "always remain, a great regional Eurasian power . . . on which the stability of the entire Eurasian continent depends." With respect to the Asia-Pacific region, Gaidar held that, because of the underpopulation and economic underdevelopment of Russia's Siberian and Far Eastern territories, China did represent a long-term threat to Russia. Therefore, it was imperative for Moscow "dramatically to strengthen the entire infrastructure and economy of the Far East and Siberia," a prescription (although, perhaps, not reasoning) close to the heart of many Eurasianists. But Gaidar veered sharply away from them when he recommended that Russia establish a close alliance with Japan. To accomplish this, he implied, Moscow should hand over the southern Kurils to Tokyo: "In view of the real significance of good relations with Japan for the development of the Far East economy, this is a small price to pay."

Significantly, Gaidar did not consistently oppose an increase in Russian military power. Since, to him, the West was friendly and benign, while China loomed as a major potential threat to Russia's security, Gaidar urged Moscow "to strengthen the military alliance with the West and switch our deterrence potential toward the Far East." He went on to note that, "traditionally," Russia had "always had sufficient military resources concentrated there. These must now be maintained at the proper level, however difficult this may be."[34] His was an unusual position. Emphasis on the buildup of Russian military power in the Far East was opposed by most liberal Atlanticists as well as by Yeltsin's Kremlin but was strongly supported by the nationalist-minded Eurasianists. At the same time, the latter rejected any notion of territorial concessions to Japan or of a military alliance with Washington and Tokyo.

The activization of Russia's policy in the Far East in the second half of 1995, marked by Yeltsin's meeting with the Chinese foreign minister, Premier Chernomyrdin's trip to South Korea, and Yeltsin's projected visit to the People's Republic of China, gave rise to speculation that the Kremlin was about to unveil a "new Asian doctrine." The critics scoffed at this notion. Konstantin Sarkisov, director of the Center for Japanese Studies (RAS), argued that, "ill-used or rejected" by the West and having no trumps to play or new ideas to present, Russia was not going to find allies in the Far East.[35] The major regional states depended heavily on the West and formed "part of the rapidly . . . [developing] global market." Moreover, politically and militarily, the United States continued to "play a pivotal role in the APR, being a guarantor of the security and stability of the majority of the countries of the region." Russia, Sarkisov implied, was simply not in the same league.

China, Sarkisov noted, was interested in a degree of rapprochement—but not in an alliance—with Russia. Beijing's "strategic interests," he explained, revolved around economic development and the dispute over Taiwan. In both those instances, "Russia's significance . . . is minimal." In contrast, "a few conciliatory steps" by Washington would suffice to persuade Beijing to distance itself from Moscow. Specifically, since most of China's trade was with the Western countries and Japan, and since $260 billion "in direct investments in the [Chinese] economy" belonged to a handful of Western or pro-Western states, no other outcome could be expected. The same was true of Japan and South Korea. "In exchanging our romantic-democratic slogans for national-patriotic ones," Sarkisov concluded, "Russia does not gain anything. It is time to go over to pragmatic conceptions of foreign policy—that is the only chance for survival."

In the fall of 1995, the opponents of Kozyrev and his foreign policy increased their attacks on the beleaguered foreign minister. In his comment on the implications of the September 1995 NATO statement outlining the conditions for the inclusion of the East European states in the military alliance, Iakov Pliais argued that the document was directed at Russia and that it "killed the pro-Western . . . foreign policy orientation of the ruling circles of new Russia." He expressed hope that the statement would also end the careers of the "architects" of Moscow's pro-Western stance: "The pragmatism of which they were trying to convince us so persistently turned out to be idealism which was . . . even more dangerous for the national . . . interests of Russia than the ideological antagonism and extremism of Soviet foreign policy."[36]

The critics got their wish. In January 1996, Kozyrev was replaced by Yevgeny Primakov, head of the Foreign Intelligence Service. A consummate politician and skillful infighter, Primakov has yet to enunciate his own foreign policy concept. However, even at his first press conference, he made it clear that Russia's foreign policy would now be based solely on the country's national interests. In this connection, Primakov singled out the following priorities: "consolidation of the country's territorial integrity"; "consolidation of centripetal tendencies in the territory of the former USSR";[37] "stabilization of the international situation on the regional level," particularly in the Commonwealth of Independent States and in the Balkans; and "development of international relations [in such a way as] to prevent the emergence of new sources of tension." Primakov added that the current "imbalance" in Russia's foreign policy would be corrected by means of "diversification." This meant that Moscow would henceforth actively pursue its interests not only in the West but also in South Asia, the Far East, and the countries of the APR. He did not elaborate.[38]

Put on the defensive, the "Westerners" attempted to fight back. In an article entitled "Partnership Must Be Saved," Sergei Kortunov (Institute of the USA and Canada) argued that U.S. and Russian interests continued to coincide in many important respects: both powers were opposed to Russia's disintegration and favored the creation of a "stable and secure system of international relations." Cooperation between them, Kortunov concluded, could not be maintained by resurrecting ideological rivalry or by setting up a worldwide "condominium." Instead, Moscow and Washington had to work out a pattern of "coordinated interaction" with respect to third countries. In so doing, they would establish what amounted to a "strategic partnership."[39] But, in 1996, few among Russia's political elite found such arguments convincing or appealing. The initiative remained with the opponents of close cooperation with the United States.

One of the more bizarre attacks on the notion of a U.S.-Russian partnership was launched by Oleg Arin. In an article devoted to U.S. foreign policy, he argued that both the Republican and the Democratic parties regarded China and Russia as Washington's potential strategic rivals. Because of Beijing's weakness and Moscow's preoccupation with domestic problems, the United States was assured a dominant global position for at least the next two decades. After that, Arin predicted, Washington's world leadership would inevitably come to an end. Equally inevitable was a clash between the United States and China. How Russia fit into Arin's scenario was not made clear. If Moscow adhered to its current policy of "reforms," it would remain weak and would not cause Washington and Beijing any problems. If, however, Russia adopted a "new model of development in accordance with the culture, history, and . . . mentality of its people, then it would be able to reclaim its global role."

In the Far Eastern setting, this meant entering into a "strategic alliance" with China—presumably against the United States. Arin believed such an outcome inevitable, caused as it was bound to be either by some future humiliation at the hands of the West and Japan or by some unexplained "geostrategic interests."[40] Be that as it may, none of these issues are likely to be resolved in the near future, and the debate about Russia's foreign policy and its national priorities is bound to continue.

Conclusion

The results of the December 1993 elections forced the Yeltsin administration to change the tenor and, to some extent, the content of Russia's foreign policy. Nevertheless, even in 1994–95, for all its Eurasianist rhetoric, the Kremlin continued to cling to its initial Atlanticist orientation. What it failed to do, however, was to prevent a significant cooling in Russian-Western relations. As Sergei Rogov saw it, the major reason for this state of affairs was the "inability of Kozyrev's diplomacy to ensure Russia's integration into the Western community as an equal participant in the decision-making mechanism." Although the Russian Federation did gain access to such important organizations as the World Bank, the International Monetary Fund, and GATT, Moscow was reduced to the "role of a supplicant, in effect receiving assistance on the same harsh terms as Third World countries." Nor did Russia succeed in joining the G-7 group of the most advanced industrial nations.[41]

But perhaps the most damaging indictment of Atlanticist diplomacy was based on the Kremlin's failure to address the fact that, in addition to being unwilling to admit Moscow to some of the institutions created during the cold war, the West has been gradually squeezing Russia out of Europe. The withdrawal from Eastern Europe and the dissolution of the Warsaw Pact led to no analogous Western concessions. Not only has NATO remained intact, but plans are being readied to expand it through the incorporation of some of Moscow's former satellites, such as Poland, Hungary, the Czech Republic, and Slovakia. To add insult to injury, the West has refused to recognize parts of the former Soviet territory as falling within Russia's sphere of vital national interests. This applies not only to the Baltic states and Ukraine but also, apparently, to Azerbaijan.

As a result, to paraphrase Yeltsin, the cold war has been replaced by cold peace.

Disenchantment with and the deterioration of relations with the West were accompanied by a growing influence of *Evraziistvo* (Eurasianism). As many of its adherents saw it, the West's refusal to embrace Russia as an integral part of its civilization and organizations left Moscow no choice but to turn away from Europe and the Atlantic and to search for its destiny in the presumably friendlier confines of Asia. However, to many Russian intellectuals and even politicians, that was a false dichotomy because, by virtue of its history and geography, Russia was both a European and an Asian power. Consequently, to choose one over the other made no sense at all. Instead, the argument ran, it should be recognized that Russia had vital interests on both continents and that it was, therefore, incumbent on Moscow to protect and advance them in Europe as well as in Asia.[42]

The Yeltsin administration has indeed attempted to do so. But its record in Europe is open to serious criticism. Its record in Asia, as demonstrated in this essay and contrary to official pronouncements, is equally bleak. Initially, Moscow dropped its former ideological allies (North Korea, Vietnam) but gained little from its limited association with Japan and South Korea, both allies of the United States. What the Kremlin lost in the process was the freedom of maneuver in the Korean peninsula. Relations with China are complicated by the fact that Beijing's own *perestroika* has proceeded at a faster, and more successful, rate than Russia's. Hence, not only does China hold the dominant position in the economic relationship between the two states, but its citizens are now crossing the porous border into the Russian Federation in droves, leading many Russian inhabitants of Siberia and the Far East to move to "more secure" areas. Relations with the other Pacific nations may well be classified as normal but do not qualify as major victories for Russian diplomacy.

It might be noted in conclusion that Russia's political and economic problems are, for the most part, of the internal variety and will eventually have to be resolved by the Russians themselves. At the same time, it is important to recognize that the West does have a role to play and that its posture will have an effect (albeit not a decisive one) on economic and political developments in Russia. Specifically, in the area of foreign policy, efforts to deny the Kremlin the respect it deserves by virtue of its great power status cannot but strengthen the ultranationalist, anti-Western voices of the extreme wings of Russia's political spectrum and, in so doing, stifle the efforts of those who are genuinely seeking to keep Russia a part of the Western world.

Notes

1 Sergei Rogov in *Nezavisimaya gazeta* (Moscow), 31 December 1994, translated in *Foreign Broadcast Information Service, Central Eurasia* (hereafter *FBIS/SOV*), 26 January 1995, 5.

2 Ibid., 6.

3 Sergei Goncharov in *Izvestia* (Moscow), 25 February 1992. For more details, see Suzanne Crow, "Russia Debates Its National Interests," *RFE/RL Research Report* 1, no. 28 (10 July 1992): 43–46.

4 Sergei Stankevich in *Nezavisimaya gazeta,* 28 March 1992, translated in *Current Digest of the Soviet Press,* 29 April 1992, 1–4.

5 For an extensive background treatment, see Milan Hauner, *What Is Asia to Us? Russia's Asian Heartland Yesterday and Today* (Boston: Unwin Human, 1990). For a recent Russian analysis, see Andrei Zagorskii and Michael Lucas, *Rossiia pered evropeiskim vyzovom* (Moscow: Mezhdunarodnye otnosheniia, 1993), 41–74.

6 Andrei Kozyrev in *Izvestia,* 31 March 1992.

7 In fact, Kozyrev toured Central Asia, the Far East, and the Persian Gulf later in 1992, saying that the Kremlin wished to establish friendly and cooperative relations with its Asian neighbors. For an account of the Persian Gulf visit, see M. Iusin in *Izvestia,* 5 May 1992.

8 What follows is taken from Andrei Zagorskii, Anatolii Zlobin, Sergei Solodovnik, and Mark Khrustalev, "Russia in a New World," *International Affairs* (Moscow), no. 7 (July 1992): 3–11, reprinted in *Foreign Broadcast Information Service, Central Eurasia, FBIS Report* (hereafter *FBIS/URS*), 10 October 1992, 62–67.

9 Sergei Rogov in *Nezavisimaya gazeta,* 31 December 1994, translated in *FBIS/SOV,* 26 January 1995, 6.

10 Iakov Pliais in *Nezavisimaya gazeta,* 16 July 1993.

11 What follows is taken from Aleksei Arbatov, "An Empire or a Great Power," *Novoye vremya* (Moscow), n.s., 49–50 (December 1992): 16–18, translated in *FBIS/URS,* 10 February 1993, 58–64.

12 What follows is based on V. Isakov in *Sovetskaia Rossiia,* 2 March 1993, translated in *FBIS/URS,* 19 March 1993, 19–21. See also Iu. Batalin and P. Filimonov in *Pravda,* 15 April 1993.

13 Iakov Pliais in *Nezavisimaya gazeta,* 19 November 1993.

14 What follows is based on Aleksei D. Bogaturov, "Russia in Northeast Asia: Setting a New Agenda," *Korea and World Affairs* (Seoul) 17, no. 2 (Summer 1993): 299, 301, 315.
15 As quoted in A. A. Muradian, "Rossiia v sisteme mezhdunarodnykh otnoshenii v ATR," *Vostok* (Moscow), no. 5 (1994): 178.
16 Sergei Rogov in *Nezavisimaia gazeta,* 31 December 1994, translated in *FBIS/SOV,* 26 January 1995, 6.
17 Viacheslav Dashichev in *Nezavisimaya gazeta,* 23 April 1994.
18 What follows is based on Andrei Kozyrev in *Rossiyskie vesti* (Moscow), 9 February 1994, translated in *FBIS/SOV,* 10 February 1994, 12–14.
19 What follows is based on Muradian, "Rossiia v. sisteme," 177–84.
20 For more details on bilateral relations, see ibid., 180–83.
21 For more details, see ibid., 183.
22 What follows is based on A. Panov, "Zasedanie Soveta po vneshnei politike pri MID RF: Problemy bezopasnosti, stabil'nosti, integratsii v ATR i interesy Rossii," *Diplomaticheskii vestnik* (Moscow), n.s., 23–24 (December 1994): 32–35, translated in *FBIS/SOV,* 23 March 1995, 2–9.
23 As later explained by one of Panov's subordinates (see n. 24 below), an "appropriate level" meant the "level of reasonable military sufficiency," a formulation first introduced during Gorbachev's *perestroika.*
24 Unless otherwise noted, the following discussion is based on Valerii Denisov in *Segodnya* (Moscow), 24 March 1995, translated in *FBIS/SOV,* 13 April 1995 (suppl.), 17–18, to which the interested reader should turn for more details. A longer version is his "Russia in the APR: Problems of Security and Cooperation," *International Affairs,* n.s., 4–5 (1995): 69–76.
25 Elsewhere, Denisov acknowledged that "the main problem of Russian-Chinese relations . . . is the illegal settlement of Russian Far Eastern regions by Chinese citizens" and added that the two governments were "working together to resolve it" ("Russia in the APR," 74).
26 Elsewhere (ibid., 75), Denisov described South Korean investments in the Russian economy—slightly more than $50 million—as unsatisfactory.
27 Ibid., 76.
28 Panov, "Zasedanie," translated in *FBIS/SOV,* 23 March 1995, 6. For a thorough discussion of this topic, see Tamara Troyakova, "Regional Policy in the Russian Far East and the Rise of Localism in Primorye," *Journal of East Asian Affairs* (Seoul) 9, no. 2 (Summer/Fall 1995): 428–61.
29 What follows is based on Sergei Rogov in *Nezavisimaya gazeta,* 31 December 1994, translated in *FBIS/SOV,* 26 January 1995, 9–10.
30 In this respect, Rogov was attacking the position of Aleksei Vozkresenskii of the "Russian-China" Center (Institute of the Far East), who argued that Moscow and Beijing needed each other to counterbalance the influence of Washington and Tokyo. For details, see Vozkresenskii's articles in *Nezavisimaya gazeta,* 25 November 1993, and 27 May 1994.

31 What follows is based on A. Iakovlev, "Mezhdunarodno-politicheskaia obstanovka v Severo-Vostochnoi Azii i polozhenie Rossii v regione," *Problemy Dal'nego Vostoka* (Moscow), no. 2 (1995): 3–13.

32 For right-wing criticism of Yeltsin's Atlanticist leanings, see Nina Petrova in *Nezavisimaya gazeta,* 17 May 1995.

33 What follows is based on Egor Gaidar in *Izvestia,* 18 May 1995, translated in *FBIS/SOV,* 23 May 1995, 22–24.

34 See also Aleksei Arbatov's interview with Vadim Egorov in *Nezavisimoe voennoe obozrenie* (supplement to *Nezavisimaya gazeta*), 14 December 1995.

35 What follows is based on Konstantin Sarkisov in *Moskovskie novosti,* 1–8 October 1995, translated in *FBIS/SOV,* 9 November 1995, 19–20.

36 Iakov Pliais in *Nezavisimaya gazeta,* 13 October 1995. See also Aleksei Puchkov in ibid., 16 November 1995.

37 Primakov explained that this did not mean the resurrection of the Soviet Union but referred to efforts at "serious economic integration of the [former Soviet] republics."

38 Dimitrii Govnostaev and Mihail Karpov in *Nezavisimaya gazeta,* 13 January 1996.

39 Sergei Kortunov in *Nezavisimaya gazeta,* 26 January 1996.

40 Oleg Arin in *Nezavisimaya gazeta,* 30 January 1996.

41 Sergei Rogov in *Nezavisimaya gazeta,* 31 December 1994, translated in *FBIS/SOV,* 26 January 1995, 7. See also Aleksei Arbatov, "Rossiia: Natsional'naia bezopasnost' v 90-e gody," *Mirovaia ekonomika i mezhdunarodnye otnosheniia* (Moscow), no. 7 (1994): 5–15.

42 On this point, see Iakov Pliais in *Nezavisimaya gazeta,* 19 November 1993.

STEPHEN J. BLANK

Russia and China in Central Asia

If we view Russian policy toward Central Asia in an Asian, rather than a purely Russian, context, we avoid the misleading approach that separates this area from Asia. We also see, then, that Central Asia is not just dependent on Moscow, not merely an object of Russia's or other states' designs. We thereby obtain a richer, more nuanced sense of local realities and the factors influencing Russia's policy and Asian international relations.

Although Russia openly pursues hegemony, if not reunion, using the full range of economic, political, and military instruments at its disposal, Central Asian states are resisting Russia's drive. Grasping Russia's aims and potential, they are diversifying the number of states with whom they maintain relations. Even when seeking Russian military and/or economic assistance, they have initiated broader trading and economic ties with China, Japan, Korea, India, Pakistan, Israel, and the United States, each of which has its own motives for supporting these ties.

The foreign policies of Central Asian states are diverse and protean. Precisely because these states are weak, they must diversify the policy of importing the means to assure their security from among competing stronger states to expand their range of choices, escape the political conditions attached to those imports, and win greater autonomy and security.[1] Therefore, their autonomy limits Russia's ability to establish its hegemony and freeze the local status quo. And their search for diversified relationships encourages the growing Chinese and even U.S. interest in Central Asia. The interplay and context of Russian–Central Asian relations reflects both Russia's objectives and its limited ability to realize them in the new Asia.

The rise of these states to sovereignty has opened important issues for Asian security. Russia and China cooperate in trying to contain expressions of religious or political nationalism in Central Asia. Yet China could well become a rival in importing energy products originating there, which it needs for its own vital economic and political interests.[2] The issue, however, is greater than one of simple importation, encompassing as it does basic issues of Asian security, namely, China's interest in the oil-rich Spratly Islands.[3]

Thus, the control of energy is a fundamental regional issue, and Central Asian states' basic sovereignty hinges on their ability to avoid dependence on any one state with ports and pipelines. Russia's efforts to extort preferential rights in all areas of these states' energy economy are nothing more than blatant economic warfare or blackmail. Russia's reluctance to accept international consortium agreements, in which it participates, that diversify pipelines across Russia, Turkey, and the Transcaucasus shows that it continues to believe in its "proprietary" relationship with Central Asia and that its energy policy is little more than a protection racket. Energy policy is also part of a larger overall Russian policy aimed at keeping Western states, especially the United States, out of Central Asia, preserving the area as an exclusively Russian sphere of influence.[4]

Consequently, it is not surprising that Central Asian states seek other alternatives and that foreign states support them. Turkmenistan pursues a sophisticated energy strategy intended to overtake Russia as an exporter and as the creditor of the energy debts of the Commonwealth of Independent States, thereby obtaining points of economic leverage in Russia.[5] Kazakhstan, China, and Japan are conducting feasibility studies for pipelines running from Kazakhstan to China, Japan, and Korea to satisfy Asia's ravenous hunger for energy.[6] In 1994–95, Washington too drew nearer to Uzbekistan and Kazakhstan and proclaimed its opposition to any Russian sphere of influence over Central Asian and Caspian Sea energy. By 1996, the Tajik civil war was on its agenda with Moscow.[7] Therefore, Russian policy toward Central Asia can be understood only in an Asian, indeed, an international, context.

Russian Policy

Russia most recently formalized its Central Asian policy in President Boris Yeltsin's edict no. 940 of 14 September 1995 on relations with members of the Commonwealth of Independent States.[8] As then Foreign Minister Andrei Kozyrev stated, that edict directly continues policies going back to 1994, when Russia's policy of coercive reintegration of the Commonwealth of Independent States was already well established.[9]

This edict is both a new point of departure and a summation of past policies meant explicitly to guide all executive agencies in their future activities. Significantly, the edict expressly states that such unification is a factor helping prevent separatist forces from gaining power in Russia itself. Thus, expansion abroad is necessary to safeguard Russia's own integrity.

The edict proclaims as its main goal an economically and politically integrated association of states that support Russian interests. Government agencies are directed to ensure the stability of the Commonwealth of Independent States, promote the interests of other friendly states, and consolidate Russia "as the leading force in the formation of a new system of inter-state political and economic relations on the territory of the post-Union space; to boost integration processes within the CIS." Relations within the Commonwealth of Independent States assume primacy since Russia's "main, vital interests" in defense, security, economics, and the rights of Russians abroad are concentrated there. Defending those interests "constitutes the basis of the country's national security."[10] Since only Russia can guarantee the security of the Commonwealth of Independent States, it must act alone in its own vital interest, as the 1993 foreign policy concept stated and the edict reaffirms.[11]

It is particularly noteworthy that the edict states that "mutually advantageous economic cooperation, not military-political integration, is the fundamental prerequisite for resolving the entire set of issues concerning CIS states' mutual relations." Russia proposes a customs union, economic integration, converging standards of international economic legislation, a payments union, integration of production in science and technology (and the defense industry), common legal conditions, and a common capital market. While adopting Russia's model is not essential, states' attitude toward that model is crucial and an "important factor determining the scale of economic, political, and military support by Russia."[12]

This linking of economics to all other issues dates back at least to 1993, when Moscow tried to force these states into a Russian-dominated economic system that would also exempt Moscow from future subsidies to them.[13] Then Vice Premier Aleksandr' Shokhin stated that Russia would use every economic instrument available to force Central Asia into an exclusive relationship with Russia and to preserve the privileged rights of Russians. He stated that the issue of Russian speakers (not just Russians) abroad would appear in all economic discussions with Central Asia and members of the Commonwealth of Independent States generally.[14]

This led to many Kazakh, Uzbek, and Kyrgyz charges that Russia was exporting its inflation to them, not paying debts for goods obtained from Central Asia, holding Central Asian oil pipelines hostage, etc. But because Russia could not and would not subsidize Central Asian states and demanded that they reform their currencies, it may paradoxically have strengthened those states' subsequent ability to resist Russian pressure and gain some fiscal stability.[15]

Shokhin also stated that Central Asia could not join other foreign economic organizations and retain Moscow's subsidies.[16] The same pressures and policy lines have continued since then. Prominent officials from Yeltsin on down steadily maintain that the integration of the Commonwealth of Independent states requires a single economy and defense and, ultimately, reunion.[17] Nor is the belief in the ability of economic leverage as a means to compel reintegration new. For Russian elites, those factors objectively impel reintegration.

Policy makers openly use economic advantages for political ends but decry other states' efforts to do the same and the refusal of Central Asian states to follow this "objective logic" since CIS countries are generally reorienting their trade away from Russia. As one reporter commented about this trend, "Thus Russia is also being deprived of real levers of influence over the non-economic processes in the CIS, and this is fraught with unpleasant surprises of a geopolitical and strategic defense character for the Russian Federation."[18] Then Vice Premier Sergei Shakhray said in 1994, "The difficult situation in the economy, the impossibility of defining borders and establishing customs control to protect the country's economy, and the undeveloped state of the budget, taxation, and banking systems mean that the factors of economic reintegration are being turned into a platform for internal political struggle in Russia and in other countries of the CIS."[19]

Shakhray also claimed that Russia bears international legal responsibility for Russians abroad. Until their legal status is fixed, "we will be at the stage of a transitional period, and the methods and forms of Russian guardianship of compatriots will largely correspond to the quality of this 'transience.'"[20] Russia supports this claim by asserting the right to use force throughout the Commonwealth of Independent States, and even the Baltic states, to defend Russians abroad. Yeltsin's former chief of the Department of Citizenship Affairs, A. Mikitaev, warned that states who "abuse" the rights of Russians will soon face growing demands for the creation of autonomous Russian territories in their homelands.[21] Russian statements in April and June 1995 about possible military intervention were seen abroad as efforts to thwart Central Asian economic independence and regional economic integration.

At the 1993 Ashgabat CIS summit, Moscow fought for a dual citizenship clause for Russians abroad. Russia also insisted that Central Asian states join the Conference on Security and Cooperation in Europe (CSCE) so that they could be arraigned there, if need be, for not protecting Russian nationals' civil rights.[22] In April 1995, Yeltsin's commission for questions of citizenship, helped by the Ministry of Foreign Affairs, drafted an edict on guidelines for Russian policy toward CIS states where Russians live. The draft strictly tied Russian economic and military cooperation with CIS countries to the defense of their Russian communities' rights and interests. Talks on establishing Russian-language radio and television service should be conducted. Firms with Russian workers and public organizations of Russian communities should receive support. Some share of Russian credits to CIS members should support "Russian" factories.[23] This policy essentially revives the nineteenth-century imperialist policy of extraterritoriality.

Oil and Gas Politics

More tangible oil interests are also at stake across Central Asia and the Transcaucasus. Lukoil's president, Vagit Alekperov, observed that, if Russia does not take control over the Caspian shelf, it "risks losing its positions on the Caspian Sea."[24] Russia and Iran argue that the Caspian Sea is subject to international laws and treaties that rule out littoral states' independent action to explore for oil there.[25] If they win their point, Russia and Iran could then strangle the oil-dependent littoral states' economies. Clearly, Russia will "blackmail" local producers unless it is brought into any deal.[26]

Russia's tactic has been to get Central Asian and Transcaucasian oil producers "by their pipelines."[27] Exploiting Central Asian dependence on Russian-controlled transport routes, Moscow systematically blackmailed Kazakhstan and Turkmenistan, making it difficult, if not impossible, for Western investors to maintain their stake. This policy had considerable success: by mid-1994, Kazakhstan's oil economy was virtually shut down. Accordingly, in October 1994, Kazakh President Nursultan Nazarbayev yielded and let Russia into a series of oil and gas deals that have been negotiated since then.[28] Kazakhstan now welcomed Russian participation in the economy and accepted that it is too dependent on Russia to make a clean break.[29] Indeed, Deputy Prime Minister Nyghmetzhan Yesengharin talks of a military-technical alliance and of an alliance between both states' financial-industrial groups.[30]

The same story applies to Turkmenistan, Russia having cut off its gas exports to Europe and tried to force its way into future energy projects. However, having connections to Iran and being less dependent on Russia, Turkmenistan has had more success in averting excessive Russian pressure. It sees itself as forming, with Iran, essential parts of triangles in all regional deals and as the juncture of regional and interregional interests. For now, Irano-Turkmen friendship serves both states' basic economic and political interests very well, and, if both remain stable (by no means a certain proposition), their amity will grow even greater.[31] This friendship, and President Sapurmurad Niyazov's broader policy of "positive neutrality," limits Russia's ability to destroy, not just Turkmenistan's oil and gas sectors, but also its overall economy. As Niyazov recently observed, the point is to prevent any one state from trying to usurp Turkmenistan's riches and sovereignty.[32]

These economic maneuvers suggest that Russia will play a large role in Central Asia but that it cannot control the region or offer it anything positive. Russia can only exert pressure and try to restore the Soviet-style integration that ruined the region. Russian reasons for economic integration resemble Soviet rationales for empire in Central Asia. V. Serov, Russian minister of cooperation, the operational coordinator for implementing edict no. 940, stated that reintegration is vital for Russia: "We need cotton, supplies for defense industry (without them we are powerless to manufacture new weapons for the army), aluminum raw material, and joint labor in nuclear power engineering which is assuming an ever greater role. Without the joint participation of all the former republics of the USSR in an upturn in Russia's fuel and energy complex, a further downturn, signifying a crisis for the whole of the CIS awaits it. The same applies to the unified railroad, meteorological, and radar systems of the former USSR."[33]

Serov's answer is Yeltsin's edict. To prevent CIS states from importing foreign mechanical engineering products, Russia should tie their credit to CIS buyers, who remit it back to Russia. Similarly, to relink the Urals' iron and steel industry with northern Kazakhstan's raw materials, Russia must block Japan from investing in Kazakh chromium. To stop Kazakh "rapacity," S. Afonin, head of Russia's Committee for Metallurgy, said that Russia had to "put the squeeze on Almaty," in other words, no electricity unless we get the chromium.[34]

The new union's outlines conform to Russia's perception that, if it fails to dominate Central Asia and the Caspian Basin, it will lose regional political influence and "forever" lose its energy position and resources.[35] Despite reunion's "objective" basis, Russia can realize its interests only by state action that excludes other states and limits Central Asian sovereignty.

Not surprisingly, Central Asia has found ways to resist Moscow. Nazarbayev's awareness of his precarious ethnic balance and Russia's capacity for wrecking his rule did not stop him from inviting Japan and China to conduct feasibility studies on building pipelines from western Kazakhstan to China, not Russia.[36] Also, Shanghai is Kazakhstan's main port, which gives Kazakhstan and its neighbors ample incentive to explore alternatives to Russia. Furthermore, Kazakhstan recently opened all its oil and gas resources to development by foreign and local companies on an equal and competitive basis, a deliberate move to weaken Russian firms, which cannot compete on equal terms with Western ones.[37]

Kazakhstan is evidently subtly inducing Russians to return to Russia and moved its capital from Almaty to Akmola to forestall Russian designs on northern Kazakhstan.[38] Kazakhstan also hosted a meeting of Caspian littoral states from which Russia was conspicuously absent. At the meeting, Almaty presented a draft accord on the use of the Caspian Sea, proposing the demarcation of each state's territorial waters and rejecting Russia's concept of joint ownership, by which no state could act without the unanimous consent of the others. Deputy Foreign Minister Vyacheslav Gizzatov rejected Russia's position because "common means no one's and the world practice does not have such a precedent."[39]

Russian policy also stimulated open U.S. opposition to its efforts to monopolize Central Asian oil and gas. Glen Rase, head of the State Department's energy policy section, rejected Russian efforts to dominate the Caspian, stating that Russian talk of condominium there was "a guarantee of inaction." Russia's views "must not be imposed on the states that prefer a more normal division of the Caspian," and Washington "does not recognize any spheres of influence."[40] Russian heavy-handedness has brought about Moscow's worst nightmare, a continuing Western presence that promotes interests directly counter to its own in Central Asia.

Defense and Political Integration

The same process appears in political and defense integration issues. Russia aims at a collective security system based on the 1992 Tashkent treaty. Signatories should be encouraged to unite in a defensive alliance based on shared interests and military-political goals. Members should keep their alliance pledges, increase cooperation on maintaining border security, and accept Russia's Law on the State Border, which defines Russia's borders, while Moscow should all the while remember that open borders across the Commonwealth of Independent States is its long-term goal: "Practical work should be guided by differentiated approaches toward individual sectors of the Russian Federation State border depending on the state of bilateral relations with different states."[41]

Finally, CIS states must collectively support Russian peacemaking operations. While this cooperation should occur under the auspices of the United Nations or the Organization for Security and Cooperation in Europe (OSCE), whose presence is welcomed in settling conflicts in CIS territories, these agencies and CIS states must accept Russian primacy. The Commonwealth of Independent States should also gain international recognition as a regional organization equal in status to other such organizations.[42]

The reality of the situation is, however, vastly different. Chechnya and other current conflicts show that no one is willing to uphold the collective security pact or any other CIS treaties and that the Commonwealth of Independent States functions very badly indeed as a security organization.[43] Even as Russia's General Staff organizes a movement of CIS militaries to resist NATO expansion, Lieutenant General Leonid Ivashov, secretary of the CIS Council of Defense Ministers, admitted that Russia can no longer pressure CIS members to send troops to Tajikistan's civil war. Rather, it is "heeding a balance of interests" among CIS members and wants Dushanbe to act more effectively to stabilize the situation.[44]

The military dimensions of Russian neoimperialism comprise the war in Chechnya, the introduction of Russian troops into Tajikistan's civil war, and "peace operations" in the North Caucasus and Abkhazia. All these operations point to the aggrandizement of Russian influence and the aggravation of regional instability as objectives, tactics, and outcomes. Moscow's common threat assessment is the fear of movements inspired by and governments based on Islamic fundamentalism, the contagion of which would spread from bases in Iran, Afghanistan, and Pakistan throughout Central Asia and then into Russia—a contemporary Russian version of the domino theory. In order to contain this threat, Russia views a continued military presence in Central Asia and the Caucasus, except for Azerbaijan, as necessary. The Gulf, Caucasus, and Central Asian routes would be sealed off by military force, and people would understand that Russia is a great power that cannot be trifled with.[45]

Russia's entry into the Tajik civil war legitimated its continued military presence in Central Asia to secure the border troops' and the army's lines of communication and logistics. But it has weakened Russia's ability to portray itself as an impartial mediator and prevented Russia from persuading Dushanbe to enact political reforms that would ease the conflict. Russia is also carrying out Uzbekistan's former policy here, for Uzbekistan was very anxious lest this war spill over into Tajik-inhabited areas of Uzbekistan or Uzbek areas of Tajikistan, outcomes that would oblige Tashkent to act.[46]

But here too Russia is failing. Russia could not appear as mediator there and is clearly perceived to support the present Tajik regime.[47] By the spring of 1995, it became clear that this war could lead Russia into an ever greater investment of men and resources and that it was inexpedient to have intervened on behalf of Uzbekistan, which now feared that the war would spread from Tajikistan's Uzbeks and Tajiks to their kinsmen in Uzbekistan. Russian costs in men and resources were already growing, no end to the fighting was in sight, its client in Dushanbe was unwilling to make the concessions needed to recast the Tajik government, Tajik military forces were fighting each other, and Russia's army and border troops could neither stop the war nor share assessments of the war's course. Russo-Tajik relations were deteriorating as Tajik soldiers deserted in droves and both sides blamed the other.[48]

Already, in 1994, Russia had sought Indian and Iranian support for its mediation efforts. Now it has also appealed to Turkmenistan to mediate between Moscow, Kabul, and, implicitly, the Tajik rebels. Meanwhile, Uzbekistan has also approached India in an effort to fend off Moscow's imperial pretensions.[49] It is apparent that Moscow alone cannot police Central Asia, a fact that Moscow evidently recognizes since the multilateral support that it is seeking is clearly premised on Russo-Irano-Indo-Chinese control of the area, effectively undercutting Central Asian states', especially Uzbekistan's, freedom to maneuver. In 1995, Defense Minister Pavel Grachev proposed that Russia and China share "policing" tasks in Asia. This proposal could only mean Russian hegemony over Central Asia, with Indian, Iranian, and Chinese support.[50]

Here, too, Russian policy provoked a reaction. Tashkent reached out to the world financial community and the United States, asking for help developing Uzbek energy deposits, thereby allowing it to achieve energy independence from Moscow. It then hosted Defense Secretary Perry in Tashkent.[51] Uzbek president Islam Karimov also revived the idea of Central Asian unity and economic integration to counter Moscow and show his concern over Russian policy. Not only is Uzbekistan encouraging Western investment, but it has initiated reforms and in 1994 was one of two CIS member states whose GDP actually grew. Equally important, Uzbekistan is exchanging oil and gas for Ukrainian pipes, a move designed to strengthen both states against Russian pressure for CIS integration, which menaces them both. Foreign Minister Abdulaziz Kamilov voiced concern over the move toward CIS integration and the binding decisions being passed at CIS sessions. He said that, by not signing the CIS treaty on border protection and by not attending the CIS interparliamentary session in St. Petersburg, Uzbekistan meant to show its concern about Russian domination.[52] Karimov told Dushanbe to negotiate with the rebels, warned about Russian and Iranian policy, and indicated that the threat posed by those two countries justified a reorientation toward the United States.[53]

Karimov's tilt toward Washington coincided with newfound U.S. concern about Russian domination of Central Asia and the Caucasus.[54] Perry visited Uzbekistan and Kazakhstan to reorient the Uzbek and Kazakh militaries along Western lines, arrange for further NATO training of officers, and communicate U.S. support for Tashkent's and Almaty's independence. Washington now also shows interest in the Tajik civil war.[55] Perry's visit to the area evidences the reinvigorated and growing U.S. interest in the Caspian Sea area, which has helped block Russian aspirations there. Recently, Undersecretary of State Strobe Talbott, the Clinton administration's point man on Russia policy, placed Russia's relations with the Commonwealth of Independent States squarely on the U.S. agenda. He said that "Russia is stepping up its call for economic and political integration among the former Soviet republics. In Eurasia, as in other parts of the world, we oppose coercion and intimidation of neighboring states. We will endorse regional cooperation only so long as it is truly and totally voluntary and only if it opens doors to the outside world."[56] By invoking the open door, the hoariest and most venerable of U.S. foreign policy metaphors, Talbott signified to Russia that Washington will now play a role commensurate with its interests in Central Asia and not let that area become part of an exclusive sphere of Russian influence.

Foreign and internal resistance, Russia's instability, demographic catastrophe, poverty, and an inability to fund Central Asian development will probably accelerate Russia's gradual retreat from the region. Central Asian states already resist making further contributions to the armies fighting in Tajikistan and are reorienting their trade wherever possible to the world rather than Russia, policies that suggest the limits of Russian power there.[57] But, unless Russia fits its ends to its means and recognizes the inevitability of the end of empire, it could easily provoke major regional crises. Indeed, the discrepancy between Russia's ambitions and its means is today the greatest standing threat to Eurasian security since Moscow seems determined to assume the neoimperial mantle and the associated burdens, which it cannot afford. A strategy based on such overreaching has, in the past, invariably brought about the downfall of the Russian state. And, since Russia cannot stop the Central Asian states from looking elsewhere—especially the Far East and the United States—for support, new imperial projects risk another crash of the Russian state and those near it. As a result, in Central Asia, as in East Asia, a balance among rivals is emerging in the region's international politics.

China and Central Asia

Chinese policy too must be viewed in the Asian context. China's policies in Central Asia dovetail with its policies in South Asia and Russia, the common objective being to stabilize its Muslim provinces. During 1995, China mounted a steady propaganda campaign to warn about possible violent attacks across the border and within Muslim areas, denounce separatists, and showcase regional economic successes, thereby signaling that nationalism is no longer relevant to local peoples.[58] A recent agreement with Kazakhstan explicitly forbade agitation among China's Muslims yet did not compel China to cease nuclear testing, which alarms Kazakhstan for ecological and security reasons.

Almaty has also had to yield to Chinese economic power and adopt a one-China policy, ruling out recognition of Taiwan.[59] This pattern, repeated in Kyrgyzstan, suggests that China's economic power is a key element in its Central Asian strategy and further that its policies show scant regard for those states' interests. While Beijing supports Russian efforts to maintain stability in Central Asia and a common animus against Islam binds it, Moscow, and Delhi for now, China pursues a much broader strategy meant to obtain long-lasting economic and political leverage in Central Asia.

China is also Russia's most likely and strongest competitor for future influence in Central Asia. There are signs that this potential rivalry is already making itself felt in the region. Recently, Kyrgyzstan's foreign minister, Roza Otumbayeva, stated that her government was seeking "reliable guarantees of our national security" from states other than those party to the CIS collective security treaty of 1992. Otumbayeva refused to renounce NATO as an option, despite Russia's resistance to NATO expansion. She then described China as "far less aggressive than Russia in attempting to influence Central Asia" and as a "most serious factor" in the region.[60] Otumbayeva's remarks reflect the fact that all the Central Asian states are aware of the expanding range of options available to them, including cooperation with neighboring states.

Given China's actual and potential influence in Central Asia, it is easy to see why Russian and Western observers understand that China has many important advantages in the contest. A recent Russian analysis concludes that, having gradually taken the lead in the struggle for influence in the post-Soviet era, China has the critical geographic advantage of bordering directly on the area. It has far fewer limitations than its Middle Eastern or South Asian rivals (Turkey, Iran, India, Pakistan). A regulated economy, which is more compatible with the economies of the Central Asian republics, a secular state, and ready financial backing also weigh in its favor. China offers the Central Asian states direct access to the Pacific, the Far East, and Southeast Asia.[61]

More important, China has a mature, well-thought-out strategic concept of its interests and goals in Central Asia, one that revolves around the questions of trade routes, transportation networks, Islam, and energy. China aims to preclude Islamic or nationalist agitation among Muslim peoples (Kazakhs, Kyrgyz, Uighur) in Xinjiang and its western provinces that border Kazakhstan and Kyrgyzstan.

China recognizes that it can achieve this goal only if it can establish intimate trading ties in Central Asia, support existing governments and their relationship with Russia, and greatly upgrade Xinjiang's economic development and integration with eastern and coastal provinces of China. The goal is to reestablish the old silk road, in the process turning it into a modern trade route that integrates Central Asia, western China, the interior, and coastal China as a single network. Xinjiang is to "tilt to the west." Developing Xinjiang's enormous Tarym Basin energy deposits becomes vital given that China was forced to start importing energy in 1993.

But China's outlook and its aim of stabilizing Central Asia mean that it also opposes any manifestation of Islamic nationalism and any decline in Russia's position lest the backlash spill over its frontier. It hopes to defend Russia's formal position in Central Asia while building its own assets and influence through trade and expanded energy and transportation links, exactly the same instruments that Russia, India, and Pakistan all employ. Furthermore, China seeks a voice in every major Asian economic and political organization—for example, the Economic Cooperation Organization (ECO)—in order to influence regional trends. But at the same time it will not compromise on its key interests, nuclear testing, its own colonialist policies in Xinjiang and Tibet, or obtaining new energy outlets.

Thus, China's strategy for Central Asia is actually part of its overall strategy for Asia. Muslim nationalism is to be checked even if that erodes the alliance with Pakistan. Russia is to be upheld as a weaker power in Asia and a stabilizing force in Central Asia, even while allowing Chinese influence in the area to grow and threats to China's stability that Russia has habitually exploited to diminish. Border treaties with Russia help it protect its security, which has obviously become a troublesome issue as open economies mean less control of movement of people, goods, and ideas.[62]

This sophisticated pan-Asian strategy is particularly visibly implemented in China's energy policy. Since the demand for and the consumption of energy are growing rapidly, stability in Xinjiang and Central Asia is not just politically desirable but essential for China's continued economic growth and modernization.[63] Otherwise, China's autarkic posture and ability to sustain its own growth, deal with the growing decentralization of power and economic imbalances among regions, and curb ethnic unrest will come into question. Projects linking Turkmen and Kazakh energy deposits to pipelines running through China rather than Russia are therefore to be encouraged.[64]

China has good reason to fear Islamic unrest. In 1990, owing to the widening division between the coast and the periphery in economics and the devolution of power to regional governments, western Xinjiang, bordering Central Asia, became a center of uprisings, undoubtedly inspired by the separatist tendencies already visible across the border. China had to send 200,000 troops there. That revolt evidently was the culmination of a series of spreading annual uprisings since 1980.[65] Unrest has not abated, and Chinese officials vigilantly oppose efforts to incite Muslims in Xinjiang.[66] Given the oil deposits, the close proximity of the Lop Nor nuclear center, and Beijing's ever-anxious political situation, this threat must be curbed. Strong ties with Russia and support for its policies in Central Asia are one way to achieve this aim. Trade with Central Asia and development of Xinjiang's economy and oil deposits are other policies that abet China's larger international strategy.[67]

Therefore, integrating any aspect of Central Asia's considerable deposits with China's would reduce pressure on the Tarym Basin, further stimulate the regional and political integration of both Central Asia and Xinjiang with China's coastal provinces and Beijing, and ease ethnic tensions.[68] Vice Premier and Political Bureau Member Zou Jiahua tied all this together when he observed that increased production, particularly in energy, played a significant role "in promoting the sustained growth of China's oil and gas production; as well as in stimulating Xinjiang's economic development, consolidating the frontier, and enhancing unity among nationalities in the region."[69]

China's strategic profile in Xinjiang is also intimately tied to the larger problems of China's role in Asian security and its intense search for hegemonic positions in the offshore oil deposits located in the South China Sea, as noted above. As a Japanese analysis observes, if China is to play a constructive role in Asia, it must stabilize its oil supply. Otherwise, it might well be tempted to seize the Spratly Islands to satisfy its vital interests and thereby jeopardize Asian security in general.[70]

Since China and Russia claim that the threat posed by Islamic nationalism could overturn basic strategic objectives and political structures, their collaboration in Central Asia can be expected to continue for some time to come. Kozyrev stated that China "has a better understanding" of the problem there than other states do.[71] This common perception of threat reveals a basic harmony in views and strategic interests, a harmony that has led to a Sino-Russian partnership in Asia. Russia and China also share with India a desire to keep Islamic nationalism under control. Thus, each has approached Delhi accordingly.[72] China therefore also strongly opposes Kashmir separatism, even if it weakens India because of its appeal to Islam.[73]

Accordingly, China is not in the foreseeable future a potential ally in opposition to Russian policies in Central Asia. Yet, given its weight, its growth, the urgency of its interests, its ability to influence events, and its determination to play a role in the area, China is likely to emerge in time as the great counterbalance, the Central Asian states' alternative to exclusive reliance on Russia.

As China's and Asia's need for energy grows, China's need to stabilize Central Asia and prevent disruptions in the flow of energy and trade will grow. Since Central Asia's need for investment and trade far surpasses Russia's ability to furnish those resources, China will inevitably become more deeply involved in the region. Ultimately, this will lead it to invest ever-greater political and economic resources in the area, and its influence will grow accordingly. That this analysis is valid is already apparent in the growth of trade between China and Central Asia and the Central Asian states' search for alternatives to Russian energy sources. As China's interest in and relations with Central Asia grow, so will its leverage. Ultimately, this cannot but diminish Russian influence, especially if Russia cannot match China's rapid economic growth and worldwide competitiveness.

While the existing infrastructure and past relations make Russia an attractive partner for Central Asian states, continuing the relations of the past will inevitably siphon resources out of the area. China's attraction, however, is based on a self-sustaining dynamism that sees that it is to its advantage to develop Central Asia and truly integrate it into China's sphere of economic influence. Although China and Russia are now allies, it is likely that the relationship will cool in the long term. In fact, it is probable that they will become rivals in Central Asia since only China has the resources and the ability to challenge Russian neoimperial pretensions there.

Conclusions

Slowly, but visibly, Central Asia is coming to be a source of contention among Russia, China, and even the United States, not to mention smaller regional powers like Iran and Turkey. Central Asian states have adroitly played on these rivalries and in so doing have managed to escape exclusive dependence on any one state. But this rivalry is interesting not only because of what it tells us about Central Asia but also because of what it tells us about Russia and Asia.

In Central Asia's dynamic growth, the ability of a government to marshal the traditional instruments of power—economic resources, sound policies ably implemented, and, ultimately, force—is as decisive as in East Asia's, albeit for different reasons. Russia's efforts to compel reintegration demonstrate its understanding of the need to deploy all these instruments of power. But the chronicle to date also shows us that Russia, as in East Asia, cannot do so. Indeed, the very effort to undertake such policies invariably calls in Russia's greatest rivals from outside Central Asia and undermines its position in the region. Moreover, Russia cannot even begin to reintegrate Central Asia in any way that could prove durable or legitimate to the local inhabitants and elites. The immensity of Central Asia's needs precludes Russia's capability to dominate it, let alone reconstruct it. Instead, Russia's attempt to do so has already called down U.S. opposition and triggered resistance from Central Asian states. And, in the future, China may well mount an even greater challenge to Moscow there.

The main U.S. interest is a fair settlement of the energy issues in Central Asia both because of the immense size of the deposits and because of the threats to Russian and Asian security if ethnopolitical conflict breaks out or nuclear nonproliferation goes awry. Washington has already committed itself to preventing the region from falling under Russia's sphere of influence. In doing so, it aims not so much at democracy as at economic opportunity and a regional balance of power. The United States and its allies are well positioned to offer the trade, aid, and investment that are essential to regional reconstruction, while Russia's only advantage is close proximity. Thus, U.S. policy is ultimately tied to its ambitions vis-à-vis Russia, the Commonwealth of Independent States, and Asia. U.S. Central Asian policy cannot succeed without also responding to China's and South Asia's needs for growth, tranquillity, and stability. It does no good to block Russia and ignore those problems. Central Asia is part of both the new Middle East and Asia, and it can be helped only as part of a broader policy embracing each region.

Thus, its interest in energy and stability inevitably imposes on the United States the task of forging a strategy for engagement with the Commonwealth of Independent States and for both the Middle East and Asia. At stake in Central Asia is more than merely regional resistance to Russia or a new East-West rivalry. If Central Asia and U.S. policy are to have a chance at success, then the United States and its rivals there must see the area as something other than a pawn in international or internal, ethnic rivalries. In short, the area's Asian context must be taken into consideration.

Accordingly, it must be realized that Russia has no choice economically or strategically but to pursue an active role in Central Asia. It cannot walk away from the region's economic and political problems or its ethnic conflicts without negative consequences. That means that U.S. policy should not aim at making Central Asia a new line in the sand against Russia. Unfortunately, certain misguided voices are calling for the United States to confront Russia politically and militarily in order to safeguard energy deposits. Thus, Senator Robert Dole, the 1996 Republican presidential nominee, stated, "The security of the world's oil and gas supplies remains a vital interest of the United States and its major allies. But its borders now move north, to include the Caucasus, Siberia, and Kazakhstan. Our forward military presence and diplomacy need adjusting."[74]

This program quickly leads to a militarized reenactment of the cold war in Central Asia, crippling the region's prospects for economic development and political stability, the correct goals of U.S. policy. This program would also inadvertently undermine the movement toward democracy in Russia. It is precisely to prevent such potential rivalry, militarization, or strife in Central Asia that we must strengthen the region's ability to defend itself and, by cooperative economic ventures with Russia and other Asian countries, reinforce the diversity of influences on the region as it develops. Only by seeing the picture in the larger international context will we be able to ask the right questions about Central Asia. And, in policy, as in life, asking the right questions is the necessary precondition, not just for getting the right answers, but also for developing a sound program of action.

Notes

The views expressed here do not necessarily reflect those of the U.S. Army, the Department of Defense, or the U.S. government.

1 Beverly Crawford, "The New Security Dilemma under International Eco-

nomic Interdependence," *Millennium: Journal of International Studies* 23, no. 1 (1994): 48–50.

2 Stephen Blank, *Energy, Economics, and Security in Central Asia* (Carlisle Barracks, Pa.: Strategic Studies Institute, U.S. Army War College, 1995), 26–30.

3 Ibid., 28–30.

4 *Monitor,* 26 October 1995; Steve LeVine, "Moscow Pressures Its Neighbors to Share Oil, Gas Revenues," *Washington Post,* 18 March 1994, A24. For an early description of this proprietary attitude and local observers' use of the term *blackmail* to describe Russian policy, see Lev Klepatsky and Valery Pospelov, "Maneuvering Round the Caspian Sea," *International Affairs,* nos. 11–12 (November–December 1995): 61.

5 *Rossiyskaya gazeta* (Moscow), 14 October 1995, translated in *Foreign Broadcast Information Service, Central Eurasia* (hereafter *FBIS/SOV*), 17 October 1995, 66–67.

6 *Foreign Broadcast Information Service* (*FBIS*), *Pacific Rim Economic Review,* 10 August 1994, 13–15; "Central Asia Is Drawing Closer to Japan Than Russia," *Current Digest of the Post-Soviet Press* (hereafter *CDPP*), 27 September 1995, 35.

7 "If We Clash It'll Be on the Caspian," *CDPP,* 21 June 1995, 21; Steven Erlanger, "Russia Wants No Return of Cold War, Christopher Is Told," *New York Times,* 11 February 1996, 14.

8 *Rossiyskaya gazeta,* 23 September 1995, translated in *FBIS/SOV,* 28 September 1995, 19–22.

9 Interfax (Moscow), 3 October 1995, reprinted in *FBIS/SOV,* 4 October 1995, 16.

10 *FBIS/SOV,* 28 September 1995, 19.

11 "Yeltsin Okays Foreign Policy Concept," *CDPP,* 26 May 1993, 14.

12 *FBIS/SOV,* 28 September 1995, 19–20.

13 Blank, *Energy, Economics, and Security,* 8–10.

14 Fiona Hill and Pamela Jewett, *"Back in the USSR": Russia's Intervention in the Internal Affairs of the Former Soviet Republics and the Implications for United States Policy toward Russia* (Cambridge, Mass.: Strengthening Democratic Institutions Project, John F. Kennedy School of Government, Harvard University, 1994), 36.

15 Ibid., 30; Blank, *Energy, Economics, and Security,* 9–10; Lynda Maillet, "New States Initiate New Currencies," *Transition* 1, no. 9 (9 June 1995): 44–49, 56.

16 Hill and Jewett, *"Back in the USSR,"* 34–36.

17 Russian Television Network (Moscow), 15 July 1992, translated in *FBIS/SOV,* 16 July 1992, 21; *FBIS/SOV,* 28 September 1995, 19–22; John Lloyd, "Slav States Pledge Economic Union," *Financial Times,* 12 July 1993, 2.

18 Vitaly Naumkin, "Russia and the States of Central Asia," in *Damage Limitation or Crisis: Russia and the Outside World,* ed. Robert D. Blackwill and Sergei A. Karaganov, CSIA Studies in International Security no. 5 (Washington, D.C.:

Brassey's, 1994), 199; *Rossiyskaya gazeta,* 7 October 1995, translated in *FBIS/SOV,* 11 October 1995, 20; *Monitor,* 11 October 1995.

19 *Novaya yezhednevnaya gazeta* (Moscow), 6 July 1994, translated in *FBIS/SOV,* 8 July 1994, 1; *Trud* (Moscow), 6 July 1994, translated in *FBIS/SOV,* 14 July 1994, 10.

20 Ibid.

21 Radio Free Europe / Radio Liberty, email bulletin, 13 December 1994.

22 *Kazakhstanskaya Pravda* (Almaty), 21 January 1995, translated in *FBIS/SOV,* 26 January 1995, 67–68; ITAR-TASS (Moscow), 8 July 1994, reprinted in *FBIS/SOV,* 8 July 1994, 10.

23 *Kommersant-Daily* (Moscow), 29 July 1994, translated in *FBIS/SOV,* 1 August 1994, 1; *Rossiyskie vesti* (Moscow), 16 August 1994, translated in *FBIS/SOV,* 17 August 1994, 12–13; *Rossiyskaya gazeta,* 22 September 1994, translated in *FBIS/SOV,* 27 September 1994, 1–4.

24 *Segodnya* (Moscow), 6 July 1994, translated in *FBIS/SOV,* 6 July 1994, 5.

25 Klepatsky and Pospelov, "Maneuvering Round the Caspian Sea," 59–65; *Monitor,* 26 October 1995. On Iran's position, see Edmund Herzig, *Iran and the Former Soviet South* (London: Royal Institute of International Affairs, Former Soviet South Project, 1995), 40–42.

26 LeVine, "Moscow Pressures Its Neighbors," A24.

27 Ibid.; see also J. Robinson West, "Pipelines to Power," *Washington Post,* 8 June 1994, A23.

28 Blank, *Energy, Economics, and Security,* 12–14.

29 *Trud,* 18 November 1994, translated in *FBIS/SOV,* 21 November 1994, 57–58; *Obshchaya gazeta* (Moscow), 16 December 1994, translated in *FBIS/SOV,* 9 January 1995, 63–65.

30 *Bizness klub* (Almaty), 30 June 1995, translated in *FBIS/SOV,* 5 July 1995, 55–57.

31 Blank, *Energy, Economics, and Security,* 14–15; Interfax, 30 June 1995, reprinted in *FBIS/SOV,* 5 July 1995, 75–76.

32 ITAR-TASS, 28 September 1995, reprinted in *FBIS/SOV,* 29 September 1995, 69.

33 *Rossiyskaya gazeta,* 26 September 1995, translated in *FBIS/SOV,* 2 October 1995, 43–44.

34 Ibid.

35 *Segodnya,* 8 September 1995, translated in *FBIS/SOV,* 28 September 1995, 9–12.

36 *Kazakhstanskaya Pravda,* 21 January 1995, translated in *FBIS/SOV,* 25 January 1995, 40–41; *Kazakhstanskaya Pravda,* 18 February 1995, translated in *FBIS/SOV,* 27 February 1995, 66–68; *FBIS/SOV,* 30 June 1995, 55–57; *FBIS, Pacific Rim Economic Review,* 12 January 1994, 6–7, 10 August 1994, 13–15, and 24 August 1994, 8.

37 *Monitor,* 21 July 1995.
38 Interfax, 5 July 1995, reprinted in *FBIS/SOV,* 7 July 1995, 2–3; *Turkish Daily News* (Ankara), 14 June 1995, reprinted in *Foreign Broadcast Information Service, Western Europe* (hereafter *FBIS/WEU*), 21 June 1995, 51.
39 Interfax, 26 September 1995, reprinted in *FBIS/SOV,* 27 September 1995, 91; *Segodnya,* 28 September 1995, translated in *FBIS/SOV,* 5 October 1995, 69.
40 "If We Clash It'll Be on the Caspian," 21.
41 *FBIS/SOV,* 28 September 1995, 20.
42 Ibid., 21.
43 *Segodnya,* 30 September 1995, translated in *Foreign Broadcast Information Service, Military Affairs* (hereafter *FBIS/UMA*), 25 October 1995, 61.
44 Interview with Lieutenant General L. G. Ivashov, secretary of the CIS Council of Defense Ministers, Carlisle Barracks, Pa., 26 July 1995.
45 *Mirovaya Ekonomika i Mezhdunarodnye Otnosheniia* (Moscow), no. 1 (January 1995), translated in *FBIS/SOV,* 23 March 1995, 11–16; Hannes Adomeit, "Russia as a 'Great Power' in World Affairs: Images and Reality," *International Affairs* 71, no. 1 (January 1995): 61; S. Neil MacFarlane and Adalbert Schnabel, "Russia's Approach to Peacekeeping," *International Journal* 50, no. 1 (Spring 1995): 295–324.
46 Rajan Menon, "In the Shadow of the Bear: Security in Post-Soviet Central Asia," *International Security* 20, no. 1 (Summer 1995): 161–63; Barnett Rubin, "Tajikistan: From Soviet Republic to Russian-Uzbek Protectorate," in *Central Asia and the World,* ed. Michael Mandlebaum (New York: Council on Foreign Relations Press, 1994), 207–24.
47 Akbar Turajonzoda, "Tajikistan-Politics, Religion, and Peace: A View from the Opposition," *Problems of Post-Communism* 42, no. 4 (July/August 1995): 24–28; "Tajikistan," *CDPP,* 24 May 1995, 21–22.
48 Sherman W. Garnett, "The Integrationist Temptation," *Washington Quarterly* 17, no. 2 (Spring 1995): 40; Sanobar Shermatova, "Tajik Crisis Splits Former Allies," *Moscow News,* 21–27 April 1995, 4, and "Russian Rivalries Echo in Tajikistan," *Moscow News,* 5–11 May 1995, 5–6; *Pravda,* 23 May 1995, translated in *FBIS/SOV,* 23 May 1995, 75; Radio Tajikistan Network (Dushanbe), 5 April 1995, translated in *FBIS/SOV,* 6 April 1995, 70–71; Interfax, 22 May 1995, reprinted in *FBIS/SOV,* 23 May 1995, 75; *Literaturnaya gazeta* (Moscow), 25 January 1995, translated in *FBIS/SOV,* 16 February 1995, 71–75.
49 "Turkmenistan," *CDPP,* 14 June 1995, 19; ITAR-TASS, 26 June 1995, reprinted in *FBIS/SOV,* 26 June 1995, 88; Voice of the Islamic Republic (Tehran), 22 August 1994, translated in *Foreign Broadcast Information Service, Near East and South Asia* (hereafter *FBIS/NES,* 22 August 1994, 52; Ramesh Thakur, "Russian Policy toward India: A Relationship on Hold," in *Russian Foreign Policy since 1990,* ed. Peter Shearman (Boulder, Colo.: Westview, 1995), 235–36.
50 *Rossiyskaya gazeta,* 23 May 1995, translated in *FBIS/SOV,* 24 May 1995, 6–7.
51 "Credits: West Will Help Uzbekistan," *CDPP,* 24 May 1995, 27; *Kommersant-*

Daily, 8 April 1995, translated in *FBIS/SOV,* 11 April 1995, 78; Interfax, 6 April 1995, reprinted in *FBIS/SOV,* 7 April 1995, 74–75, 77; Uzbekistan Television (Tashkent), 6 April 1995, translated in *FBIS/SOV,* 7 April 1995, 75–77.

52 *Open Media Research Institute, Daily Digest* (hereafter *OMRI Daily Digest*), 9 May 1995, 26 February 1996; *Narodnoe Slovo* (Tashkent), 30 May 1995, translated in *FBIS/SOV,* 31 May 1995, 83; *Ukrayina Moloda* (Kiev), 23 June 1995, translated in *FBIS/SOV,* 30 June 1995, 46–48.

53 Shermatova, "Tajik Crisis," 4; *FBIS/SOV,* 7 April 1995, 74–77.

54 Ibid.; *FBIS/SOV,* 11 April 1995, 78; "Val's Letter from Moscow," *Asian Defence Journal,* July 1995, 74; Strobe Talbott, "Terms of Engagement," *New York Times,* 4 February 1996, E13.

55 "Val's Letter from Moscow," 74; Talbott, "Terms of Engagement," E13; Erlanger, "Russia Wants No Return," 14.

56 Talbott, "Terms of Engagement," E13.

57 *Monitor,* 11 October 1995.

58 For two examples, see *Renmin Ribao* (Beijing), 31 July 1995, translated in *Foreign Broadcast Information Service, China* (hereafter *FBIS/CHI*), 27 September 1995, 70–73; and *Guofang* (Beijing), no. 6, 15 June 1995, translated in *FBIS/CHI,* 25 August 1995, 36–38, 109. See also ITAR-TASS, 12 September 1995, reprinted in *FBIS/SOV,* 13 September 1995, 77.

59 Irina D. Zviagels'kaia, "Central Asia and the Caucasus: New Geopolitics," in *Central Asia and Caucasia: Ethnicity and Conflict,* ed. Vitaly Naumkin (Westport, Conn.: Greenwood, 1994), 133.

60 *The Monitor,* 21 February 1996.

61 *FBIS/CHI,* 25 August 1995, 36–38.

62 Ross H. Munro, "China's Waxing Spheres of Influence," *Orbis* 28, no. 4 (Fall 1994): 585–606; Keith Martin, "China and Central Asia: Between Seduction and Suspicion," *RFE/RL Research Report* 3, no. 25 (24 June 1994): 31–34; Lilian Craig Harris, "Xinjiang, Central Asia, and the Implications for China's Policy in the Islamic World," *China Quarterly,* no. 133 (March 1993): 111–29; J. Richard Walsh, "China and the New Geopolitics of Central Asia," *Asian Survey* 33, no. 3 (March 1993): 272–83; Gaye Christoffersen, "Xinjiang and the Great Islamic Circle: The Impact of Transnational Forces on Chinese Regional Planning," *China Quarterly,* no. 133 (March 1993): 130–51.

63 Harris, "Implications for China's Policy," 113–18.

64 Ibid.; Christoffersen, "The Great Islamic Circle," 136–51.

65 *FBIS/CHI,* 27 September 1995, 70–73, and 25 August 1995, 36–38.

66 Harris, "Implications for China's Policy," 118–30; Christoffersen, "The Great Islamic Circle," 136–51; Walsh, "China and the New Geopolitics," 279–81; Munro, "China's Waxing Spheres of Influence," 598–605; *Nezavisimaya gazeta,* 3 August 1994, translated in *Foreign Broadcast Information Services, Central Eurasia, FBIS Report* (hereafter *FBIS/USR*), 15 September 1994, 1–5, 118.

67 Blank, *Energy, Economics, and Security,* 26–30.

68 Xinhua Domestic Service (Beijing), 26 July 1994, translated in *FBIS/CHI,* 26 July 1994, 18; see also Gao Anming, "Plan for Xinjiang Outlined," *China Daily,* 3 October 1995, 1–2.

69 Ibid.

70 Ikuo Kayahara, "Will China Succeed in Implementing Energy Strategy?" *Sekai Shuro* (Tokyo), 10–17 May 1994, translation provided by the U.S. Embassy, Japan.

71 *Izvestia,* 1 February 1994, translated in *FBIS/SOV,* 1 February 1994, 11.

72 Interfax, 30 June 1994, reprinted in *FBIS/SOV,* 1 July 1994, 96; Interfax, 30 June 1994, reprinted in *FBIS/SOV,* 1 July 1994, 4; *Rossiyskaya gazeta,* 31 July 1992, translated in *FBIS/USR,* 24 August 1992, 45; S. Nihal Singh, "Indo-Russian Goals for Central Asia," *International Herald Tribune,* 22 September 1993, 8. Ali Abbas Rizvi, "ECO: From Geopolitics to Geonomics," *Asian Defence Journal,* March 1995, 25.

73 Ibid. It is also worth noting that at least one Indian analysis openly calls for supporting Russia's leadership here and cooperation among India, Russia, and China to stabilize Central Asia (see P. Slobdan, "International Aspects of the Conflict Situation in Central Asia," *Strategic Analysis* [Delhi] 16, no. 3 [June 1993]: 265–81). 69. Walker, "Caspian Oil," 8.

74 Martin Walker, "Caspian Oil and Pipeline Diplomacy," *Moscow Times,* 29 September 1995, 8.

Russia and China

STEPHEN J. BLANK

Russia Looks at China

The Russo-Chinese relationship is one of Asia's fundamental relationships. The bilateral normalization that Brezhnev began in 1982 and Gorbachev completed affected relations among states all over Asia: it induced Indian and Vietnamese rapprochements with China, helped end Cambodia's civil war and Vietnam's intervention there, and reduced North Korea's ability to manipulate Beijing and Moscow. Normalization has also prevented Central Asian states from playing China off against Russia and encouraged China to support Russia's interests there even while enhancing its own position.[1]

This last point underscores normalization's importance for Beijing. Once the cold war ended, normalization freed China from leaning to the United States and allowed it to pursue a more independent and assertive foreign policy, as befits a rising power. But for Russia the relationship frames the limits of its possibilities in Asia. Today, Russia needs China more than China needs Russia, a reversal of which the full implications are only now emerging because Russia remains unstable.

Official programmatic documents indicate that China is Russia's most important Asian partner. Two Russian diplomats recently wrote, "It will be no exaggeration to say that the Chinese dimension of Russia's foreign policy is hardly second to any other, and is perhaps at the cutting edge in some respects."[2] The Russian Federation Security Council's 1993 Security Concept concluded that Russia's potential influence and actual influence on world affairs make it a great power. It is responsible for the post-1991 world order and for the system of relations among the former Soviet republics, which it guarantees. Any threat to that system is a threat to Russia. Russia must play a greater role in international organizations to ward off such threats.[3]

Russia also faces the economic threats of being relegated to an inferior, noncompetitive industrial status and a colonial position as a purveyor of fuels and raw materials. The security concept claims that, on the basis of common interests in strategic stability, nuclear nonproliferation, and the prevention of regional conflicts, Russia's status in Asia and Europe is equal to that of the United States. The security concept advances a hierarchy of the countries important to Russia in Asia: "Our foreign policy priorities include the development of balanced and stable relations with all countries, especially such key states as the US, China, Japan, and India, and the establishment of multilateral cooperation in strengthening security. In this context, it is urgent to consolidate the breakthrough achieved in relations with China—from our standpoint—the region's most important state in geopolitical and economic terms."[4] In short, Moscow's China policy is intended to help Russia enhance its status and avert its exclusion from such key Asian organizations as the Organization for Asian-Pacific Economic Cooperation (APEC), its relegation to an inferior colonial economic position, instability in Central Asia, and its marginalization in the process of maintaining security in Asia.

China's historically central strategic position in Moscow's Asian policy derives from its proximity to Russia, which puts China in a position that makes it a potential threat to Russia's integrity. As China is a rising economic-political power in Asia, friendship with it is even more vital to Russian security. Yet, among Russian observers, there is considerable ambivalence about China. Nor is friendship with China entirely risk free for Russia. Aleksei Arbatov warns that Russian theater-level conventional war games are conducted against China because China is regarded as the only power that might actually threaten to invade.[5] Christoph Bluth also notes that, "for Russian strategic planners, the future relationship with China in an environment in which the military-strategic balance and the relative economic potential is changing substantially, remains potentially the most troublesome. For all these reasons, they perceive the need to guard against nuclear attack or nuclear blackmail in the future."[6] Mikhail Titarenko, director of the Institute of the Far East, warns about the potential threats to China's own stability from its ecological and demographic crises and from the impending struggle over succession.[7] Vladimir Miasnikov, deputy director of the institute, further claims that, despite the consonance of many joint Sino-Russian interests, China already is and will continue to be a rival, if not a threat, to Russia:

Few Russians yet realize the enormity of the Chinese challenge to Russia's long-term political and economic interests. Attempts have already been made, both by China and by the United States, to exclude Russia from the discussion of Asia-Pacific issues vital to its national security. — China would prefer that the United States deal primarily with Beijing with regard to economic and strategic planning in the Pacific Rim, and envisions that the Russian-American dialogue will be replaced by the Chinese-American dialogue in U.S. national security. In such an arrangement, U.S. relations with China would largely determine the United States' political, economic, and military engagement in the region as a whole over the long term.[8]

Both the threat posed by China and the need for continued relations are a product of Russia's domestic crises, political instability, incomplete economic transition, and pervasive feeling of weakness and insecurity. Notwithstanding the visible ambivalence about China, policy decisions have been made on the basis of Russia's sense of weakness, its desire to act independently of Washington, and its nationalist conception of its interests. The outcome is an Asian-Pacific policy that centers almost exclusively on China.

The Context of Russia's China Policy

Despite the ambivalence, friendship with China atypically commands support across Russia's political spectrum.[9] China assiduously courts people across that spectrum, and reformers and conservatives alike positively assess China's achievements and often wish to copy them at home.[10] Their differences lie in the weight each Russian side attaches to China. Russian conservatives even talked of alliance in 1991–93.

But, while consensus exists that China must be a partner and friend of Russia's it appears that Moscow's 1992 decision to focus its Asian policy on China and forgo rapprochement with Japan represents more than a bow to the conservative agenda. This decision signified a strategic choice undertaken for domestic and foreign policy reasons, which Yeltsin has built on and extended beyond Gorbachev's vision of a fundamental rapprochement with China. Gorbachev liquidated Soviet threats to China in Southeast Asia and Afghanistan and terminated the military-political encirclement of China that typified Brezhnev's policy. He also encouraged key Asian states, like India, to follow suit, and they did so.[11] He opened up trade with China, allowed favorable analysis of Chinese reforms as part of *perestroika,* and refused to criticize the 1989 Tienanmen Square massacre.

While in the past normalization has benefited both sides equally (even though it was largely a Chinese victory), today's relationship is much more one-sided. Not only is China the superior party in terms of power, stability, and clarity of goals, but it also benefits more than Russia does from these ties. This does not mean that Russia gains little from the relationship. China is an important counterweight to the United States, and the relationship allows Russia to escape some risks of its alleged "subordination" to Washington. Today, it is Russia that seeks to manipulate the "triangle" to maintain a balance between China and the United States and thereby enhance its freedom of action. In economics, friendship with China offers Russia markets for its otherwise uncompetitive products, a major arms buyer, and support for Moscow's hegemony in Central Asia, which depends on those states not having an alternative foreign patron. When the Soviet Union collapsed, the possibility of nationalist religious or ethnic uprisings in Central Asia and the subsequent collapse of Russia arose. But China has supported Yeltsin's regime (while hoping for a more ideologically congenial partner) and not challenged Russia in Central Asia. Thus, China earned Russia's visible gratitude.[12] Finally, friendship with China is crucial to stabilizing Northeast Asia and eliminating threats to Russia's integrity or security.

Both states are pursuing mutual but unilateral conventional disarmament as well as projects designed to build mutual confidence, such as hotlines to local regional commanders.[13] This lets China retire obsolete forces while upgrading its forces in southern and eastern China, more important potential theaters of war. Chinese friendship with Russia reduces the threat from the north, puts pressure on Japan, allows China to manipulate Japanese fears of an Asian anti-Japan bloc, keeps the United States in Japan, and prevents Pyongyang from playing Russia and China off against each other or provoking trouble. Russia is also no longer a potential rival of China's in India and Vietnam, forcing these countries to deal directly with Beijing. This entente also keeps Russia at a distance from the United States, which China considers a political and ideological threat. Finally, a Russia that needs China cannot offer itself as a viable ideological alternative to the Chinese leadership, which feels threatened by any hint of reform. Thus, China gains greatly from this relationship and wants it to continue.

These mutual benefits show how mutual comity prevents other states from acting against Russian and Chinese interests. But a deeper analysis suggests that the actual result of the relationship has been ultimately to threaten Russia's position in Asia.

The Domestic Bases of Russian Policy

That Russia's position is more problematic than China's is due to the protracted crises that it has experienced. Although friendship with China has obvious benefits, it also comes at a considerable cost. First, Russia still lacks a coherent policy-making process, let alone coherent policy, so, instead of pursuing ways to enhance Central Asian stability and better its position in Asia, it allows domestic political and economic concerns to drive its overall security policy.[14] Indeed, to become fully accepted in Asia, it needs China to act on its behalf, and Beijing knows it. Li Jingjie, deputy director of the Chinese Academy of Sciences' Institute of East Europe, Russia, and Central Asia, writes, "Moscow's current leaders surely know that only by maintaining good relations with China can the new Russia secure a smooth path to a bright future in the Asia-Pacific region."[15] Accordingly, state incapacity and instability directly marginalize Russia in Asia, show the risks in not developing an effective state, and make Russia dependent on China's support for entry into Asia (e.g., membership in APEC).[16]

This underdeveloped state capacity appears in conflicts in procedural and substantive issues that hold security policy hostage to domestic politics. Many conflictual aspects typify foreign and defense policy.

First, no standard procedure or institutional basis exists for formulating security policy. Rival ministries, the Security Council, the legislature, the president's and the premier's personal administrations, interest groups in and out of government, etc., all can express their views and have them heeded without regard for order and context.[17] In May 1995, the minister of defense, Marshal Pavel Grachev, offered China a collective security scheme for jointly "policing" Asia and then falsely claimed that Beijing had accepted it.[18] Unfortunately, such episodes characterize too much of Russian foreign policy.

Since all chains of policy and command are vertical and end in Yeltsin's office or person, the absence of horizontal, integrating structures makes all politics a contest among rival factions for access to Yeltsin.[19] Although Yeltsin placed the Ministry of Foreign Affairs directly under him in 1995 to coordinate and monitor other agencies' actions and thereby ensure unified policy, such decrees come and go.[20] Even before that particular decree could be implemented, Yeltsin fired Foreign Minister Andrei Kozyrev and replaced him with Yevgeny Primakov, head of Russia's Foreign Intelligence Service (SVR), who clearly understood that his mission was to take control of and coordinate foreign policy. Nevertheless, absent a true rule of law, no ground rules for relations among the various departments and branches of government exist.[21] The Ministries of Defense and Atomic Energy still act autonomously.[22] For Russia to regain power and influence, it must reverse this process of "deinstitutionalization."[23]

Since decrees are not necessarily obeyed and Yeltsin's periodic decrees to end confusion in policy making have had the opposite effect, new decrees will change nothing. Nor is it necessarily the case that personalities are decisive since traditionally Russian foreign ministers are advocates, not shapers, of their government's foreign policy. Nor are debates over foreign and defense policy necessarily or exclusively concerned with institutional interests of turf and budget. Instead, major ideological differences over national identity and interest have coexisted with bureaucratic politics since 1991, when Russia came into being.

Second, executive branch discord parallels similar substantive discord with the parliament over fundamental rules of the game. Again, absent the rule of law, we find a free-for-all where anyone can and does unrestrainedly attack anyone or any foreign, defense, or overall security policy. Although the parliament's power is limited, it nonetheless has significant control over the purse and treaties, so it is not a wholly negligible factor.

Third, intense discord over general and specific policies exacerbates conflicts. While Russia swaps arms for debt to South Korea, other elites openly urge new arms sales to North Korea, illustrating that Korea policy remains a battleground.[24] The diversity of opinion on China's prospects cited above shows this uncertainty in China policy too. These debates evoke an uncertain, even confused policy abroad.

A fourth destabilizing factor is Yeltsin's frequent actions against his ministries or without their knowledge. His gratuitous insults of Japan when discussing relief for Sakhalin's earthquake victims are one of many cases where Yeltsin intervened without prior policy coordination.[25] The upshot is that policy emerges from intense institutional and personal struggles, despite a working strategic consensus since 1993 that Russia must have a free hand throughout the Commonwealth of Independent States (CIS) to reunite the region. Inter-institutional conflicts no longer begin exclusively over Russia's basic objectives, as in 1992. The conservatives won that argument. Rather, conflicts frequently revolve around the modalities of expressing the consensus abroad and bureaucratic politics.[26]

These institutional deficiencies and inadequate constraints on political participation also allow military leaders freedom to agitate publicly and even defy state policy. This legitimates the military's politicization and efforts to usurp control of foreign policy.[27] Kozyrev claimed that the Ministry of Defense (MOD) and intelligence agencies seek such control and told U.S. audiences that failure to support him on major issues meant that he would be speaking to us "from the Gulag."[28] This apocalyptic and hysterical rhetoric underscores Russia's weakness and uncertain policies.

Grachev's 1993 remarks in Seoul about relations with South Korea—that soldiers could find common ground between their states even if politicians and diplomats could not and that he was ready to exchange views and cooperate with all Asian states and military leaders toward that goal—confirm Kozyrev's fears.[29] Similarly, the issue of returning the Kuril Islands to Japan in 1992 allowed Valentin P. Fyodorov, governor of Sakhalin, and military leaders to organize a loud and unpunished public opposition to Yeltsin's policy that led to the cancellation of Yeltsin's state visit to Japan.

Thus, Russia's domestic chaos permits civilians and military leaders to forge opportunistic alliances with impunity to check central policies deemed to be against their interests. This episode had profound repercussions. Quite probably, it helped persuade the government to adopt a viscerally anti-Japanese policy and an assessment of threat based on a worst-case analysis of U.S.-Japanese military plans for the Asia-Pacific region. This victory allowed the armed forces to retain their "hammerlock" on the Far East and prevent the normalization of Russo-Japanese relations. Instead, the government has slowed economic reform and adopted a joint posture with China against Japan and the United States. Thus, Russian thinking about Asia reflects above all geopolitical and military rather than economic factors when conducting a strategic assessment.[30] By renouncing Japan, Russia must depend exclusively on China and consider Tokyo and Washington military rivals in Asia, not potential partners.

Regional Separatism and Russian Policy toward China

These trends in civil-military relations reflect broader trends toward the fragmentation of policy making in the body politic. In February 1995, Yeltsin conceded the failure to build effective, coherent, and legitimate state institutions to preserve central authority in security policy when he told the Duma, "The institutions of state power have yet to accumulate sufficient weight to ensure that *force does not have to be applied to restore Russian sovereignty on their territory.* Today, the state has to resort to the exercise of its right to use strong-arm methods in order to preserve the country's integrity."[31]

At about the same time, Yevgeny Nazdratenko, governor of Russia's Maritime Province (Primorskii Krai), unilaterally attempted to undo the 1991 border treaty with China, a major policy achievement, and restrict Chinese immigration to his province.[32] Nazdratenko's challenge reveals the general weakness in Asia policy. Recent reports show that Primorskii Krai is increasingly pressuring to have its relation with Moscow changed from a federal to a confederal one, that is, from nominal to real federalism. This demand unites republics, districts, and regions, reflecting local elites' ambition to control their own resources.[33] Western observers worry about Russia's disintegration into many states and warlordism; Siberia and Primorskii Krai are particular potential trouble spots, but even central provinces like Bashkortostan are demanding more autonomy.[34] If central power is curtailed despite Moscow's best efforts, the security implications for Russia, China, and Asia will be enormous.

That trend would stimulate international rivalry for influence along Russian and CIS Asian frontiers and validate Russia's most alarmist worst-case scenarios. Russia's instability also shows that it can offer Asia only force of questionable utility. Therefore, Russian power and influence are retreating from Asia.[35] Already some sectors of both civilian and the defense industry either work directly for Chinese consumers or producers or are exquisitely susceptible to Chinese preferences.[36] Failure to strengthen Russia's cohesion will intensify the negative potential in such relationships. On the other hand, if Russia regained stability and once again began to move forward, it could immediately begin to develop and implement a stronger, more coherent, confident, and effective foreign policy.

Nazdratenko's insubordination thus reflects a broader struggle for power. Kozyrev admitted that he and Yeltsin never went to China, Japan, or Korea without consulting with the appropriate regions on all issues to be discussed.[37] Thus, Asian policy has been held hostage to domestic struggles. Fyodorov showed that enterprising regional governors can join with key lobbies like the military to constrain Moscow's policies and that no barriers restrain open military participation in politics.

Claims that the Russian state is "weak and irrelevant," decaying, dying, or disintegrating are probably excessive.[38] But the evidence suggests that Moscow and the regions are each too fragmented internally to act unilaterally. Certainly, constant struggle pervades Primorskii Krai's and Siberia's relations with Moscow.[39] Crosscutting cleavages among political actors, lobbies, and factions impede the resolution of many issues and could trigger demands for immediate recentralization, regional secession, a more stable devolution of power, or other, unforeseeable outcomes.

Domestic Politics and Arms Sales

These internal factional rivalries directly affect China policy, particularly arms sales, a key aspect of that policy. Many reports indicate the large size and scope of Russian arms transfers to China.[40] Not only is China interested in obtaining weapons platforms, like other Asian states, but it also wants production techniques and state-of-the-art technology, that is, offsets. Many in the Russian military were reluctant to provide offsets, for obvious reasons. Yet the constant pressure of arms industries who benefit from the sales and military figures who support the idea (also a sign of the military's factionalism) prevailed, so in at least some cases China is obtaining offsets.[41] Thus, in February 1996, China not only bought forty-eight more SU-27 fighters but won the right or license to produce them with Russian offsets. This agreement also suggests China's continuing ability to come out ahead in bilateral negotiations with the Russians.[42]

The fact that arms sales is among the most corrupt and corrupting sectors of Russian business is also an important factor in the decision-making process. Already in 1993 Russia had no idea how many scientists were working in or for China and could not control the arms sales process. Andrei Kuzmenko said then, "The producers are now more or less independent. And they have their own independent lobby."[43] This is even more true today, for, in mid-1995 and again in February 1996, Yeltsin allowed arms producers to sell directly to buyers.[44] Thus, that arms sales are unregulated and unrestricted carries potential domestic and foreign dangers to Russia's overall Asia policy.

In 1993, then Vice Premier Aleksandr' Shokhin admitted that many design bureaus and enterprises were seeking private deals with China.[45] Other reports then confirmed Kuzmenko's remarks and blasted the sales to China because they were largely paid for by consumer goods instead of cash, for example, atomic reactors to be built in China.[46] These trends in bilateral relations suggest that, in many ways, Russia or key economic, military, scientific, and political elites could become hostage to Chinese policies and developments, a trend that will severely limit, if not undermine, reform. The implications for Asian security from the U.S. standpoint are equally negative. Already we can see the threat posed by a rearmed China in its blustery and confrontational actions vis-à-vis Taiwan and ASEAN in the South China Sea.

Russian arms sales to China thus bridge domestic policy and security concerns and pose considerable risk and cost to Russia. Since China is Russia's most prominent partner in Asia, the volume of arms sales to China makes those sales critical policy instruments that affect all Asia.

The systems being sold and the linkages established may thereby exert major influence on Russia's future domestic and foreign policies. The profitable arms trade with China and Asia stimulates and justifies defense industry demands to control arms sales and its new freedom to sell abroad. The importance of arms sales similarly attracts both the MOD and the Ministry of Foreign Affairs (MFA) as well as the defense industry, each wanting to control the process and policy.[47] Thus, a full-scale turf battle occurs among the groups that want to control the overall arms sales program for their own benefit.

The defense industry's main aims are direct control over foreign currency and operating freedom. But it also wants a privileged relationship with the government and continued preferential treatment through subsidies. It and its allies view arms sales as a way either to avoid or to fund conversion based on dual-use industry's priority. Thus, conversion for the new military-industrial-complex lobby is a nonstarter to be avoided, whereas arms sales justify its continuing production, under state protection, of weapons.[48] That would continue the defense industry's privileged position, which ruined Soviet military power. Continued large sales to China are a most crucial element in this process.

Viktor Glukikh, former chairman of the State Committee on Defense Industry, admitted that there is no alternative to arms sales to fund investment in the defense industry since procurement has been radically slashed since 1991.[49] Similarly, this lobby's leaders continually broadcast their plight to demand more and more state support lest the industry go bankrupt. These pleas have received government support as key officials pledge that support will be coming, and it now looks like Yeltsin will increase defense spending. The recent liberalization of the rules for arms sales signifies that support. But even that failed to satisfy the many defense industrialists who unanimously supported the League to Support Defense Industry Enterprises' April 1995 call for their own political party and for stripping the MOD of some power and reassigning it to Glukikh's committee.[50]

Meanwhile, responding to Kozyrev's efforts to introduce some sense of state (and the MFA's) interest into the program, Marshal Grachev has often reiterated that the MOD should control the program.[51] However, Pavel Felgengauer, the defense correspondent of *Segodnya,* reports that the MOD opposes even selling individual models of high-tech, state-of-the-art weapons.[52] Undoubtedly, he is right about the General Staff's successful opposition to the sale of such models abroad, but other observers charge that the MOD is dangerously willing to sell such models through companies it set up or controls. Grachev and the MOD have tried to find autonomous sources of funding that would be under Grachev's exclusive control and that would evidently be for this purpose.[53] Recently, military space authorities sold three of Russia's most advanced upper-stage rocket engines to China in violation of the Missile Technology Control Regime but did not go through NPO Energomash, the only entity licensed to sell this engine legally.[54]

The dangerous implication of such actions and organizations and the rivalry among defense industries to sell abroad subject to state licensing is that Russia has no export control law. Exports are controlled by presidential decree, and those desires are subject to change at any time. Since the government is notoriously corrupt and the defense industry is increasingly tied to it through large financial-industrial cartels dependent on bank capital that the state controls, possibilities for "privatization" and corruption of arms sales by selfish interests are very great. When state officials have a pecuniary interest in allowing sales to proceed and can act with impunity, state control is a non sequitur.

Thus, there are many domestic risks in the extensive arms trade with China. China reportedly acts clandestinely, deals directly with military producers rather than through Moscow, and squeezes every available technology out of its partners by apparent sharp practices.[55] For the Chinese to have such covert influence on policy impedes civilian control of the military and the defense industry in Russia and could also corrupt Russian politics across the board. Even where Moscow knows about the deals being made, it is unclear whether it controls the policy or the process, as noted above. In the SU-27 case, for example, although Russia will receive royalties for every Chinese modification of the design of the plane, sooner or later China will be able to sell its version of the plane at a lower cost.[56] Russia or key political elites could become hostage to Chinese policies and developments, a trend that will limit, if not undermine, reform. That consideration does not even begin to broach the international security issues raised by these sales.

Not surprisingly, these trends concern many military men and civilians. For example, hundreds of Chinese technicians now work at Russian aerospace institutes. One reporter noted that Chinese delegations of highly skilled specialists are "wandering around the defense enterprises and negotiating on the conclusion of contracts. They are being shown and told practically everything in the hope that we might obtain if only some orders." While Russian specialists travel to China in groups of two to three, China sends ten at a time, gets this free reconnaissance, and orders little. Moreover, "It has even reached the point of our specialists' development of models of military equipment adapted to the production possibilities of the plants of the Chinese military-industrial complex being planned."[57]

This happened in 1994 in St. Petersburg and Nizhny Novgorod, where shipyards producing Kilo-class "Varshavyanka" submarines have no other work. One plant director complained that the Chinese somehow obtained secret specifications for Kilo-class submarines for the Russian navy and demanded that China receive exactly the same subs. But, once that happens, the plant will be out of work.[58] The unspoken implication is that, without Chinese orders, this plant (and presumably others, too) dies. Since then, six such submarines were sold to China. While Washington viewed this sale calmly, Rear Admiral V. D. Ryazantsev, the Pacific Fleet's deputy commander in chief for combat training and chief of the Fleet's Combat Training Directorate, observed, "Of course, today six 'Varshavyanka' Class submarines will not substantially change the naval might of the Chinese Navy. But that is today. But tomorrow when China's shipbuilding industry has mastered the technologies of the construction of the lowest-noise diesel submarines and when they rearm those submarines with cruise missiles and missile-torpedoes of their own design? And if they also adapt to them a relatively small nuclear electrical power source?"[59]

These concerns led some military men to argue against providing state-of-the-art weapons. But they lost the battle to restrain the defense industry. Nor are the armed forces united. In March 1995, a military spokesman said that Russia had no objection in principle to China buying licenses to manufacture the SU-27 but would prefer that China (which probably has insufficient cash for this) bought 100–150 such aircraft. Arguably, this would benefit Russian industry and China.[60] Presumably, firms would get orders and cash, thus easing rising unemployment, their gravest fear. In the end, of course, China did get the license, a sign of the successful pressure to sell arms regardless of the risks. Indeed, Alexander Kennaway of the Royal Military Academy at Sandhurst, an expert on the defense economy, said in 1994 that, owing to such fears, Russian policies "are moving back to the aims and methods of the old command economy.—Almost every pronouncement, publication, and discussion—especially in the military press—in Russia about the defense industries insists that they must be retained in their present form and size and that further conversion would be a crime."[61]

Thus, there is a community of interest between military men and those who want to and can sell to China with minimal restrictions. Since they have political leverage, through their financial ties to banks, control over company towns and labor, and access to key policy makers, they constitute a formidable domestic bloc in Russia's China and Asia policy. But they have little or no concern for the strategic implication of arms sales.

The Strategic Implications of Sino-Russian Arms Deals

Space precludes a detailed list of what China has bought, is talking about buying, and would like to obtain, through purchase or otherwise.[62] But China's purchases to date and ongoing discussions bespeak its ambition to field an integrated land/sea/air defense system using Russian air and missile systems. Indeed, there are reports that China has recruited from Russia a whole cruise missile research-and-development team that is now helping China develop cruise missiles.[63] Combined with the naval air platform that China seeks from either Russia or Ukraine, these capabilities would give China a formidable air and air defense system extending far beyond its borders. China is evidently creating the infrastructure for a mobile and expanding offensive air, air defense system, and integrated carrier battle group. It is not mere coincidence that these systems are precisely those that China needs successfully to wage the kinds of wars it expects to fight.[64] Nor are these conventional systems the only causes for worry. Even more alarming is China's desire to obtain the long-range TU-22M Backfire bomber. It has a dual-use, four-thousand-kilometer unrefueled range and is far more advanced than China's principal bomber, the H-6. Although spare parts may prove to be a problem, mere possession of this system, let alone possible production capability, will likely frighten all China's neighbors and heighten the alarm that leads to intensified arms buying across Asia.[65]

Not only does Russia argue its need for revenues from arms sales and good relations with China. It also claims to take precautions to ensure that the weapons are not deployed against Russia, where most Chinese land forces are still deployed, and that China does not get the most technologically sophisticated models of the platforms it buys from Russia.[66] Russia also says that it sells only defensive systems, not, for example, air-to-ground missiles.[67] Nonetheless, the extensive subsidies to China, the transfer of production technology, and China's ability to form direct links to defense producers who are desperate for customers weaken Russia's claims and suggest the many great dangers accruing from these sales and China's military buildup, which facilitates China's policies to realize its military doctrine and security goals in Asia.

Equally important, the Russian military knows and publicly discusses Chinese developments in doctrine and force planning. Therefore, it is impossible to believe that Russia is unaware of those plans. In fact, "As Russians see it, there will be a battle to dominate the region, fought between China and Japan. In this, the principal feature will be Chinese plans for the creation of a carrier group in the South China Seas. As well as ships, China's US$4–6 billion project will call for long-range air supersonic TU-22."[68]

Russian arms sales to China could encourage Chinese coercive diplomacy or worse, degrading Asian security and spurring a brisk regional arms race. Russia's risks thereby now include other Asian states—Taiwan, Southeast Asia, possibly even Japan and both Koreas—not to mention the United States. In 1993, Japan's Miyazawa government increasingly tied arms sales to China to the return of the Kuril Islands as a precondition for aid to Russia and rightly saw these sales as anti-Japanese.[69] Developments in 1995 further heightened Japanese alarm over arms sales to China since the dispute between Tokyo and Beijing over the Senkaku Islands remained unresolved.[70] Russia is also offering arms across Southeast Asia and to South Korea but is not concerned that these states are among the most suspicious of China's aims and could easily become involved in a local war against China, forcing Russia to make uncomfortable policy choices.

Arms sales of sophisticated weaponry, often at fire-sale prices, also allow China to circumvent post-1989 Western and U.S. restrictions and continue anti-Western policies. Nor do Chinese appetites stop at what they have already acquired. U.S. officials have charged that China is considering acquiring weapons of mass destruction, missile guidance systems, and nuclear fusion technologies on top of the aircraft already sold or under consideration, rumored sales of T-72 tanks, air defense equipment, electronics, and carriers.[71] Such acquisitions not only enhance China's capabilities but also intensify the sense of a major shift in the Asian balance of power. Asian states customarily regarded U.S. power as the best check on Japan and China. Our drawdown of forces now heightens local fears of instability. Thus, Asian capabilities and arms races, China's power, and Russian sales grow together.

But Moscow sees arms sales to Asia as a major instrument of a new Russian standing and presence there. Therefore, strong political pressure exists to continue them. Kozyrev told ASEAN's 1993 annual ministerial meeting (AMM) and postministerial conference (PMC) that Russia views arms sales as a way to enter Asia's security agenda and restructure its security order, for example, by establishing an arms trade code.[72] In 1995, he went so far as to propose a code of conduct for Asian security, a proposal that undoubtedly also includes arms sales.[73] Since Russia cannot soon revive its economic standing and partnership with Asia, arms sales play a disproportionate role in assuring consideration of Russia's interests. So the failure of economic transformation and the structure of Asian interstate relations drive Russia to sell arms to China and other Asian states.

China's own growing role as an arms exporter also heightens this subject's importance since joint-venture or coproduction accords could lead China to produce Russian systems or foster joint production for reexport abroad, despite foreign pressure. Since Chinese arms sales firms are lucrative preserves of key leaders' relatives and essential for military modernization, strong domestic pressure exists to maintain or expand China's ability to produce high-quality weapons.

Most dangerous for Russia, however, is the fact that its dependence on Chinese economic power and arms purchases robs it of flexibility in Asia. It has renounced normalization with Japan, used ties with China to resist U.S. pressure and assert its independence in world affairs, and is no longer available to counterbalance China's influence in Asia. And the security cooperation inherent in large-scale and continuing programs of arms and technology transfer is only enhanced by the other forms of military and defense cooperation with China, including military intelligence and the GRU (the Russian military intelligence). This intelligence cooperation could be used against Asian and U.S. targets, most likely defense and dual-use technologies. Thus, Russian arms sales contribute heavily to a policy that contradicts and endangers Russian interests in Asia.

The Bilateral Economic Relationship

Economics are the most important day-to-day aspect of Russo-Chinese relations. That is not surprising, given that China is growing spectacularly and East Asia is the most dynamic sector of the world economy while Russia struggles merely to achieve an end to depression. Russia needs buyers for its manufactured goods and technology, which generally surpasses China's, and China needs customers for its less competitive sectors, new niches in world trade, and arms and technology transfers. China has already begun investing in Russia. But, since it needs massive foreign investment to sustain its own growth, China, too, recently urged Russians to invest in China, especially in nuclear and large-scale hydroelectric energy projects like the Three Gorge project.[74]

China's needs for a stable customer, external investment outlets for its businessmen, and foreign investment in China are enhanced by its concerns about Russia's economy. Russia, too, is eager to overcome all barriers to expanded economic intercourse with China because many Russian figures believe that there is an objective Sino-Russian economic complementarity that impels them to close ties.[75] And, because its strategic plan for economic revitalization in Asia rules out normalization of relations with Japan, Russia can turn only to China. Furthermore, these plans condemn Siberia and Russian Asia to remain sources of exportable raw materials to China and other states. Accordingly, those regions depend on reasonably cheap Chinese consumer goods and barter trade with China since they lack investment capital.[76]

Thus, Russia's overall and regional economic strategies point—

perhaps unconsciously—to an increased need for and dependence on Chinese buyers and investors if they are to succeed. Arguably, because of the unbalanced traditional regional policy stress on China, Siberia and Primorskii Krai might not develop rapidly without substantial Chinese trade.[77] This trend is recognized locally, constitutes a major source of regional anger against Moscow, and hinders relations and trade with China. Indeed, this anger at the alleged Chinese "invasion," to use Grachev's term, finally led the government, in August 1995, to consider measures to settle Russians in the Far East.[78]

The bilateral trade structure confirms Russia's dependence. Raw materials constitute 84 percent of Russian exports, machinery and equipment 16 percent.[79] More specifically, "With a few major exceptions relating to arms sales and nuclear energy, current bilateral trade is an extension of pre-existing patterns of trade in general commodities rather than an accelerated interdependence in high-tech co-operation and technical trade which characterizes the dynamic sectors of the Asia-Pacific region."[80]

Therefore, the fall in bilateral trade in 1994 by one-third (from $7.6 billion to just over $5 billion) triggered considerable high-level alarm in both governments. Chinese premier Li Peng's visit to Moscow in June 1995 focused on ways to overcome barriers to trade. But, if trade is to return to its accelerating trajectory after 1994's disappointing figures, China claims that Russia must do more and tactfully but firmly points this out. While China calls on its textile and light industry to make their goods competitive in terms of quality and style, Russia is called on to make fundamental changes in policy. Russia is urged to improve price competitiveness, delivery dates, and after-sales service, foster a favorable investment environment, bolster Chinese investors' confidence, provide reliable legal and social protection for China's legitimate production and operating activities, and invest in China.[81] Although the joint communiqué spoke in more tactful and restrained terms about what both sides must do, this article, coming out a week later from China's government newspaper, suggests who has the upper hand in the relationship and what China wants in economic terms.

The problem for Russia is that it cannot control the political or economic situation in the Far East. The opening up of the area after 1990 has triggered a massive influx of Chinese immigrants, workers, and small businessmen, which has in turn triggered great local resentment. Nazdratenko has used this xenophobia to strengthen his political position and join with other regional governors who are similarly suspicious of China to compel more side payments and freedom from Moscow.[82] This two-level game—replete with Nazdratenko's unilateral actions to restrict immigration, resist the terms of the border agreement with China, agitate in the Duma for a referendum on "ceding Russian land," and close the border to "illegal" immigrants—not only precipitated the fall in trade in 1994 but also threatens to "explode" the bilateral relationship, according to MFA officials who strongly oppose revising the border treaty.[83]

To the extent that he and other regional governors can mobilize organized political opposition to the policy, Russia's Far East and Russian Asia will stagnate because these forces, along with the security services (and the military), equally staunchly oppose normalization with Japan. Xenophobia, great power nostalgia, opposition to economic reform, interdependence, and development and personal rivalries already inhibit Russia's ability to function as an Asian power and fully participate in Asia's dynamic transformation. This attempt to have large state enterprises, not enterprising small businessmen, control Russo-Chinese economic ties means more mercantilistic foreign economic relations and less openness, reform, and liberalization. It also enhances the role of security services on both sides of the border as they patrol it more vigorously.

Ultimately, therefore as Gaye Christoffersen wrote in 1994,

> Chinese influence will not encourage reform but rather will encourage Primorye's [the Maritime Province–Nazdratenko's bailiwick] state enterprises, the association that represents the military-industrial complex, PAKT [the association representing local military industry and security forces and which controls local government, i.e. Nazdratenko's bloc], and increased dominance by security forces. The local population's strong support for Zhirinovsky's LDP during the December [1993] elections confirms the overall direction Primorye is taking.[84]

This evidence also confirms that the Russian Far East regards economic integration with China and Asia as just another strategy to siphon off regional wealth, withhold the subsidies needed to convert the defense industry and develop, stunt regional development, subordinate the region to China and Chinese influence, and circumscribe the region's freedom of action in Asia.[85] This antagonism has triggered a local gridlock that reflects Yeltsin's broader failure to create effective, viable, and legitimate state institutions. By 1994, in the regional-central relationship threats of secession, appropriation of state property, the local government's forging of alliances with foreign states against Moscow, and acts of violence against potential foreign allies of the center were predominant. Moscow employed equally desperate actions like closing the local Soviets. All this attests to the failure not only to develop a viable central-local bargaining relationship but also to go beyond personalities to stable governing, policy-making institutions that command authority and legitimacy.[86] Of course, this also shows Russia's inability to devise an effective strategy for economic recovery and participation in Asia.

To the extent that this failure persists, the consequences for Russia are grave. Russia will then harvest only a fraction of the benefits of opening to Asia in general, and China in particular, but will incur much hostility from China and continue to incur hostility from Japan. Its economic and political reform pattern will stagnate, with grievous implications for domestic stability, that is, continuing long-term domestic political and economic crisis. Russia will then also be further marginalized in Asia and will be able to play only the military or the arms sales cards in the Sino-Russian poker game. If Sino-Russian relations fail to meet their economic potential, states are still seeking secure borders, and China needs high-tech arms, Russia and China will then share only a military agenda, with unforeseeable consequences for them and Asia.

Alternatively, if opposition from governors, local populations, and their allies in the Duma and the government can force a referendum on the issue of ceding Russian land and win, or if progress with China can be blocked, Sino-Russian relations would explode. Thus, Sino-Russian ties depend on Yeltsin's future ability to build viable state structures and policies and on local political emotions. While here, too, all politics is local, the implications for Asia are anything but.

Political and Military Relations

Despite concerns about Chinese aims, Russia has unreservedly opted against Japan and for China. The Security Council Concept Paper and the Defense Doctrine of November 1993 demonstrate both this choice and the prevalent viewpoint, consonant with China's, that sees security essentially in military and realpolitik terms. The concept paper denigrates Japan's largely economic power even as it claims that progress toward normalization is very important. This stress on military threats also downgrades Japan, economic power, and economic relationships in general.[87]

That the Security Council sees Japan and foreign investment in general as an economic threat to Russia reveals an inherent contradiction in the realpolitik view. Russian economic recovery is thereby precluded and its most promising region in terms of international economic integration condemned to being the very domestic colony that policy makers fear Russia will become.[88] Unfortunately, as noted above, the risks to domestic stability stemming from this strategy already loom large on the horizon.

As China poses the key potential threat to Russia in Asia, the current bilateral relationship is mutually beneficial because, for over a decade, both states have engaged in matching but unilateral disarmament on the border and a series of confidence-building measures, including redeployment away from the border and a redrawing of the boundary. While the border issues are highly technical and disputed, both governments support efforts to reduce tensions and establish mutual confidence-building measures (CBMS) in the borderlands. And these efforts are to be formalized in the treaty signed in March 1996 by China, Russia, Kyrgyzstan, Tajikistan, and Kazakhstan.

Nevertheless, Russia's current military policy also reflects some of the unresolved antimonies of this relationship. Except for Aleksei Arbatov, most analysts wrongly ignored the defense doctrine's implications for Russia's strategic posture in Asia. The doctrine displays the military's regained supremacy in making threat assessments and policy and reflects a decidedly one-sided approach to Russian security issues. Of particular relevance in Asia are statements about nuclear options, dangers, and threats to Russia. Those threats are

—territorial claims by other states on Russia;
—existing and potential local wars on Russia's borders;
—the possible use of weapons of mass destruction;
—the proliferation of nuclear and other weapons of mass destruction

and delivery systems and state-of-the-art production techniques in conjunction with certain states, organizations, and terrorists to fulfill their military and political aspirations;

- —threats to strategic stability by a violation of international arms treaties;
- —attempts to destabilize the Russian Federation or interfere in its internal affairs;
- —the suppression of the rights, freedom, and interests of Russian citizens in foreign states;
- —attacks on Russian military installations abroad; and
- —expansion of military blocs and alliances against the interests of Russia's security.[89]

Those dangers become threats when forces build up on Russia's borders to the point of disrupting the correlation of forces or of attacking installations and the border. Similarly, threats also appear when troops are trained in Russia or its allies' territory, actions are taken that hinder Russian strategic systems for supporting nuclear forces, state military C2s or, above all, their space component, and foreign troops are introduced without UN sanction into neighboring states.[90]

According to Russian doctrine, if command and control, nuclear, chemical, power, or electric installations are attacked, even by conventional weapons, Russia will consider first use of nuclear weapons. Russia will not use strategic systems against a nonnuclear party to the nonproliferation treaty of 1968 unless it participates as an ally with a state having nuclear weapons or carries out joint actions with that state to support an invasion of Russia's territory, armed forces, other troops, or allies.[91]

As Arbatov observes, these "nuclear-first" threats and the expansive definition of dangers and threats to Russia are, in Asia, clearly aimed at Japan, which is vulnerable to nuclear strikes, to which it would open itself merely by supporting purely conventional U.S. forces in operations against Russia. He also warns that this threat of a nuclear response, which supposedly also deterred China from theater conventional operations against Russia, was particularly threatening to China, which, alone among the nuclear states, publicly adheres to a no-first-use doctrine. If China grasped the doctrine's implicit threat and realized that Russia's nuclear strategy is directed against it, it could follow suit and revise its own doctrine. This is especially the case since its forces will be inferior to Russian and U.S. forces for the next decade. Nuclear containment in the Far East would then fail, or would be more likely to do so. But China can become a threat to Russia only if it keeps getting high-quality, Russian conventional weapons and technology.[92] Many Russian officers discount this possibility, even though it happened in the 1960s, and cite the nuclear nonaggression pact that Kozyrev negotiated in 1994.[93] But that pact and the earlier 1992 bilateral treaty with Beijing signified China's ability to gain leverage in Russian policy and amend the doctrine's implications.

Article 4 of the 1992 bilateral treaty stated, "Both parties will not participate in any form of political or military alliance which is directed against the other party, and will not conclude any form of treaty of agreement with a third country which jeopardizes the national sovereignty and the security interest of the respective other party; no party shall allow a third country to use its territory in a manner which threatens the national sovereignty and the national security interest of the other party."[94]

The nuclear nonaggression pact of 1994 corrects the loophole in Russia's nuclear doctrine and goes further along the lines of the 1992 treaty to state that neither side will attack, collude against, or use first strikes against the other.[95] But, although this policy upholds the nuclear-first scenarios and holds that China is the most important country both to deter and to maintain friendly relations with, it is inherently contradictory. Russian doctrine's expansive defense requirements against very broad threat assessments will not assure nonproliferation or strategic stability in Asia. But, taken in tandem with the priority of friendship with China and efforts to reduce U.S.-Japanese strategic superiority, those requirements already constrain Russian policy. U.S.-Japanese superiority is regarded as the main destabilizing factor in the Pacific to be removed, supposedly by collective security regimes there.[96] This is the only option open to Russia because it cannot afford a strategic naval and antisubmarine warfare (ASW) arms race with the United States. But the constant raising of such one-sided proposals only hinders Russia's integration into Asia. Furthermore, given the shifting balance of power, it is the stable U.S.-Japanese relationship that also deters China from thoughts of going north in the not-so-distant future, a fact that seems to be lost on Russian analysts.

Even if Russia could afford an arms race with the United States, any buildup of Russian antimissile, ASW, and air defense measures weakens the strategic equation with China and threatens to undo the positive achievements in Sino-Russian relations. Thus, collective security and U.S. disarmament to the Russian level — a self-evidently bad move for all Asia — becomes the only way Russia can see to assure security and strategic stability.[97]

Thus, the China-first policy leaves Russia without viable proposals for Asian security or its own strategic stability and also renders Russia's strategic force modernization hostage to China's future political and strategic developments. Nuclear force modernization is inhibited, lest it antagonize China. Precisely because too many elites remain fixated on strategic competition with the United States and Japan, Russia's Asian policy leads to a dead end.

Nor do close ties with China resolve Russia's problems with ethnic wars in Asia. Grachev's proposal for joint "policing" of Asia probably means some sort of condominium in Central Asia now and possibly sphere-of-influence peacemaking in future conflicts.[98] China wisely evaded this proposal because it chains Beijing to defending Moscow's interests and goes against the grain of Chinese unilateralism and flexibility. China will not pull Russian chestnuts out of the fire. But this proposal itself bespeaks Moscow's weakness across Asia because it made analogous diplomatic proposals to Turkmenistan, India, and Iran.[99] Here, too, refusal to work with Japan, dependence on China for all strategic goods in Asia, pursuit of an unsustainable hegemony over the Commonwealth of Independent States, and lack of control over the MOD are leading Russia's Asian and China policies into a dead end. The sheer strategic incoherence of Russian policy in Asia stems directly from its unsettled internal conditions and leads steadily to a Russia that is increasingly marginalized in Asia.

Conclusions

There are signs that some policy makers sense the problem. Kozyrev's last security proposals to ASEAN's annual Regional Forum in 1995 were seen as an effort to regain lost ground in Southeast Asia and limit China's growing influence.[100] The 1961 treaty with North Korea is also being renegotiated, and this may generate new policies. However, today Russian foreign policy from Bosnia to Korea manifests an undeniable sense of failure and incoherence. In China policy, as Sergei Blagovolin warned, Russia is in danger of becoming China's junior partner by virtue of its excessive closeness to China.[101] Although Russia's China policy derives from strategic and geographic realities, analysis of that policy nevertheless displays a state whose ability to plan, formulate, and implement national security policies is low and perhaps still declining. As Andrei Bouchkin also warned, Russian foreign policy in Asia is in danger of being captured by the military-industrial complex and essentially "privatized" despite the risks of building up a likely military-political rival.[102] Until and unless Russia overcomes its structural problems—and that it will do so is not a foregone conclusion—it will play an increasingly marginal global role. This is unhealthy for Russia, China, and other interested parties.

That is particularly true for the United States, even though U.S. Asian policy utterly marginalizes Russia's Asian position.[103] That policy drives Russia to China, making them both more anti-American and belligerent on a host of issues, with the baleful political, ideological, and military outcomes for both states suggested here. U.S. policy and Russia's marginalization create a vacuum in Asia. And, since nature abhors a vacuum, creating one in Russia's Asian position encourages Asia's overall insecurity.

Friendship with China is essential to Russian security on defense, economic, and political grounds. The problem today is that Moscow is leaning excessively toward China. This robs it of the flexibility it needs to realize its true interests in Asia. Russia need not have to choose between China and Japan to have security. Indeed, by doing so, it diminishes its security and flexibility, at home and abroad. Moreover, leading policy makers seem to believe that an alliance or a reciprocal spheres-of-influence deal with China or a joint collective security scheme such as Grachev prematurely proclaimed will safeguard Russian hegemony in the Commonwealth of Independent States and thus its position in Asia.[104] Nothing could be farther from the truth. Actually, even in Central Asia, China could become Russia's only real rival for influence.[105]

Therefore, Washington should consider launching a strategic initiative to broker Russo-Japanese normalization, thereby giving Russia options other than China and allowing Russia's internal forces to argue more freely for an Asian balance that benefits all Russian interests. This balance will somewhat restrain China's international truculence because Russia will have other options, as will the United States and other Asian states.

Precisely because the Sino-Russian bilateral relationship fundamentally shapes Asian international relations, it facilitates mutual cooperation against threats to common interests and security and induces India, Vietnam, and North Korea to draw closer to China. That is to everyone's benefit. But this relationship could also then restore Asian bipolarity. Russia is wrong to believe that it must frown on Tokyo to smile at Beijing. That belief locks Russia into a self-perpetuating cycle of enmity with Japan, excludes it from the explosive Asian-Pacific economy, and ties the rest of Asia into a bloc with the United States and Japan opposing Russia, China, and perhaps North Korea, in other words, a renewed bipolarity.

For Russia's recovery, bipolarity is contraindicated. Neither does it help Washington. China cannot assume the role that Japan must play in Russia's economic recovery. It engages Russia mainly in barter trade and is accused of sharp dealing and exchanging inferior goods for arms.[106] Nor does China seek Russia's economic restoration, and it is less able to invest in Russia than Japan and the West are. Too close ties to China prevent Russia from gaining strategic stability in Asia and contributing meaningfully to Asian security. Thus, Russia pays dearly for security in Asia.

Another consideration is that this relationship is at best a temporary marriage of convenience, given both sides' deep-rooted mutual ambivalence. That is especially true since China is now undergoing a profound leadership and political crisis. The closer Russia is to any one faction or government in China, the less it can extricate itself easily from unpredictable situations. Enmity may quickly replace amity.

Finally, the excessively close ties to China reinforce, in both states, the dominance over security policy of precisely those, like the defense industrialists and the military, who adhere to traditional positions that inhibit domestic reform and democracy. The longer this approach predominates, the longer Russia will find itself facing other states' permanent hostility, and the longer the democratization of China will be delayed. Furthermore, this vision of world politics relates directly to failed Russian reform and economic integration with Asia. Ties with China have profound global and domestic significance for Russia and should be built on a healthy domestic foundation. While Russo-Chinese friendship serves both states' and U.S. interests, Russia's "leaning to one side" and renewed Asian bipolarity, with China now in the driver's seat on the other side, serves nobody except both states' reactionaries and militarists. Unfortunately, as long as the foundation of Russian democracy is insccurc, and to the extent that it remains so, the structure of Russian, Asian, and U.S. security will be equally insecure.

Notes

The views expressed here do not in any way represent the views of the U.S. Army, the Department of Defense, or the U.S. government.

1 Stephen J. Blank, *Energy, Economics, and Security in Central Asia: Russia and Its Rivals* (Carlisle Barracks, Pa.: Strategic Studies Institute, U.S. Army War College, 1995), 26–30.

2 Yevgeny Afanasiev and Grigory Logvinov, "Russia and China: Girding for the Third Millennium," *International Affairs,* nos. 11–12 (November–December 1995): 46.

3 "Yeltsin Okays Russian Foreign Policy 'Concept,'" *Current Digest of the Post-Soviet Press* (hereafter *CDPP*), 26 May 1993, 14.

4 Ibid., 15.

5 "Expert on Nuclear Aspects of Military Doctrine," *Foreign Broadcast Information Service, Central Eurasia* (hereafter *FBIS/SOV*), 7 December 1993, 27–28.

6 Christoph Bluth, "The United States and Russia: Strategic Nuclear Forces and Arms Control after the Cold War," in *Brassey's Defence Yearbook, 1995* (London: Brassey's, 1995), 178.

7 Mikhail Titarenko, "China in the Post-Deng Epoch and Russo-Chinese Relations," *International Affairs,* no. 8 (August 1995): 24–33.

8 Vladimir Miasnikov, "Russia and China," in *Damage Limitation or Crisis: Russia and the Outside World,* ed. Robert D. Blackwill and Sergei A. Karaganov, Center for Science and International Affairs Studies no. 5 (Washington, D.C.: John F. Kennedy School of Government, Harvard University, and Brassey's, 1994), 232–33.

9 Report from Michael Shuster in Moscow, National Public Radio, 15 December 1992.

10 "Economist Interviewed on Sino-Russian Cooperation," *Foreign Broadcast Information Service, China* (hereafter *FBIS/CHI*), 24 May 1995, 11. More recently, in 1995 Yuri Skokov, head of the Nationalist party, Congress of Russian Communities (KRO), was invited by the Chinese Communist party to China and returned home urging an alliance with China that could become "the serious basis for a new world order, or, if you want, for the construction of the world of the future" (Sergei Grigoriev, "The China Card and Russian Roulette," *Perspective* 6, no. 2 [November–December 1995]: 1).
11 Interview with Admiral K. K. Nayyar, retired, of the Indian navy, Washington, D.C., August 1990.
12 Robert Legvold, "Russia and the Strategic Quadrangle," in *The Strategic Quadrangle: Russia, China, Japan, and the United States in East Asia,* ed. Michael Mandelbaum (New York: Council on Foreign Relations Press, 1995), 44–49; Miasnikov, "Russia and China," 231.
13 David Shambaugh, "China's Challenge to Asian Security," *Survival* 36, no. 2 (Summer 1994): 50–51. In March 1996, Russia, Kazakhstan, Kyrgyzstan, and Tajikistan signed a treaty demarcating their borders with China, a treaty that arose out of these negotiations.
14 The discussion on policy making is based on my own and several other analyses that come to similar conclusions: Stephen Blank, *Why Russian Policy Is Failing in Asia* (Carlisle Barracks, Pa.: Strategic Studies Institute, U.S. Army War College, in press); Suzanne Crow, *The Making of Foreign Policy in Russia under Yeltsin* (Munich and Washington, D.C.: Radio Free Europe/Radio Liberty, 1993), 4–12; Thomas L. Friedman, "Eyes on the Prize," *New York Times,* 10 May 1995, A24; Stephen Foye, "Whither Moscow? Domestic Politics and Russia's Assertive Diplomatic Posture," *Post-Soviet Prospects* (Center for Strategic and International Studies, Washington, D.C.) 3, no. 5 (May 1995): 3. For very valuable essays on this subject, see also Leon Aron, "The Emergent Priorities of Russian Foreign Policy," Charles H. Fairbanks Jr., "The Legacy of Soviet Policymaking in Creating a New Russia," and Mikhail E. Bezrukov, "Institutional Mechanisms of Russian Foreign Policy," all in *The Emergence of Russian Foreign Policy,* ed. Leon Aron and Kenneth M. Jensen (Washington, D.C.: U.S. Institute of Peace, 1994), 17–34, 51–66, and 67–77; and Jeffrey Checkel, "Structure, Institutions, and Process: Russia's Changing Foreign Policy," in *The Making of Foreign Policy in Russia and the New States of Eurasia,* ed. Adeed Dawisha and Karen Dawisha, Russian Littoral Project vol. 4 (Armonk, N.Y.: M. E. Sharpe, 1995), 42–65.
15 Li Jingjie, "China and Russia," in *Damage Limitation or Crisis,* 250.
16 Thus, in the communiqué of his 1995 visit to Russia, Chinese Prime Minister Li Peng pledged China's support for Russia's entry into APEC ("'Text' of Communique on Li Peng Visit Published," *FBIS/SOV,* 29 June 1995, 10).
17 Foye, "Whither Moscow?" 3; Crow, *Making of Foreign Policy,* 5.

18 "'Mystery' Surrounding Grachev PRC, ROK Trips," *FBIS/SOV,* 24 May 1995, 6–7; "Beijing Rejects Grachev's 'Alliance' Proposals," *CDPP,* 14 June 1995, 22.

19 Richard Boudreaux, "Russian Premier Takes Bold Step in Tackling Crisis," *Los Angeles Times* (Washington ed.), 20 June 1995, 1; Dmitri Simes, "Get over It! Yeltsin's in Charge!" *Washington Post* (weekly ed.), 20–26 March 1995, 23.

20 *FBIS/SOV,* 17 March 1995, 9–11.

21 Crow, *Making of Foreign Policy,* 7.

22 Foye, "Whither Moscow?" 2.

23 This term was coined by Rowland Evans and Robert Novak, "Yeltsin's New Friend," *Washington Post,* 5 January 1995, A29.

24 Alexander Zhebin, "Russia-DPRK Treaty: Is the Inherited Agreement Applicable?" *Northeast Asian Peace and Security Network Daily Report* (hereafter *NAPSNET Daily Report*), 17 August 1995. For an analysis of the divisions that still afflict Russian policy toward Korea, see Stephen Blank, *Russian Policy and the Korean Crisis* (Carlisle Barracks, Pa.: Strategic Studies Institute, U.S. Army War College, 1994).

25 Crow, *Making of Foreign Policy,* 5–6.

26 Michael McFaul virtually claims that interests alone and not ideas have become the stuff of the policy debate (Michael McFaul, "Revolutionary Ideas, State Interests, and Russian Foreign Policy," in *Political Culture and Civil Society in Russia and the New States of Eurasia,* ed. Vladimir Tismaneanu, The International Politics of Eurasia, vol. 7 [Armonk, N.Y.: M. E. Sharpe, 1995], 27–45). While this formulation seems excessive since interests are not articulated in an intellectual vacuum, it nonetheless astutely captures much of what has evolved since 1991.

27 For examples of this military participation in politics that appears to be a more general malady of incompletely democratized states, see Blank, *Russian Policy and the Korean Crisis,* 6–10. See also Edward D. Mansfield and Jack Snyder, "Democratization and War," *Foreign Affairs* 74, no. 3 (May–June 1995): 79–97.

28 Michael Dobbs, "Kozyrev Portrays Stance as Benign to Ensure U.S. Support," *Washington Post,* 30 April 1995, A28.

29 Crow, *Making of Foreign Policy,* 49–50.

30 Blank, *Russian Policy and the Korean Crisis,* 6–10.

31 "Yeltsin Annual Message to Federal Assembly," *FBIS/SOV,* 21 February 1995, 10.

32 *FBIS/SOV,* 7 February 1995, 3–4, and 9 June 1995, 38–39.

33 Susan L. Clark and David R. Graham, "The Russian Federation's Fight for Survival," *Orbis* 39, no. 3 (Summer 1995): 329–51; *FBIS/SOV,* 13 April 1995, 12–14.

34 Sergei Strokan, "Siberian Discontent," *Moscow News,* no. 16, 28 April–4 May 1995, 3; Peter Kirkow and Philip Hanson, "The Potential for Autonomous Re-

gional Development in Russia: The Case of Primorskiy Krai," *Post-Soviet Geography* 25, no. 2 (1994): 63–88; Vladimir Todres, "Bashkortostan Seeks Sovereignty—Step by Step," *Transition* 1, no. 7 (12 May 1995): 56–59.

35 Allen Lynch, "Politics without Government," *Transition, 1994 in Review* (Open Media Research Institute, Prague), pt. 2 (1995): 3.

36 Private communication from Jacques Sapir based on his research on Russian economic conditions in the Far East.

37 *FBIS/SOV,* 13 April 1995, 13.

38 Paul Goble ("Regions, Republics and Russian Reform: Center-Periphery Relations in the Russian Federation," in *The Successor States to the USSR,* ed. John W. Blaney [Washington, D.C.: Congressional Quarterly Press, 1995], 77–87) all but proclaims the death of the Russian state in making these charges.

39 Ibid., 82; Kirkow and Hanson, "Autonomous Regional Development," 63–88. It is not surprising that the Far East voted heavily for the Communists and Vladimir Zhirinovsky's Liberal-Democratic party in the parliamentary elections of December 1995. Nor is it surprising that, during the presidential campaign of 1996, Yeltsin ordered the government to remit to Primorskii Krai emergency credits guaranteed by the Finance Ministry and settling the debts of the entire federally funded sector, including the defense industry. Nazdratenko announced that the budgetary debt to his province totals 1,270 billion rubles and that decrees paying this debt going back to 1994 have not been fulfilled. According to the newspaper report of Nazdratenko's meeting with Yeltsin: "During the meeting, it was agreed that practical measures should be taken to resolve the difficult economic situation in the Far East. The political situation in the country and the upcoming presidential election were also discussed" (*Kommersant-Daily* [Moscow], 25 January 1996, translated in *Foreign Broadcast Information Service, Arms Control* [hereafter *FBIS/TAC*], 8 February 1996, 63).

40 According to recent reports, from 1991 to 1994 (the last full year for which we have data) China purchased from $4.5 to $6 billion in weapons and military equipment from Russia (Bates Gill and Taeho Kim, *China's Arms Acquisitions from Abroad: A Quest for "Superb and Secret Weapons,"* SIPRI Research Report no. 11 [Oxford: Oxford University Press, 1995], 59–70).

41 Tai Ming Cheung, "China's Buying Spree," *Far Eastern Economic Review,* 8 July 1993, 24–25. Since then, China has increased its interests in offsets and acquiring indigenous production capability, and Russian officials like Deputy Prime Minister Oleg Soskovets are arguing in favor of transferring technology and production capability to China (*Open Media Research Institute, Daily Report* [hereafter *OMRI Daily Report*], 26 July 1995).

42 *OMRI Daily Report,* 7 February 1996; *Jane's Defence Weekly,* 14 February 1996, 12. This pattern of Soviet/Russian negotiators acceding to China's preferences rather than their own was already set under Gorbachev, who overruled his military negotiators and dismissed their concerns about China's potential use of the initial SU-27s in 1990–91. His rationale was the political gains to be had from

the relationship with China. This pattern of "squeezing technology out of its trade partner" appears to be part of a broader pattern of Chinese arms-purchasing policy. (Tai Ming Cheung, "Ties of Convenience: Sino-Soviet/Russian Military Relations in the 1990s," in *China's Military: The PLA in 1992/1993,* ed. Richard H. Yang [Taipei: Chinese Council of Advanced Policy Studies, 1994], 65–66; Nigel Holloway, "Playing for Keeps," and Nayan Chanda, "Nervous Neighbors," both in *Far Eastern Economic Review,* 8 February 1996, 14–16).

43 Kuzmenko was cited in William Van Cleave et al., "U.S.-C.I.S. Relations in a Changing Global Environment," *Global Affairs* 7, no. 3 (Summer 1993): 116.

44 Anton Zhigulsky, "Russian Firms Get Approval to Export," *Defense News,* 17–23 July 1995, 1, 29; *Monitor,* 29 February 1996.

45 *FBIS/SOV,* 18 December 1992, 9.

46 Ibid., 15 December 1992, 13–15.

47 Pavel Felgenhauer, "Russia's Arms Sales Lobbies," *Perspective* 5, no. 1 (September–October 1994): 1, 7–8; *FBIS/SOV,* 17 April 1995, 11, 4 May 1995, 26, 5 May 1995, 27–28, and 11 May 1995, 40–41.

48 Stephen Blank, *Challenging the New World Order: The Arms Transfer Policies of the Russian Republic* (Carlisle Barracks, Pa.: Strategic Studies Institute, U.S. Army War College, 1993), 8–33.

49 *FBIS/SOV,* 21 April 1995, 40.

50 Ibid., 24 April 1995, 16.

51 Blank, *Challenging the New World Order,* 11–25.

52 Felgenhauer, "Russia's Arms Sales Lobbies," 7.

53 "Russian Defence Sales: The Insiders' View," *Military Technology* 8 (December 1993): 44–45.

54 Bill Gertz, "Russia Sells Rocket Motors to China," *Washington Times,* 13 February 1995, 4.

55 "Russia's Asian Arms Sales Onslaught," *International Defense Review,* May 1994, 49; *Joint Publications Research Service, Military Affairs* (hereafter *JPRS/UMA*), 1 July 1992, 5.

56 *Kommersant-Daily,* 7 February 1996; *FBIS/SOV,* 8 February 1996, 19–20.

57 *JPRS/UMA,* 12 October 1994, 45.

58 *FBIS/SOV,* 14 July 1994, 7.

59 *JPRS/UMA,* 6 June 1995, 22.

60 *FBIS/SOV,* 13 March 1995, 14.

61 Brooks Tigner, "Experts: Conversion Threatens Eastern Security," *Defense News,* 11–17 July 1994, 8.

62 Gill and Kim, *China's Arms Acquisitions,* 59–70.

63 *Lien Ho Pao* (Hong Kong), 30 July 1995, translated in *FBIS/CHI,* 29 August 1995, 33–34.

64 *China's Arms Acquisitions,* Gill and Kim, 59–70; Tai Ming Cheung, "China's Regional Military Posture," *International Defense Review,* June 1991, 618–22; Keith Jacobs, "China's Military Modernization and the South China Sea," *Jane's*

Intelligence Review 4, no. 6 (June 1992): 278–81; Paul H. B. Godwin, "Chinese Military Strategy Revised: Local and Limited War," *Annals of the American Academy of Political and Social Sciences,* no. 519 (January 1992): 191–201; A. James Gregor, "The People's Liberation Army and China's Crisis," *Armed Forces and Society* 10, no. 1 (Fall 1991): 7–28; "China's Shadow over Southeast Asian Waters," *Global Affairs* 7, no. 3 (Summer 1992): 1–13; Zhao Xiaowei, "The Threat of a New Arms Race Dominates Asian Geopolitics," *Global Affairs* 7, no. 3 (Summer 1992): 29–40; "Notes on Chinese Visit to Observe Far East Exercises," *JPRS/UMA,* 19 May 1993, 59–64.

65 Glen E. Howard, "MiGs and Mandarins: Russo-Chinese Security Relations and the Soviet Demise" (1993, typescript).

66 Ibid.; Tai Ming Cheung, "Quick Response," *Far Eastern Economic Review,* 14 January 1993, 19–21.

67 *FBIS/SOV,* 13 January 1993, 16–17.

68 "Russia's Arms Sales Onslaught," 49.

69 Blank, *Challenging the New World Order,* 56.

70 "Chinese Frighten Japanese with Russian-Made Weapons," *CDPP,* 25 October 1995, 23–24.

71 Jim Mann, "China Seeks Russian Weapons," *Los Angeles Times,* 12 July 1992, 1.

72 *FBIS/SOV,* 26 July 1993, 2–3.

73 Ibid., 1 August 1995, 8–9.

74 *FBIS/SOV,* 28 June 1995, 9.

75 Ibid., 30 June 1995, 9–10.

76 Sergei Manezhev, *The Russian Far East* (London: Post-Soviet Business Forum, Royal Institute of International Affairs, 1993), 34–35; Pavel A. Minakir, "Economic Development in Russia and the Russian Far East," in *Proceedings of the Seminar: Integrating the Russian Far East into the Asia-Pacific Economy, October 20–22, 1994,* ed. Tsuneo Akaha (Monterey, Calif.: Center for East Asian Studies, Monterey Institute of International Studies, 1995), 55.

77 Ibid.

78 *Monitor,* 25 August 1995.

79 Manezhev, *The Russian Far East,* 34; *FBIS/SOV,* 27 July 1995, 9–10.

80 Ronald C. Keith, "The Post–Cold War Political Symmetry of Russo-Chinese Bilateralism," *International Journal* 49, no. 4 (Autumn 1994): 783.

81 *FBIS/CHI,* 5 July 1995, 12–13. It is noteworthy that this article appeared in *Renmin Ribao,* the official paper of the Chinese government.

82 *FBIS/SOV,* 14 March 1995, 18.

83 "China," *CDPP,* 8 March 1995, 29. For the concept of a two-level game, see Robert D. Putnam, "Diplomacy and Domestic Politics: The Logic of Two-Level Games," in *Double-Edged Diplomacy: International Bargaining and Domestic Politics,* ed. Peter B. Evans, Harold K. Jacobson, and Robert D. Putnam (Berkeley and Los Angeles: University of California Press, 1993), 431–68.

84 Gaye Christoffersen, "Cooperation under Anarchy on the Sino-Russian Border" (1994, typescript), 30.
85 Ibid.; James Clay Moltz, "Regional Tensions in the Russo-Chinese Rapprochement," *Asian Survey* 35, no. 6 (June 1995): 511–27.
86 Gaye Christoffersen, "The Greater Vladivostok Project: Transnational Linkages in Regional Economic Planning," *Pacific Affairs* 67, no. 4 (Winter 1995): 531.
87 "Yeltsin Okays Russian Foreign Policy 'Concept,'" 14.
88 Ibid., 15.
89 "Osnovnye Polozheniia Voennoi Doktriny Rossiiskoi Federatsii," *Rossiyskie vesti,* 19 November 1993, 1–8.
90 Ibid.
91 Ibid.
92 "Expert on Nuclear Aspects of Military Doctrine," 27–28.
93 Sergei Blagovolin, "Some Aspects of Russian Strategy in the Asia-Pacific Region," in *Asia in the 21st Century: Evolving Strategic Priorities,* ed. Michael D. Bellows (Washington, D.C.: National Defense University Press, 1994), 52; Andrei Bouchkin, presentation to the Russian Littoral Project (Washington, D.C., 7 March 1994), and "Russia's Far Eastern Policy in the 1990s: Priorities and Prospects," in *The Making of Foreign Policy in Russia,* 70–71.
94 Xuewu Gu, "China's Policy toward Russia," *Aussenpolitik* (English ed.), no. 3 (1993): 293.
95 "Foreign Ministers Discuss Cooperation," *FBIS/CHI,* 27 January 1994, 10–11.
96 Stephen Blank, "The New Russia in the New Asia," *International Journal* 49, no. 4 (Autumn 1994): 874–906; Naoaki Usui, "Russia, Japan Seek Stronger Ties," *Defense News,* 7–13 March 1994, 11.
97 Major General A. B. Bolyatko (Ret.), "O Reglamentatsii Operativnoi Deiatel'nosti Strategicheskikh Sil'," *Voennaya Mysl',* no. 7 (July–August 1994): 10, and "Voenno-Politicheskaia Situatsiia i Problemy Formirovaniia Novoi Struktury Bezopasnosti v Severo-Vostochnoi Azii," *Voennaya Mysl',* no. 2 (February 1994): 6–11.
98 "'Mystery' Surrounding Grachev PRC, ROK Trips," 6–7; "Beijing Rejects Grachev's 'Alliance' Proposals," 22.
99 "Turkmenistan," *CDPP,* 14 June 1995, 19; *FBIS/SOV,* 26 June 1995, 88; "Russia Willing to Cooperate on Inter-Tajik Issue," *FBIS/SOV,* 22 August 1994, 14; "Russian Call for Cooperation on Tajikistan Noted" and "Kozyrev Letter Received," *Foreign Broadcast Information Service, Near East and South Asia* (hereafter *FBIS/NES*), 22 August 1994, 52–53.
100 *Bangkok Times,* 1 August 1995, reprinted in *Foreign Broadcast Information Service, East Asia* (hereafter *FBIS/EAS*), 2 August 1995, 4–5; ITAR-TASS (Moscow), 22 December 1995, reprinted in *FBIS/SOV,* 26 December 1995, 10.
101 Blagovolin, "Some Aspects of Russian Strategy," 52. Some go even farther.

Alexander Nemets recently stated that the trend in Sino-Russian relations is leading to Moscow's acceptance of a Chinese economic sphere of influence in Russia east of the Urals: "The main conclusion to be made from the materials given in this work, is as follows: one, rapidly rising super power (in far perspective, super empire) is establishing control, at least in economic aspect, over the large and most part of another, destroyed, broken into pieces, former super empire" (Alexander Nemets, *The Growth of China and Prospects for the Eastern Regions of the Former USSR* [Lewiston: Edwin Mellen Press, 1996], 95). These are his conclusions; the argument runs throughout the book.

102 Bouchkin, "Russia's Far Eastern Policy," 70–73.

103 Vladimir I. Ivanov, "Russia and the United States in Northeast Asia and the Russian Far East: Economics or Defense" (in *Proceedings of the Seminar,* 121–24) is the most recent compilation of sources showing U.S. disregard for Russia in Asia.

104 "'Mystery' Surrounding Grachev PRC, ROK Trips," 6–7; "Beijing Rejects Grachev's 'Alliance' Proposals," 22.

105 Blank, "Energy, Economics, and Security in Central Asia," 26–30.

106 "MFA Official, Commentary Assess Chinese-Russian Relations," *Foreign Broadcast Information Service, Central Eurasia, FBIS Report,* 16 February 1994, 36.

BRUCE A. ELLEMAN

Russian Foreign Policy in the Chinese Context

The 9 January 1996 announcement that Yevgeny Primakov had been selected to be Russia's new minister of foreign affairs further undermined the pro-Western policies that Andrei Kozyrev had championed during most of his five-year tenure as foreign minister. On the following day, Primakov unequivocally stated that his top priorities included reuniting the CIS states and strengthening ties with Russia's eastern neighbors, specifically China, Japan, India, and the countries of the Middle East. The goal of Primakov's new Eurasian foreign policy is to distance Russia from the West by carving out its unique niche as the economic and political intermediary between Europe and Asia.

At the heart of Russia's new Eurasian foreign policy is China. The dissolution of the Soviet Union in 1991 provided Beijing with an unexpected opportunity to extend China's economic and political influence throughout Northeast Asia. This region includes not only the vast territories adjoining the lengthy Russo-Chinese border but also the newly democratized government of Mongolia, formerly a Soviet puppet state. During the past five years, commerce along the Russo-Chinese border has already been dominated by China, while Mongolia's bilateral trade with China has mushroomed. In economic terms, therefore, a huge swath of Northeast Asia has already shifted from Russia's sphere of interest to China's.

In political terms, however, this picture is far less clear. Although Moscow has conducted a series of border talks with Beijing, attempts to delimit Russia's borders with China have stalled. In fact, the final demarcation, based on a treaty announced with great fanfare in September 1994 and finally ratified on 5 July 1995, has largely bogged down. Russian provincial governments throughout Siberia have protested these Russo-Chinese border treaties and have taken measures to ensure that the boundary does not change. For example, in a direct return to imperial traditions, Cossacks have been sent to live in disputed territories in the Maritime Province, thus ensuring that China will not be able to assume control. Furthermore, on 17 October 1995, Russian and Chinese negotiators acknowledged that their dispute over certain sections of the border—most notably three islands in the Amur and Argun Rivers—was irreconcilable, leaving to "future generations" the final demarcation of the Russo-Chinese border.[1]

Moscow has also continued to sponsor close diplomatic relations with Mongolia, while Ulan Bator, faced with an ever-weakening Russia to the north, in sharp contrast to a rapidly growing China to the south, has attempted to achieve a delicate balance with its immediate neighbors by turning to the United States for help. Washington has provided wholehearted support, sponsoring increased Mongol-American trade, joint ventures, and high-level diplomatic contacts. Hillary Rodham Clinton's visit to Ulan Bator during September 1995 highlighted the importance that the State Department attaches to Mongolian independence. U.S. efforts to back Mongolia's fledgling democracy might eventually sour Sino-American relations, however, should China ever attempt to increase its political influence over Mongolia.

Meanwhile, Mongolia's attempts to open relations with Taiwan have complicated the resumption of official Sino-Mongolian relations. In 1991, Taiwan's president, Li Teng-hui, offered to recognize Mongolia's independence. This proposal repeated an offer first made by the Nationalists in 1946 but later renounced in 1952, after which Taiwanese maps once again included Mongolia as an integral part of China. To counter Taipei, Beijing apparently resorted to its nuclear card: on 30 April 1994, Premier Li Peng publicly announced that the People's Republic of China (PRC) would never use nuclear weapons against Mongolia. In return, Ulan Bator was forced to acknowledge that Beijing was the only legitimate Chinese government and promised never to open diplomatic relations with Taipei.[2]

Finally, Moscow's decision to increase its sales of advanced military equipment to China, including SU-27 jets and Kilo-class diesel submarines, has dramatically increased China's ability to threaten Taiwan. This issue, in conjunction with sharp differences over trade and human rights, has further complicated Washington's relations with Beijing. On

26 June 1995, Prime Minister Viktor Chernomyrdin and Premier Li Peng jointly criticized outside—presumably American—interference in the two countries' domestic affairs.[3] Yevgeny Primakov's adoption of a stronger Eurasian foreign policy, a policy that might even lead to the formation of a Russo-Chinese alliance, will undoubtedly exert even greater diplomatic pressure on Washington policy makers.

The essay will attempt to provide historical background on the recent changes in Russia's foreign policy; identify the most important Russo-Chinese geostrategic tensions in northeast Asia; review economic and political developments that could affect Russo-Chinese relations; evaluate the U.S. role in Mongolia; and assess the possible future effect of a Russo-Chinese alliance on Sino-U.S. relations.

This essay will conclude by offering four possible scenarios. The first proposes an aggressive Beijing that decides to reconquer those areas stripped from China by imperial Russia and the Soviet Union. The second postulates an aggressive Russia that once again adopts an expansionist foreign policy in Northeast Asia. The third suggests what might happen were Siberia to carry out its threats to secede from Russia. Finally, the fourth, and perhaps the most important, scenario will assess the effect on Washington should increasing cooperation between Moscow and Beijing—either real or merely perceived—lead to an anti-Western Russo-Chinese alliance.

The Evolution of Russia's Foreign Policy in Asia

Since 1991, Russia's foreign policy has shifted from an actively pro-Western to a mixed policy that can most aptly be called Eurasian. During most of his five years as foreign minister, Andrei Kozyrev supported a close strategic partnership with the United States; this was perhaps most clearly shown during the Persian Gulf War, when Russia refused to take the side of its former ally, Saddam Hussein. But, spurred by disagreements with the West over Bosnia and NATO expansion as well as by domestic accusations that Moscow was ignoring Russia's national interests in the Far East, Yeltsin agreed to replace Kozyrev and stated on 29 December 1995 that his government would support a "balanced" foreign policy with the East as well as the West. Only two weeks later,

Yeltsin's handpicked replacement for Kozyrev, Yevgeny Primakov, went on to announce that Moscow's Eurasian goals included strengthening ties with China, Japan, and India as well as the Middle East.

Primakov, formerly head of the Oriental Studies Institute of the Soviet Academy of Sciences and deputy head of the Institute of International Economy and International Relations, was one of the most accomplished Asian specialists in the Soviet era. During the fall of 1991, Primakov was appointed by Mikhail Gorbachev to be the director of the Russian Foreign Intelligence Service, the successor to the KGB, and was retained in this post by President Boris Yeltsin in December 1991. Primakov demonstrated his opposition to the CIS states' national self-determination in September 1994 when he publicly argued that the future reintegration of the Soviet Union was "inevitable and consistent with Russian national interests."[4] From an early period, Primakov also advocated paying more attention to Russia's national interests in Asia and the Middle East.

Primakov's decision to emphasize Russia's historic relations with China should not be viewed as an entirely new and unique policy: during the 1920s, with its foreign policy toward Europe also in shambles, the Soviet Union turned to Asia and promoted close relations with China.[5] Although the Soviet Union's attempt to foment a socialist revolution in China suffered a dramatic defeat in 1927, the Chinese Communist movement, which was set up with Moscow's assistance during 1921, eventually came to power in China in 1949 and produced a second period of Sino-Soviet alliance. Primakov's background as an Asian expert has undoubtedly convinced him that Russia can play a major, if not a leading, role in the Far East.

Primakov clearly does not stand alone with this opinion. Following the announcement of Primakov's nomination as foreign minister, Gennady Zyuganov, leader of the Communist party of the Russian Federation, praised Primakov's appointment for demonstrating that Yeltsin was making "open political efforts to protect Russia's national interests which were sacrificed to enemies of our state"; meanwhile, the ultranationalist leader, Vladimir Zhirinovsky, vocally predicted that Primakov would "turn Russia's foreign policy toward the Arab world, India, and China."[6]

In fact, signs suggesting a major shift toward Asia were soon apparent. For example, Primakov's deputy foreign minister, Boris Pastukhov, is well known as the former Soviet ambassador to Afghanistan from 1989 to 1992.[7] Perhaps even more important was the rapid announcement that Primakov's replacement as head of the Russian Foreign Intelligence Service would be Vyacheslav Trubnikov. According to news reports, Trubnikov is also an "Asian specialist who speaks Hindi and English."[8]

Russian foreign policy is experiencing a shift toward Asia. China will undoubtedly be tempted to exploit this circumstance by adopting more friendly relations with Russia in order to exert pressure on the United States to back down on a wide range of issues, including U.S. diplomatic support for Taiwan, condemnation of Chinese human rights violations, and criticism of China's heavy-handed policies in Tibet, to name just a few. To Russia, a temporary diplomatic alliance with China would also be tempting since it would strengthen Moscow's weak hand vis-à-vis the West. But the major stumbling blocks to this alliance are the tense political disputes over the Russo-Chinese border and over Mongolia, two issues that will be discussed in greater detail below.

Russo-Chinese Border Negotiations

Fundamental disagreement over the location of the Russo-Chinese border has festered for over a century, ever since imperial Russia forced China to sign a series of treaties ceding it vast territories. According to the most definitive book on this topic: "For China, the physical territorial losses were enormous: an area exceeding that of the United States east of the Mississippi River officially became Russian territory or, in the case of Outer Mongolia, a Soviet protectorate."[9] Therefore, it should come as no surprise that the September 1994 announcement of what was then touted to be the definitive Russo-Chinese border treaty seemed overly optimistic. In fact, since the signing, the actual demarcation of the new Russo-Chinese border has deadlocked, leaving to "future generations" decisions on the most divisive sections of the border.

During the early 1990s, Sino-Soviet border negotiations had progressed to the point that, on 16 May 1991, the two countries signed an agreement detailing most of the eastern section of the border adjoining Russia's Maritime Province. This treaty was subsequently ratified by the

Russian parliament in 1992, and three islands seized by the Soviet Union during the mid-1930s were returned to China. During February 1994, however, it was reported that border negotiations on sections further west had bogged down over the status of several strategic islands in the Amur River, located not far from Khabarovsk. China agreed to allow Russian farmers to continue cultivating the land until a final settlement was reached.

In early September 1994, Jiang Zemin, chairman of the People's Republic of China and general secretary of the Chinese Communist party Central Committee, visited Russia. At this time, a second treaty was signed demarcating the western section of the border. Although Moscow publicly announced that 99 percent of the far western section of the border had been settled, it conceded that disputes still existed over several islands near Khabarovsk as well as over another island in the Argun River. By adopting a policy known as a "border with holes," Russia hoped that these final disputes could be resolved gradually, thus allowing for the treaty on the eastern sector to come fully into effect.

It is important to note that these Russo-Chinese treaties called for the complete demarcation of the border by 1997. However, the process of surveying and marking the Russian side of the border bogged down, owing mainly to local leaders in Siberia, who have protested against the treaty and refused to abide by its terms. Most important, on 10 February 1995, it was reported that Yevgeny Nazdratenko, the governor of the Maritime Province, publicly denounced Russia's border treaties with China. Specifically, Nazdratenko accused Moscow of signing treaties that ceded Russian territory in the Khanka, Ussuri, and Khasan districts to China.

By March 1995, virtually all the Far Eastern and Transbaikal members of the Russian Federation had joined Nazdratenko in denouncing the new borders. These local officials even went so far as to accuse Foreign Minister Kozyrev of supporting "antistate activity."[10] In addition, the Far Eastern and Transbaikal military districts voiced their opposition to ceding several hundred strategic islands. Finally, Anatoli Dolgolaptev, the deputy speaker of the Council of the Russian Federation, claimed that the new borders with China were unfair to Russia.

In a notable return to imperial Russian practices, in March 1995, Nazdratenko took matters into his own hands, ordering that all Chinese traders and laborers should be expelled from Vladivostok. Soon afterward, in May 1995, Nazdratenko put disputed territory near the town of Khasan under the control of local Cossacks.[11] This was a risky move since the 1991 Sino-Soviet treaty apparently stated that this area, located about seventy miles southwest of Vladivostok, was to be turned over to China. Although the survey of the final segment of disputed territory in the Maritime Province was completed on 30 November 1995, Nazdratenko has publicly denounced Russia's transfer of almost four thousand acres to China and reportedly plans to use this border dispute as a central issue during his 1996 reelection campaign.[12]

Moscow was clearly concerned that interference by local governors might eventually lead to a resumption of Russo-Chinese border tensions. Therefore, Moscow worked hard to silence local Siberian authorities. As early as September 1994, Vladimir Lukin, chairman of the state Duma's Committee on International Affairs, cautioned that Moscow had to resolve "the strange attempts of some members of the Russian Federation to conduct their own 'China policy.'"[13] In February 1995, Deputy Foreign Minister Aleksandr Panov further warned these local leaders that this issue might cause Russo-Chinese relations to "explode" once Beijing's patience ran out.[14]

Meanwhile, Sergei Rogov, former deputy director of the Institute of the USA and Canada, stressed the overwhelming importance of the Far East. In a lengthy article published in late 1994, Rogov presented a startling reversal of the Soviet Union's earlier cold war strategic objectives: he argued that while the primary Russian sphere of interest must remain the Commonwealth of Independent States, the next area of importance was the Far East, followed, in descending order of importance, by the Middle East, Eastern Europe, and only then the West.[15]

Although Rogov may have been expressing only his own views, other important Russian leaders appeared to agree with him. For example, in an interview published on 14 March 1995, Lukin emphasized the importance of the Russo-Chinese border: "I just visited the border with China, and it's a calm border, thank God. So long as our mighty local politicians don't turn it into a conflict-ridden border. But there too, the border troops find themselves in a very serious situation: They are underpaid and are being disbanded—even very strong units, including aviation. The border is becoming symbolic. And this is no laughing matter."[16] The 25–31 May 1995 issue of *Obshchaya gazeta* also warned that, although China would never dare attack a unified Russia, "anything can happen if the Far East becomes a separate and independent entity."[17]

During an April 1995 trip to China, Andrei Kozyrev reassured Beijing that Moscow would stand by its treaties. On 5 July 1995, Russia's Federation Council finally ratified the September 1994 treaty. But, on 17 October 1995, it was reported that, because China and Russia could not agree on sovereignty over three islands in the Amur and Argun Rivers, they had decided that these issues would be put aside and decided later. Although Moscow and Beijing declared that the process of demarcating the border was now complete, clearly this was an attempt to save face.

Perhaps Beijing did not publicly protest Russia's refusal to return these three islands to China because it hoped to discourage Moscow from taking a firm stand on the equally complicated issue of Chinese immigration into Siberia. In this matter, Chinese controls are clearly lax, as shown by a February 1994 report estimating that as many as two million Chinese were living, many illegally, in Russia.[18] Later, an article published during February 1995 warned that this number might even be closer to five million.[19] Chinese immigrants already outnumber ethnic Russians in some areas in the Russian Far East.

For some time, the Russian government has been threatening to take action against these illegal Chinese aliens. In September 1994, Lukin stated that one of the most important problems facing the Russian Far East was "the illegal 'squatting' on our territory of an as yet undetermined number of Chinese citizens."[20] On 1 March 1995, the Interfax news agency reported that more than one thousand Chinese citizens had been expelled from Russia because they had counterfeit passports or expired visas.[21] Finally, on 23 August 1995, Russia and China signed a border-policing agreement that clamped down on illegal immigration. But the Russian defense minister, Pavel Grachev, was still quoted as warning: "Persons of Chinese nationality are trying to conquer the Russian Far East by peaceful means."[22]

Although the large number of illegal Chinese aliens in Siberia gives Russia some political leverage with China, it may also offer Beijing a pretext for demanding more border concessions in the future. This possibility was raised at the October 1994 Pacific Rim Forum by Andrei Maximov, president of the Moscow-based East Consultancy Company. According to Maximov: "The settling of Chinese on Russian territory in the immediate proximity of the border with China may serve as an extra argument for confronting Russia with appropriate territorial claims."[23] Thus, the enormous flow of Chinese immigrants into Russia's Far East may eventually work to China's advantage.

Beijing may also be hesitant to raise territorial issues too directly because of the enormous success of its economic policies along the border. Beginning in the late 1980s, China has tried to develop a series of "open belts" in the border regions like its coastal trade zones. Inner Mongolia represents one such belt. From 1985 to 1990, its trade with Mongolia and Eastern European nations jumped sevenfold from $27,500,000 to $186,400,000.[24] As for bilateral trade between Russia and China, this hit a high of $7.8 billion in 1993, mainly as a result of small-scale trade along the border regions.[25]

Thereafter, when Beijing began to expand cross-border highways with all fifteen of its neighbors in the early 1990s, it focused on building roads to Russia, Mongolia, Kazakhstan, and Kyrgyzstan.[26] During Beijing's 1994 negotiations with Uzbekistan, Prime Minister Li Peng specifically stressed the need for a "new Silk Road" between China and the Central Asian states.[27] Border tensions would undermine this lucrative trade and would also inhibit the rapidly growing commercial dependence on Chinese goods throughout the border regions. This growth is taking place primarily at Moscow's expense.[28]

In the foreseeable future, the border will continue to be at the center of China's relations with Russia. Although both countries may claim in public that the Russo-Chinese border has been settled, in fact, Beijing and Moscow have merely agreed to disagree. Moreover, Beijing knows that its economic and demographic position in Siberia is continuing to strengthen every year. For this reason, it can afford to wait and reap future benefits from these economic and demographic trends. Conversely, Russians fear these trends but feel powerless to stop them.[29] For all practical purposes, therefore, the Russo-Chinese border regions have already shifted away from Russia and are well on their way to becoming integrated into China's sphere of economic, if not political, influence.

Russo-Chinese Relations and Mongolia

For a whole variety of reasons, Mongolia threatens to become the most divisive issue in Russo-Chinese relations. Not only do many Chinese still consider czarist Russia's and the Soviet Union's efforts to separate Mongolia from China to be imperialistic, but, during the early 1940s, the Soviet Union's secret diplomacy with Japan led to extensive changes in Mongolia's southern and eastern borders at China's expense. Aware of its precarious position as a buffer between a declining Russian empire to the north and a strengthening Chinese empire to the south, the Mongolian government has advocated an "open door" policy to form closer diplomatic ties with Western countries, most notably the United States. When Taiwan offered to recognize Mongolia, however, the People's Republic compelled Mongolia to renege.

In order to understand Mongolia's contemporary importance, it is helpful to know how Russia took Mongolia from China. In 1915, imperial Russia, Outer Mongolia, and China signed a tripartite treaty by which Outer Mongolia recognized the *suzerainty* of China in exchange for Chinese recognition of Outer Mongolia's *autonomy*. Even though Moscow publicly renounced Russian imperialism in 1919, Soviet diplomats signed a secret agreement with China during 1924 that reaffirmed the terms of this treaty.[30] From 1924 to 1945, the Soviet Union guaranteed Outer Mongolia's autonomy from China by claiming that the terms of the 1915 unequal treaty were still valid. This made possible the formation of the Mongolian People's Republic (MPR) on 25 November 1924, when a socialist constitution was adopted and the name of the capital was changed from Urga to Ulan Bator.

During the 1930s, the Mongolian People's Republic underwent a long period of political purges, linking it more firmly to the Soviet Union. The Mongolian historian Dorjnamjiliin Tod has estimated that, "by 1940, 35,000 people were purged and 20,000 executed" and that, from 1930 to 1934, more than twenty thousand Mongolians fled the country.[31] Similarly, Mongolia's secret service, patterned after the Soviet NKVD and called the State Security Organization, was purged during the 1930s. It has been estimated that 57 percent of all of its ministers, 100 percent of all vice ministers, 60 percent of department chiefs, and over 20 percent of officers were executed.[32]

During the early 1940s, the Soviet Union and Japan conducted secret negotiations to define their spheres of interest in Northeast Asia. These talks led to the Soviet-Japanese nonaggression pact of 13 April 1941. This pact also stipulated that a mixed commission would redraw Mongolia's border with the Japanese puppet state of Manchukuo, which resulted in territorial gains for the Mongolian People's Republic at the expense of Manchukuo.[33] Although the Soviet Union denounced this pact on 5 April 1945, Mongolia retained all new territories instead of returning them to China.

Until 1945, Soviet diplomats publicly recognized that Outer Mongolia remained an integral part of China. During Sino-Soviet negotiations held in 1945, Stalin not only obtained China's official recognition of the Soviet Union's sphere of interest in Mongolia but also retained the territory that Mongolia had earlier gained from Manchukuo. Granting the Mongolian People's Republic its independence meant much more to China than simply losing control over Mongolia's territory; it also meant sanctioning Mongolia's control over territory in Manchuria and Inner Mongolia that had traditionally been considered part of China. With Soviet backing, over 120 countries eventually recognized Ulan Bator, and, after more than twenty unsuccessful attempts to overcome Washington's opposition, Mongolia succeeded in joining the United Nations.

After China's 1949 revolution, Beijing protested the Mongolian People's Republic's inclusion in the Soviet sphere of interest and denounced Soviet encroachments on Chinese territory. Moscow's refusal to negotiate the Sino-Mongolian border eventually led to a series of border clashes during the 1950s and early 1960s. Although the Sino-Mongolia border was finally resolved during 1962, Mao Zedong publicly criticized Moscow during 1964: "The Soviet Union, under the pretext of assuring the independence of Mongolia, actually placed the country under its domination."[34]

The bitterness surrounding the Soviet Union's policies in Mongolia all but guarantees that this issue will remain a sore point for China. Beijing officials undoubtedly watched with interest the creation of the Mongolian Democratic party on 10 December 1989, the convening of the Mongolian Democratic Union's first congress on 18 February 1990, and the March 1990 hunger strike by democratic reformers that forced the resignation of the pro-Soviet Mongolian People's Revolutionary party (MPRP) Political Bureau. Although the MPRP won the elections in August 1990, the rapidly changing political climate forced Moscow to pull all remaining Russian troops out of Mongolia by 15 September 1992.

During the early 1990s, Mongolia had little choice but to continue close relations with Russia; in 1992, for example, Russia accounted for 85 percent of Mongolia's foreign trade. In addition, Mongolia accounts for approximately one-sixth of all the foreign debt owed to Russia, or about ten billion rubles. But many Mongols dispute the amount of their country's debt to Russia. During January 1992, a Mongol reporter, Namdagiin Sharov, presented three reasons why Russia's debt figures were inaccurate and should be ignored: (1) during the last fifteen years, while the price of Soviet goods rose by 230 percent, Mongolia's goods increased only by 36 percent; (2) inflated Soviet construction costs accounted for an extra one billion rubles of foreign debt; and (3) "land and minerals of Mongolia were exploited in a predatory manner without any compensation from the Soviet side."[35]

Since Mongolia does not want to become a protectorate of either Russia or China, Jagvaralyn Hannibal, minister of foreign relations, announced on 3 March 1992 that Mongolia would adopt an "open door" policy. This policy would entail forming closer ties with the United States and Japan and also joining the nonaligned movement and the Group of 77.[36] On 18 August 1992, President P. Ochirbat announced that Mongolia would "conduct a pragmatic policy of neutrality based on a 'multi-support doctrine,'" by cultivating relations with Russia, the People's Republic of China, the United States, and Japan.[37]

As a direct result of this new policy, Ulan Bator turned sharply away from Moscow. On 19 January 1993, B. Dash-Yondon, secretary general of the MPRP, reaffirmed that "the past 70 years of Mongolia-Soviet relations can be characterized as being unequal and perverse." He then stated that the safety of the "sovereignty and independence of Mongolia lies in having good relationship[s] with our two great neighbors [Russia and China]. While maintaining relationship[s] with different countries, it is difficult to give priority to any one of them."[38]

The new policy of the Mongolian government to increase its ties with Western countries, and especially with the United States, has led to greater financial aid, foreign investment, tourism, educational exchanges, and increased bilateral trade.[39] But the primary purpose has been to use Washington to counterbalance Beijing. Mongolia's goal was perhaps best summarized by a Russian diplomat who, in November 1991, candidly explained that Ulan Bator was afraid that "China would try to creep in to replace [the] Russians" and that in sponsoring relations with the United States "the West was bound to off-set Chinese claims and help keep their passion under control."[40] Or, as one official from the Asian Development Bank in Ulan Bator put it: "The main thing is to make sure this country doesn't fall into China's hands after having rid itself of Moscow's influence."[41]

To date, the United States has proved itself to be one of Mongolia's greatest supporters. There have been frequent high-level diplomatic contacts, including a much-publicized trip by Secretary of State James Baker in 1991. Most recently, in September 1995, First Lady Hillary Rodham Clinton made a special effort to visit Ulan Bator, immediately after delivering a speech critical of China's forced abortion policy to the United Nations Fourth World Conference on Women in Beijing. The political significance of this visit could not have been lost on the People's Republic; for example, L. Galbagrakh, an adviser to the Mongolian president, emphasized: "Mongolia is situated between two giants, therefore our cooperation with the United States is very important from the point of view of security as well as our progress toward democracy."[42]

Although Mongolia's open door policy has been successful in preserving its independence from China, the pro-Western bias undoubtedly disturbs Russia. In a particularly candid interview, Yuri Kruchkin, a Russian diplomat in Ulan Bator, pointedly reminded his hosts of the rationale underlying many years of Russo-Mongolian cooperation: "Like Mongolia, Russia is doomed to have China as a neighbor."[43] Another diplomat, Maxim Ilonov, then warned that in the future only "Russia will play the role of the basic safeguard of Mongolian security and sovereignty."[44] On 19 January 1993, Sergei Razov, Russia's ambassador to Mongolia, suggested that "Russia, by virtue of its geopolitical position, is both a Eurasian and European state and we must look toward both west and east," and he advocated developing Mongolia's and Russia's "traditional relations in the political, economic, commercial, military and humanitarian spheres."[45]

Clearly, Russia has not yet become reconciled to its loss of influence over Mongolia; Russia was Mongolia's primary trade partner through the early 1990s, and this trade is still important.[46] But this situation has changed rapidly as Chinese goods have entered Mongolia for the first time in decades. In addition, the People's Republic has attempted to use economic aid and foreign trade to gain a foothold in Mongolia: in 1991, Beijing agreed to postpone Mongolia's payments on all remaining debts from the 1960s. By 1992, the People's Republic was Mongolia's sixth highest provider of foreign aid, estimated at $9.6 million.[47] And, by January 1993, the number of permanent Chinese residents in Mongolia had surpassed the number of Russians for the first time since the 1920s, a strong indicator of China's growing influence over Mongolia.

Beijing's diplomatic policies, however, have not been as successful as its economic policies. As early as May 1992, both Li Peng and Jiang Zemin publicly promised to respect Mongolia's independence and sovereignty. But Mongolia's leaders seemed hesitant to believe Beijing's words, perhaps taking China's treatment of Tibet as an indication of what could happen if Beijing had free reign. On 19 January 1993, D. Ganbold, leader of the Mongolian National Democratic party, cautioned that, "lately, China has been showing a keen interest in Mongolia."[48]

To help counterbalance Beijing, it was Ulan Bator that initially promoted friendly relations with Taipei. During 1991, President Li Teng-hui responded, promising to recognize Mongolia's independence as part of a proposed agreement to open Mongol-Taiwanese relations. Taiwanese politicians openly acknowledged that Taipei and Beijing were "competing over Mongolia," and Taipei tried to support Taiwanese businessmen in Mongolia. During 1993, Taiwan's Tibetan and Mongolian Affairs Commission used $770,000 in outside donations to organize a "private" foundation in Ulan Bator. According to one report, Ulan Bator has reciprocated Taipei's friendly gestures, and "Mongolia has encouraged Taiwan to push for a UN seat."[49]

These warming relations were interrupted, however, by a series of treaties that Mongolia signed with Russia and China. On 21 January 1993, Mongolia and Russia signed a bilateral treaty that did not guarantee Ulan Bator's security, as earlier Russo-Mongolian treaties had done. Instead, it merely stated that neither country would sign any agreements that would interfere with the "sovereign interests and independence" of the other or participate in any military-political alliances directed against the other.[50]

This shift in Russo-Mongolian relations left Ulan Bator vulnerable and eventually led to the signing of a Sino-Mongolian treaty on 30 April 1994. In this bilateral agreement, Beijing announced that it would never use nuclear weapons against Mongolia, while Ulan Bator agreed that the People's Republic was the only legitimate Chinese government and promised not to open relations with Taiwan.[51] When one recalls that it was Mongolia that had initially sought to open relations with Taiwan, it is difficult not to suspect that the People's Republic's decision to include this provision on nuclear weapons was used to pressure Mongolia into renouncing relations with Taiwan. No longer able to rely on Moscow for support, Ulan Bator was forced to capitulate.

With Western financial aid and political assistance, Ulan Bator hopes to chart a delicate course between Moscow and Beijing. To date, Mongolia's open door policy has been successful, with the notable exception of its failure to open relations with Taiwan in order to counterbalance the People's Republic's growing political influence throughout Northeast Asia. Mongolia's diplomatic standing in this region will remain relatively weak, however, since Ulan Bator's fate will be determined more by Moscow's and Beijing's future policies than by its own internal initiatives.

Conclusions

In the foreseeable future, the Russo-Chinese border regions will become ever more closely tied to China's economic sphere, while Mongolia will continue its struggle just to retain its political independence. But Ulan Bator would surely fail were it to face an aggressive Beijing determined to reconquer those areas stripped from China by imperial Russia and the Soviet Union. Likewise, it might also falter should Moscow once again adopt an expansionist foreign policy in northeast Asia. Finally, if the United States were to become Mongolia's sole protector against any future Russo-Chinese alliance, this would undoubtedly have a negative effect on Sino-American and Russo-American relations.

Four possible scenarios on the future of Northeast Asian relations will be presented below. On the basis of the history of the Russo-Chinese border and Mongolia, these scenarios will take for granted that both China and Russia would like to expand their economic and political spheres of influence. Scenario 1 will discuss the possible consequences of an aggressive China, while scenario 2 will examine those of an aggressive Russia. Scenario 3 will show what might happen were Siberia to break with Russia and form either one or more independent states. Finally, scenario 4 will speculate on what might happen should Russia and China choose to form a political alliance directed against the United States.

Scenario 1

By far the greatest threat to the status quo in Northeast Asia is China. The Chinese have not forgotten their enormous territorial losses in the nineteenth century—primarily to Russia—and have taken a firm stand on such recent territorial issues as sovereignty over Hong Kong, Macao, the Spratly Islands, and Tibet. On 31 August 1995, while preparing for the thirtieth anniversary of Tibet becoming an autonomous region, Beijing officials attacked critics of their Tibetan policies by insisting that Tibet had been a part of China since the "13th century."[52] Beijing's use of this type of historical argument has a direct bearing on disputed Russo-Chinese territories and on Mongolia since during the thirteenth century China was ruled by a Mongol dynasty, the Yuan, which was based in territory that is currently part of Mongolia and which had conquered much of Russia. By extension, therefore, this same historical argument could be used to claim Chinese sovereignty over Mongolia and, indeed, over much of the Russian Far East.

It is almost certain that China will continue to extend its influence over Northeast Asia, but it seems likely that Beijing will rely mainly on economic, not military, methods. A military solution would be too costly since it would risk war with Russia and would threaten China's lucrative trade with the West. If Beijing proves able to assert economic control, however, it might use its economic leverage to gain political control, perhaps even through such seemingly democratic methods as a plebiscite. China would not hesitate to use such a policy in Mongolia.

Beijing's desire to increase its economic and political influence is not lost on Ulan Bator. According to one foreign diplomat in Mongolia: "Every step the Mongolians take is done with a nervous look over the shoulder towards China." This same diplomat concluded: "The Mongolians have seen what's happened to Inner Mongolia and Tibet. . . . They know that there is precious little they can do to keep out the more powerful and much more numerous Chinese once the Russians are gone."[53]

In the near term, Washington will remain the most powerful guarantor of Mongolian independence. Although Japanese financial aid to Mongolia dwarfs that from the United States, most of its funds are earmarked for developmental projects. By contrast, Winston Lord, the assistant secretary of state for East Asian and Pacific affairs, recently pledged $10.8 million in U.S. aid to Mongolia specifically for "strategic interests and democracy."[54]

Beijing is certainly unhappy with Washington's role as Mongolia's protector. But it will probably tolerate this arrangement through the summer of 1997, when Hong Kong will return to Chinese control, and perhaps even through 1999, with the return of Macao. After 1999, however, should Beijing's goal to retake Taiwan be thwarted, attention might easily shift north to Mongolia.[55] If this occurs, the Mongols will be hard pressed to fend off China.

Scenario 2

Russia would also like to reassert predominant control over the Russo-Chinese border regions and Mongolia, but—unlike China—Moscow does not have a choice between using economic and using military means. Historically, Russia's influence in the Far East has been primarily military. Now, Russia's economic collapse is so complete, especially in the Far East, that it might well take decades to recover. Therefore, there is no real economic option.

Recently, Russia has taken the first step toward adopting a more aggressive military policy. On 6 July 1995, Kozyrev proclaimed to the Russian Federation Council that Russia's foreign policy was once again to "gather together the former Soviet republics."[56] As part of this effort, Kozyrev expressed an eagerness to establish Russian military bases in those CIS states facing external threats. Although China was not specifically mentioned as one of these "external threats," it clearly remains one of Russia's most important rivals in the Far East; for example, on 13 October 1995, Russia specifically offered to help Kazakhstan defend its border with China by providing a portion of the fifteen thousand border troops along the one-thousand-kilometer-long Sino-Kazakhstani border.[57]

Since taking over the duties of foreign minister, Primakov has emphasized his goal of strengthening Russia's territorial integrity and fostering the reintegration of the CIS governments into the Russian Federation. Beginning in January 1996, Primakov undertook a series of trips to observe and negotiate with the CIS governments in Central Asia. Following a three-day trip to Tajikistan and Uzbekistan, which Primakov described as the strategic "underbelly" of Russia, he promised to retain Russian troops in these Central Asian states, warning that without Russian support "a wave of destabilization would sweep across all Central Asia."[58] Carrying through on offers to protect CIS governments from Chinese pressure, Primakov announced immediately after concluding a trip to Kazakhstan during February 1996 that Russia and Kazakhstan had agreed to hold joint talks with China during April 1996 on the Sino-Kazakhstani border disputes.[59]

Primakov's announcement was almost certainly intended, in part at least, to placate those Russians living in the Far East who are concerned about China. These fears became extreme in the Maritime Province, as reflected in Nazdratenko's March 1995 order to expel all Chinese from Vladivostok. One Western commentator has even compared the contemporary anti-Chinese mood to Russia's xenophobic "yellow fever" of the late nineteenth and early twentieth centuries.[60] In one extreme Russian reaction to this immigration, the director of Russia's Federal Migration Service even suggested counterbalancing the Chinese by developing a program to settle "Russian-speaking people in Far Eastern regions."[61]

Another hint that Moscow may intend to reassert military influence in the Far East was dropped by Defense Minister Pavel Grachev when he visited Beijing during May 1995 to discuss demilitarizing the Russo-Chinese border. When China proposed that the two countries carry out a 50 percent reduction of both weapons and military equipment within a one-hundred-kilometer-wide zone on each side of the border, Grachev refused. According to Grachev, if this proposal were carried out, then

Russia's "security in the Asian-Pacific region would be significantly impaired."[62] Meanwhile, Grachev proposed the formation of a new security system in Northeast Asia. But his membership roster included only Russia, China, the United States, Japan, North Korea, and South Korea. The exclusion of Mongolia suggests that Grachev still considers Mongolia to be firmly within Russia's sphere of military, if not economic, influence.

If Russia attempts to reassert predominance over either the Russo-Chinese border regions or Mongolia by resorting to military means, however, it would probably face an armed response by China. Since Mongolia is a member of the United Nations, other countries, perhaps including the United States, might even assist China in repelling Russia. Control of these territories is not worth such enormous risks. Therefore, it seems highly unlikely that Moscow would ever adopt this military option.

Scenario 3

Time and time again, Russian republics in the Far East have threatened to declare independence. Generally speaking, these threats have been made to force Moscow to pay more attention to Far Eastern concerns. But it is conceivable that conditions could deteriorate so drastically that these threats might one day become reality. In this case, China would have an unparalleled opportunity to extend its economic and political influence throughout the Russo-Chinese border regions and Mongolia.

Ever since the Soviet Union's dissolution in 1991, Moscow's apparent inability to respond to the needs of the Far Eastern republics has caused increasing frustration and anger. Moscow owes trillions of rubles to local governments throughout Russia. In 1994, the Far Eastern situation had become so bad that over 100,000 Russians felt compelled to leave, most of them choosing to move back to European Russia.

In February 1995, Russia's Far East and Baikal regions signed an ultimatum threatening to "break away" from Moscow if their needs were not met.[63] Since February 1995, conditions throughout Siberia have worsened dramatically. This prompted a series of hunger strikes that crippled the coal-mining industries in the Maritime Province, Sakhalin, and the Khabarovsk territory. In almost all cases, the strikers' major demand was to be paid the many months of back wages owed them.

Moscow has responded by signing a series of special treaties with the Far Eastern republics and territories. To date, over ten such treaties have been signed. Although the terms of these treaties grant certain economic rights to the local governments, they have been criticized for being far too general. To obtain the promised funds requires personal connections in Moscow. According to one Far Eastern leader, the effectiveness of these treaties depends "exclusively on the level of influence and pertinent experience of a given regional leader."[64]

If Russia's Far Eastern republics ever do declare independence, they would become easy economic prey for China, which could immediately supply them with all the daily necessities that Moscow lacks. Almost overnight, Beijing could extend its economic influence throughout the Russian Far East and, by doing so, might be able to surround and eventually isolate Mongolia politically as well. How Moscow would react to such an eventuality is impossible to predict. Should civil war ensue, however, China could always secretly exchange arms with the combatants in return for economic and political concessions, thus presenting Moscow with a fait accompli.

Scenario 4

As happened during a short period in the 1920s and then during a much longer period in the 1950s, Russia and China might decide to form a political and/or military alliance directed against the United States. This possibility is of much greater concern today than it was a year ago because both Moscow and Beijing have a long list of grievances against Washington; in Moscow's case, this includes Bosnia and NATO expansion, while, for Beijing, it includes a more vocal human rights policy by the United States, a wide variety of trade frictions, and Washington's decision to issue Taiwan's president, Li Teng-hui, a visa to visit the United States. If such a Russo-Chinese alliance were ever concluded, the United States might soon discover that it would hinder American foreign policy worldwide.[65]

Evidence that just such an alliance is being considered is readily available. First and foremost are Russia's increased arms sales to China, which can now be measured in the billions of dollars. These sales include as many as ten Kilo-class submarines, a reported seventy-two high-performance SU-27 jet aircraft, and the transfer of licenses to China enabling it to build the SU-27 domestically.[66] Moscow's ulterior motive for these arms sales is to redirect Beijing's attention to the south, away from the Russo-Chinese border and Mongolia.[67] Taiwan, for one, protested Russia's sales as undermining its security and creating "instability throughout Southeast Asia and Asia."[68]

Perhaps more to the point, if Moscow feels sufficiently rebuffed by the West because of NATO's planned expansion or its policies in the former Yugoslavia, then Russian leaders may feel the urge—as they have during other periods of tension with the West—to ally with China. On 16 October 1995, Andranik Migranyan, a former Yeltsin adviser who is now aligned with the "My Fatherland" bloc in Russia, accused Foreign Minister Kozyrev of driving Russia "into a corner" with its unrealistically optimistic policy toward the West.[69] Responding to criticisms of this type, President Yeltsin announced that he intended to replace Kozyrev. His decision to appoint Primakov was intended to placate the conservative opposition and to push Russia away from Kozyrev's pro-Western policies. Most important, during Yeltsin's spring 1996 visit to Beijing, Russia and China plan to sign at least ten agreements on a wide range of subjects, including new security accords and an agreement to a pullback of border troops.[70]

It should also be recalled that, while anti-Western criticisms such as these were being aired, Russia and China publicly claimed that all their border problems were solved. Although this claim is patently untrue—instead, some of the most difficult disputes have merely been postponed for a future decision—this announcement paved the way for rapidly improving Russo-Chinese relations. Even though these relations might be only superficially friendly, the very existence of a Russo-Chinese alliance would still serve to direct diplomatic pressure against the United States.

It has been postulated in the first three scenarios discussed above that China will rely mainly on its increasing economic power throughout Northeast Asia while Russia will have little choice but to fall back on its ever-declining military might. In scenario 4, however, Beijing's enormous economic potential would be joined with Moscow's military strength in a Russo-Chinese alliance.

If just such a Russo-Chinese bloc ever does appear, it is important to remember how fragile its foundations will be; similar alliances during the 1920s and 1950s were relatively short-lived. The current tensions underlying Russo-Chinese relations are enormous and include differences of opinion and policy on territorial, immigration, and economic questions. While those factors that are pushing Russia and China to cooperate are significant, they revolve mainly around their respective diplomatic tensions with the United States. Therefore, if Washington takes care to balance its bilateral relations with Moscow and Beijing so as not to promote a premature adoption of this alliance, it should be able to avoid facing the consequences of any anti-Western bloc.

Another important factor is the possibility of future political turmoil in Russia. By all accounts, Yeltsin's government appears to be weakening, and a more radical leadership may take power after the elections. Although it is difficult to predict what effect this new leadership might have, one scholar has suggested that a "radical regime in Moscow most likely would pay less attention to East Asia than to other regions where there are large Russian populations living in other former Soviet republics."[71]

If the formation of a Russo-Chinese alliance is successfully countered, then it has been hypothesized that the two most likely alternatives for Northeast Asia would be either the formation of an economically defensive "macroregion" in which Japanese investment would predominate or a more open "melting pot" in which U.S. economic interests would also play an important role.[72] Clearly, it should be Washington's goal to promote the latter course. To do so requires the active economic involvement of the U.S. government in all aspects of Northeast Asia.

As shown in the above-mentioned scenarios, it will be the United States that will need to act as Mongolia's primary protector. This will necessitate continued political support for Mongolia's democratic government as well as coordinated diplomatic support, particularly with the United Nations, to bolster Mongolia's national security. The ultimate goal of this policy should be to help Mongolia construct a complex network of diplomatic contacts with as many countries as possible so that it will not be isolated by its much larger neighbors to the north and south.

But it is important to note that, while the United States might be able to organize an international coalition to oppose any overt military offensive against Mongolia, its ability to oppose a more gradual economic threat would be severely limited. This suggests that Washington's policies will ultimately be much more effective against Moscow than against Beijing. It would appear to be simply a matter of time, therefore, before China achieves its ultimate goal of reasserting, first, economic control and, later, political control over much of Northeast Asia, possibly even including Mongolia.

Notes

1 From an ITAR-TASS news agency report summarized in the Open Media Research Institute's *Daily Digest of News on Russia, Transcaucasia, Central Asia, and the CIS* (hereafter *OMRI Daily Digest*), no. 202, 17 October 1995.
2 "Zhongmeng liangguo Zongli Huitan" (Talks between the premiers of china and mongolia), *Jiefangjunbao* (PLA press), 30 April 1994.
3 During December 1995, the official Chinese journal *Outlook* complained that the United States wanted to stifle China and accused Washington of seeking "more containment than cooperation with China and Russia" (*International Herald Tribune,* 12 December 1995, 4). Later that month, Steven Erlanger reported that, to offset poor relations with Washington, Beijing was engaged in a policy of using improved relations with Moscow to strengthen China's international position ("Russia and China Getting Together Again," *International Herald Tribune,* 30–31 December 1995/January 1996, 1).
4 *Jamestown Foundation Monitor* 2, no. 7 (10 January 1996).
5 Bruce Elleman, "Soviet Diplomacy and the First CCP/GMD United Front in China," *Modern China* 21, no. 4 (October 1995): 450–80.
6 *OMRI Daily Digest,* no. 8, 11 January 1996.
7 Ibid., no. 26, 6 February 1996.
8 *Jamestown Foundation Monitor* 2, no. 8 (11 January 1996).
9 S. C. M. Paine, *Imperial Rivals* (Armonk, N.Y.: M. E. Sharpe, 1996).
10 Oleg Kryuchek, "Referendum on Demarcation of Russian-Chinese Border Proposed—Far Eastern Officials Seek to Oust Andrei Kozyrev," *Segodnya,* 25 March 1995, 2, as reported in *Current Digest of the Post-Soviet Press* (hereafter *CDPP*), 19 April 1995, 25.
11 The Khasan district was the scene of an armed confrontation between Russians and Chinese on 12 April 1995. According to ITAR-TASS reports, a party of three Chinese (who were hunting frogs, a great delicacy in China) strayed across the Khasan section of the border into Russian territory. When warning shots

were fired by Russian border guards, the Chinese returned fire and killed Captain Sergei Dashuk. Although two of the Chinese fled across the border, one was wounded and captured (*Foreign Broadcast Information Service, Central Eurasia* [hereafter *FBIS/SOV*], 13 April 1995). Perhaps in reaction to Nazdratenko, on 5 May 1995, Moscow protested a verbal protest to the Chinese embassy that demanded that China do more to regulate its side of the border. This protest eventually led to the signing of a Russo-Chinese border-policing agreement during August 1995.

12 *OMRI Daily Digest,* no. 233, 1 December 1995.

13 Vladimir Lukin, "Neither Fraternal Love nor Fraternal Hatred," *Moskovskie novosti,* no. 36, 4–11 September 1994, 5, as reported in *CDPP,* 5 October 1994, 14.

14 Aleksandr Platkovsky, "Border Dispute Could Explode Our Relations with China," *Izvestia,* 10 February 1995, 3, as reported in *CDPP,* 8 March 1995, 29.

15 Sergei Rogov, "Result Is Distressing, but There Is a Way out of the Impasse—Three Years of Trial and Error in Russian Foreign Policy," *Nezavisimaya gazeta,* 31 December 1994, 1–5, as reported in *CDPP,* 1 February 1995, 22–24.

16 Mikhail Karpov, "We Find Ourselves in a Very Bad Geopolitical Situation," *Nezavisimaya gazeta,* 14 March 1995, as reported in *CDPP,* 12 April 1995, 24–25.

17 *Jamestown Foundation Monitor,* 1 June 1995.

18 Vladimir Abarinov and Andrei Vinogradov, "Moscow and Beijing: Positions 'Are Close or Coincide,'" 28 January 1994, 3, as reported in *CDPP,* 23 February 1994, 28–29.

19 Yelena Matveyeva, "Massive Influx of Chinese Seen as Source of Problems, Resentment in Russia's Far East," *Moskovskie novosti,* no. 13, 19–26 February 1995, as reported in *CDPP,* 29 March 1995, 3, 15.

20 Lukin, "Neither Fraternal Love nor Fraternal Hatred," 5 (*CDPP,* 14).

21 *OMRI Daily Digest,* no. 44, 2 March 1995.

22 Sergei Zhikharev, "Russia and China Will Have Friendly Borders," *Kommersant-Daily,* 26 August 1995, as reported in *CDPP,* 20 September 1995, 26–27.

23 C-reuters@clarinet.com (Reuters), 27 October 1994.

24 "New 'Open Belt' Forms along Border Areas," *Beijing Review,* 3–16 February 1992, 5–6.

25 Valeria Sychova, "Andrei Kozyrev's Visit to China: Just Neighbors—So Far without Aspirations toward an Alliance," *Kommersant-Daily,* 2 March 1995, 4, as reported in *CDPP,* 29 March 1995, 18–19. This number dropped to $5 billion in 1994 because Russia adopted a new visa system and increased customs duties in January 1994. During June 1995, however, Yeltsin apparently agreed to ease these restrictions (by agreeing that trade should be in hard currency, not barter) in exchange for Li Peng's decision to defer Russian payment on an unspecified amount of trade credits. On 16 April 1995, ITAR-TASS estimated that this trade would once again increase in 1995 to an estimated $6 billion (*FBIS/SOV,* 19 April 1995).

26 "Cross-Border Highways Open Door Wider," *Beijing Review,* 15–21 November 1993, 5.
27 "China Prime Minister, in Uzbekistan, Calls for Renewal of the 'Silk Road,'" *International Herald Tribune,* 4 April 1994, 2.
28 Russia is clearly concerned about China's increased role in Central Asia. One article noted that the Russian Federation now ranks fifth in Kyrgyzstan's overall trade, after China, Uzbekistan, Kazakhstan, and Turkey, and advocated that Russia, not China, should build a road from Central Asia to the Indian Ocean, warning: "It's no secret to anyone, after all, that China is expanding its economic influence in both the Far East and certain Central Asian countries, and in the near future this expansion could also become political expansion aimed at forcing Russia out of Central Asia" (Azer Mursaliyev and Khasan Mustafayev, "Quiet War for Asian Lines of Communication," *Moskovskie novosti,* no. 21, 26 March–2 April 1995, 12, as reported in *CDPP,* 3 May 1995, 24–25).
29 For example, during July 1995, one article supported the development of Kamchatka for this very reason: "To leave undeveloped a large piece of our land, and land that basically is suited for people to live on (this is not Vorkuta or the Kola peninsula), and, moreover, when its next-door neighbors are demographically overburdened, could simply lead to its complete loss" (Vadim Dubnov and Galina Kovalskaya, "Kamchatka Adrift," *Novoye vremya,* no. 28, July 1995, 17–19, as reported in *CDPP,* 13 September 1995, 11–12).
30 Bruce Elleman, "Secret Sino-Soviet Negotiations on Outer Mongolia, 1918–1925," *Pacific Affairs* 66, no. 4 (1993): 539–63. As recently as April 1992, owing primarily to the secrecy that formerly surrounded the fact that Soviet-Mongolian diplomatic relations continued to rest on unequal treaties, an editorial in the *Mongol Messenger* (28 April 1992) incorrectly lauded Lenin for "abolishing all the inequitable treaties and agreements imposed on Mongolia by Tsarist Russia" as well as "exposing the true nature of Tsarist Russia's colonial policy" and making "tireless efforts to hammer home the idea that Mongolia must be an independent country." "Who was Lenin to Mongolia and what is he now?"
31 Dorjnamjiliin Tod, "Stalinist Torture and Purges," *Mongol Messenger,* 22 September 1992.
32 Dorjnamjiliin Tod, "Special Services with a Special History," *Mongol Messenger,* 18 August 1992.
33 Bruce Elleman, "The Final Consolidation of the USSR's Sphere of Interest in Outer Mongolia: The 1940–41 Soviet-Japanese and 1945 Sino-Soviet Negotiations," in *Greater Mongolia in 20th Century Northeast Asia,* ed. Stephen Kotkin and David Wolff (Armonk, N.Y.: M. E. Sharpe, in press).
34 "Mao's Statement to the Japanese Socialist Delegation," 11 August 1964, reprinted in Dennis J. Doolin, *Territorial Claims in the Sino-Soviet Conflict,* Hoover Institution Studies no. 7 (Stanford, Calif.: Hoover Institution, 1965), 43.

35 Namdagiin Sharov, "Will Mongolia's Debt Be Sold Off?" *Mongol Messenger,* 21 January 1992.

36 Jagvaralyn Hannibal, "Restructuring the Foreign Policy," *Mongol Messenger,* 3 March 1992.

37 "The Present Situation of Mongolia and Pressing Tasks," *Mongol Messenger,* 18 August 1992.

38 B. Dash-Yondon, D. Ganbold, and B. Batbayar, "Normal Relationship Is a Must," *Mongol Messenger,* 19 January 1993.

39 For example, in 1993, the IMF granted Mongolia a three-year loan of $57 million, while foreign aid to Mongolia for the year 1995 was set at $210 million ("Bare Cupboards," *Economist,* 26 November 1994, 37–38). Texas oil companies, such as Snyder Oil Corps. of Fort Worth and Exploration Associated International of Texas Inc. of Houston, have taken the lead in signing contracts with Mongolia both to restore older oil fields and to explore for new oil deposits. As for tourism, American and European hunters have been willing to pay as much as $90,000 for the chance to hunt rare Mongolian game, such as the ibex and the snow leopard. The importation of trophies of the endangered Mongolian wild sheep, called the Argal, has been limited recently by the U.S. Fish and Wildlife Service, an action that will undoubtedly cut into this important source of income for Mongolia. Finally, during 1992, with the help of Peace Corps volunteers, more than three hundred former teachers of Russian began to take classes on how to teach English instead (Enhboldyn Bilguun, "'We Must Not Give Up Russian,'" *Mongol Messenger,* 4 February 1992).

40 Maxim Ilonov, "New Relations Needed," *Mongol Messenger,* 4 November 1991.

41 Bertil Lintner, "Mongols Fear Hordes," *Far Eastern Economic Review,* 18 May 1995, 30.

42 "Mrs. Clinton's Pause at a Hearth in Mongolia," *International Herald Tribune,* 8 September 1995, 4.

43 Yuri Kruchkin, "Time for a Realistic Appraisal," *Mongol Messenger,* 7 October 1991.

44 Ilonov, "New Relations Needed."

45 Sergei Razov, "One of Russia's Priorities," *Mongol Messenger,* 19 January 1993.

46 On 9 August 1995, Mongolia signed a series of agreements with Russia's Chita Oblast, detailing trade in petroleum, petrochemicals, and electrical equipment (*FBIS/SOV,* 18 August 1995).

47 The World Bank highest at $32.45 million, while Japan is $30 million and the United States only $6 million ("International Aid Is Crucial," *Mongol Messenger,* 28 April 1992).

48 Dash-Yondon, Ganbold, and Batbayar, "Normal Relationship Is a Must."

49 Julian Baum, "Taiwan Virtual Reality Moves to rejoin UN, Recognise Mongolia," *Far Eastern Economic Review,* 13 June 1993, 15.

50 Boris Vinogradov, "Russia and Mongolia Outline Framework of Mutual Interests," *Izvestia,* 21 January 1993, 4, as reported in *CDPP,* 17 February 1993, 17. Within a day or two of this report, it was announced that China and Mongolia had opened talks on their own bilateral relations ("Xiwang Zhongment Liangguo Youhao Guanxi Jinyiby Fajan" [Hopes for further developing friendly relations between China and Mongolia]), *Jiefangjunbao,* 25 January 1993.
51 "Zhongment liangguo Zongli Huitan" (Talks between the premiers of China and Mongolia), *Jiefangjunbao,* 30 April 1994. An earlier report on Sino-Mongolian negotiations can be found in "Waijiaobu Fayanren Tan Zhongmei, Zhongde Ji Menjju Xuanbu Wie Wuhequ Wenti" (Foreign ministry spokesman discusses questions regarding Sino-American relations, Sino-German relations, and the Mongolian declaration of a nuclear-free zone), *Jiefangjunbao,* 22 October 1993.
52 "China Assails Critics of Its Policy in Tibet," *International Herald Tribune,* 31 August 1995, 4.
53 Bertil Lintner, "Mongols Fear Hordes—China Seems too Close for Comfort," *Far Eastern Economic Review,* 18 May 1995, 30.
54 Ibid.
55 See "China's 'Schedule' for Taiwan," *International Herald Tribune,* 31 January 1996, 4.
56 Yelena Tregubova, "Andrei Kozyrev: Russia Has No Imperial Ambitions, But—" *Segodnya,* 7 July 1995, 1, as reported in *CDPP,* 2 August 1995, 23.
57 *OMRI Daily Digest,* no. 201, 16 October 1995.
58 Ibid., no. 21, 30 January 1996.
59 Ibid., no. 38, 22 February 1996.
60 "Russia's Wild East," *Economist,* 25 March 1995, 54.
61 Sergei Zhikharev, "Russia and China Will Have Friendly Borders," *Kommersant-Daily,* 26 August 1995, 4, as reported in *CDPP,* 20 September 1995, 26–27.
62 Aleksandr Isayev and Natalya Gorodetskaya, "Pavel Grachev Creating Security System in Northeast Asia," *Segodnya,* 17 May 1995, 2, as reported in *CDPP,* 14 June 1995, 21–22.
63 Julie Tolkacheva, "Report: Siberia Threatens Split," *Moscow Times,* 5 February 1995, 55.
64 Yelena Tregubova, "Buryatia Becomes the Sixth 'Special' Republic," *Segodnya,* 12 July 1995, 2, as reported in *CDPP,* 9 August 1995, 12.
65 The political columnist William Safire even warned that Primakov would soon join with China "in enlisting world support against American export of democracy as 'destabilizing'" ("It's Comrade Tough Guy at the Diplomatic Helm," *International Herald Tribune,* 16 January 1996).
66 "China Asserts Right to Acquire Arms," *International Herald Tribune,* 9 February 1996, 4.
67 One expert has hypothesized that, before Moscow agreed to allow China the right to produce the SU-27 domestically, it probably "reached an understanding

with Beijing that the planes would not be used against Russia" but would instead be directed to the east and south ("China-Russia Deal Could Fuel an Asian Arms Race," *International Herald Tribune,* 8 February 1996, 4).

68 *Jamestown Foundation Monitor* 2, no. 29 (12 February 1996).

69 *OMRI Daily Digest,* no. 202, 17 October 1995.

70 "Russia-China Ties Warm, in a Cool Kind of Way," *International Herald Tribune,* 12 February 1996.

71 Peggy Falkenheim Meyer, "Russia's Post–Cold War Security Policy in Northeast Asia," *Pacific Affairs* 67, no. 4 (Winter 1994–95): 495–512.

72 Gilbert Rozman, "Spontaneity and Direction along the Russo-Chinese Border," in *Rediscovering Russia in Asia, Siberia and the Russian Far East,* ed. Stephen Kotkin and David Wolff (Armonk, N.Y.: M. E. Sharpe, 1995), 286–87.

Russia and Japan

RAJAN MENON

Russo-Japanese Relations: Implications for Northeast Asian Security

World politics in recent years has confounded even specialists. The Soviet empire is no more; a single German state has reemerged; Yugoslavia disintegrated amid irredentist bloodletting; Nelson Mandela emerged from prison to be elected president of postapartheid South Africa; an incipient Palestinian state has risen on the West Bank and the Gaza Strip; and Russia, the successor state of the Soviet Union—for long China's implacable foe—is now its largest supplier of weapons. Old patterns are not without resilience, however, as the relationship between Russia and Japan demonstrates. Despite glimmers of hope under Gorbachev and Yeltsin, the two countries remain deeply suspicious of one another, their territorial dispute endures, and economic ties remain weak. While changes have occurred, they have been marginal, manifested more in expectations than reality. As the cliché would have it, the more things change between Moscow and Tokyo, the more they remain the same.

Yet the abundance of the improbable in the world of late suggests that the past may not necessarily be prologue between Japan and Russia. In my view, there are five preconditions for any radical improvement in their relationship. First, leaders on both sides must forge cooperative political and economic ties, with Japan demonstrating—not merely proclaiming—that its policy linking cooperation on economic and security issues with Russia to a resolution of the territorial problem has been discarded. Second, the resulting web of cooperation must bring tangible benefits to powerful institutions and interests in Japan and Russia so that they acquire a stake in better relations and are prepared to countenance the risks and sacrifices needed for a territorial settlement. Third, the payoffs from the expansion of ties must be felt by Japanese and Russian citizens as well so that public opinion ceases to impede a resolution of the territorial problem. Fourth, strong Japanese and Russian leaders must emerge capable of persuading average citizens and powerful groups that compromise is not treason and will yield long-term advantages. Fifth, Japan and Russia must develop a new conception of security that is regional and premised on cooperation between them. This new paradigm must reinforce the network of political and economic ties, thus reshaping the psychological-political dynamics of bilateral relations. Are harbingers of change in evidence? What are the impediments, and how can they be removed? What if fundamental change proves elusive? I address these questions in the following analysis of Russo-Japanese relations since 1985.

Gorbachev: Hope Unrequited

Mikhail Gorbachev's policy toward Japan had three principal goals.[1] One was to enlist Japanese capital and technology to supplement *perestroika*. To this end, he sought increased trade, aid, and investment from Japan as well as support for Soviet membership in the IMF, the World Bank, the G-7, the Organization for Asian-Pacific Economic Cooperation (APEC), and the Asian Development Bank. He understood that these benefits would not be realized if the Japanese continued to see the Soviet Union as their primary military threat. In part, the Soviet withdrawal from Afghanistan, the signing of the intermediate nuclear forces (INF) treaty (specifically the acceptance of the "global zero option," which led to the removal of Soviet intermediate-range missiles east of the Ural Mountains), the pressure applied on Vietnam to withdraw from Cambodia, the reductions in ground and naval forces from the Soviet Far East, and the proposals for regional economic cooperation and confidence-building measures (CBMS) unveiled at Vladivostok (1986) and Krasnoyarsk (1988) were meant to alter Japanese perceptions.[2] Thus, Gorbachev's second objective was to transform the political context of Soviet-Japanese relations by breaking the cold war mold in which they were shaped. The third was to end the deadlock on the southern Kurils/Northern Territories dispute.[3] Gorbachev understood that progress on this issue was a sine qua non for a new relationship with Japan. True, he publicly rejected the official Japanese position that settling the dispute over the Kunashiri, Etorofu, Habomais, and Shikotan

Islands was a precondition for cooperation on economic and security issues. But he and Foreign Minister Eduard Shevardnadze knew that the territorial problem had to be tackled.

Gorbachev failed to achieve his goals. The increase in Japanese trade and investment was modest at best. As for aid, Tokyo pledged $100 million in humanitarian assistance in January 1991 and $2.5 billion in loans in October. By the time the Soviet Union collapsed, however, none of the funds had actually been extended because of Japan's concerns over the lack of a coherent Soviet economic policy and the absence of progress on the territorial question. Within the G-7, Tokyo parried the insistence of Germany that it be more generous in view of the larger strategic imperative of averting chaos in the Soviet Union.[4]

Pace quotidian wisdom, the territorial dispute was not the sole reason for Japan's economic reticence.[5] Rather, increased trade and investment ties were unattractive for purely economic reasons.[6] A partnership between Japanese capital and technology and Soviet labor to tap Siberian natural resources proved much less attractive by the latter part of the 1980s than in the 1970s. Access to Siberian oil would have reduced the dependence on potentially unstable sources in the Persian Gulf to which Japan was connected through long, vulnerable sea lanes; but Japan was less dependent on Middle Eastern oil by 1985, its economy had a larger service sector and was more energy efficient, and nuclear power had become a more important source of energy.

The potentially vast Soviet market was no doubt alluring, but the Soviet Union's rising indebtedness and political instability raised questions about the wisdom of increasing trade and investment ties. The Ministry of Trade and Industry (MITI) was reluctant to provide insurance guarantees to cover large business ventures in the Soviet Union. And the opportunity costs of large investments in the Soviet Union were considerable inasmuch as China, Taiwan, South Korea, and ASEAN were more promising and safer economic prospects. Trade with the Soviet Union accounted for less than 2 percent of all Japanese trade in the latter part of the 1980s. Consequently, the political influence of Japanese industries and institutions with a stake in expanding economic ties proved marginal; it was easily outweighed by powerful groups and institutions (particularly the Gaimusho and the Defense Agency) that had long regarded the Soviet Union with suspicion and by the effect on Japanese public opinion of the legacy of rivalry and conflict in Russo-Japanese relations.

Gorbachev's effort to remake the Soviet image in Japan was somewhat more successful. Japanese opinion polls, scholarly writings, and press reports (and, to a much lesser extent, the pronouncements of Japanese officials) showed that a more favorable view of the Soviet Union was emerging.[7] Visits by senior Soviet leaders (Shevardnadze in 1986, 1988, and 1900, Alexander Yakovlev and Anatoly Lukyanov in 1990) and by Gorbachev himself in 1991 certainly helped improve the atmosphere. Yet ambience could not substitute for achievement. Tokyo followed Washington's lead and remained unreceptive to Soviet proposals for naval CBMS and a regional security regime. The traditionally conservative Japanese Defense Agency's annual *White Paper* failed to make any fundamental reassessment of the Soviet military threat, "New Thinking" and "reasonable sufficiency" notwithstanding. Soviet force reductions were interpreted in ways consistent with the traditional view: they were noted with the caveat that Moscow now sought smaller, but more modern, forces.[8] For all Gorbachev's efforts, by the end of his tenure, Japan and the Soviet Union had still not signed a postwar peace treaty.

The third goal—making headway on the territorial dispute—proved elusive as well. After focusing initially on relations with the United States, Europe, and China, Gorbachev became serious about Japan and took some important steps to prepare the ground for a territorial settlement involving *mutual* compromise. Visa-free visits by Japanese to the islands were approved in 1986; Moscow finally acknowledged the existence of a territorial dispute; and the Soviet-Japanese working groups set up in 1988 for negotiations on a peace treaty included the territorial problem on their agenda. Despite Gorbachev's reputation for dramatic diplomatic breakthroughs, his much-anticipated visit to Japan in April 1991 was anticlimactic and failed to unfreeze the territorial dispute. The principal reason was that conditions within the Soviet Union made it essentially impossible for him to hand over—or even agree to hand over in the future—to a historic rival territory that, so far as the elites and masses of the Soviet Union were concerned, belonged legitimately to the Soviet Union. By 1991, his political position was too precarious to disregard this sentiment. His vacillation on reform and use of force against nationalist movements had alienated the radical Yeltsinite reformers, and the political instability and economic hardship made the once-popular proponent of change widely unpopular. Political weakness made him increasingly beholden to the military, intelligence services, and party *apparat*—the very institutions stridently opposed to a deal with Japan on the islands. To these constraints was added the rising power and confidence of leaders in the union republics and provinces. Both the Russian republic under Yeltsin—by 1991 a bitter opponent of Gorbachev's—and the authorities in Sakhalin *oblast,* personified by governor Valentin Fyodorov, had for rather different reasons become important players in the territorial dispute. The leaders of the Russian Federation invoked democratic norms to reject any settlement that excluded them, thus leading Japan to question the significance of any agreement reached with a central government that seemed weaker with each passing day. In emotionally charged language that played to conservatives and statists, Fyodorov challenged Moscow's right to make any territorial concessions.

Tokyo's unwillingness to go back to Khrushchev's 1956 proposal—the return of Habomais and Shikotan in exchange for a peace treaty—also ruled out a settlement.[9] The Japanese insisted that Habomais and Shikotan be returned as part of a settlement that acknowledged Japan's sovereignty over Etorofu and Kunashiri (the larger two islands) and set a timetable for their return. The guiding assumption was that economic desperation would force the Soviet leadership to yield. What this overlooked was that by 1991 Gorbachev was politically too weak to accept so radical a proposal. Japan wanted the whole loaf—or at least half immediately with a firm promise regarding the remainder. By 1991, Gorbachev could not even deliver very many slices.

Boris Yeltsin: The Chimera of Power

Yeltsin had defined himself as a leader who, unlike Gorbachev, had the strength and vision to break new political ground. This image was initially widely accepted in Russia and the West. (Japanese officials and experts were more skeptical.) Ironically, Yeltsin quickly found himself in the same political bind as Gorbachev and was no more able to put Russo-Japanese relations on a new footing. Like Gorbachev, Yeltsin understood that increased trade and investment ties with Japan could complement economic reform by offsetting the concomitant pains with some visible gains: consumer goods, technology, investment capital, and a shot in the arm to schemes for multilateral economic cooperation like the "Sea of Japan Rim Economic Zone."[10] Like Gorbachev, Yeltsin knew that there would be no new chapter in relations with Japan unless headway were made on the territorial dispute. But the erosion of his political position at home soon made it impossible to take unpopular decisions abroad.

The parallels to Gorbachev's predicament are striking. Yeltsin too has alienated the radical reformers such as Yegor Gaidar and Grigorii Yavlinsky; he too is politically in debt to the military and the security services. And, to undercut the ultranationalists and Communists, as early as 1992 he embraced the discourse of nationalism—that great enemy of compromise—and soon became its prisoner. In these circumstances, he could not offer terms for a territorial settlement acceptable to Japanese leaders—especially as political weakness had made them risk averse as well. A stubborn recession and the fragile coalition governments that followed the end of the thirty-eight-year monopoly of power of the Liberal Democratic party (LDP) in 1993 made them fear the political fallout from the "Northern Territories," which, because of the campaigns of successive LDP governments to portray their return as a paramount national imperative, have acquired a symbolism that leaves governments, particularly weak ones, little room in which to maneuver.

It could be argued that a stable Russia is so important that Japanese leaders have a strategic rationale for extending economic assistance even without a territorial settlement. If Russia slides into authoritarianism or civil war, Northeast Asia will be a less secure place. Japan has nothing to gain if a nationalist-authoritarian regime replaces Russia's (admittedly flawed and rickety) democracy; the chances for a territorial settlement would diminish sharply, as would Japan's security. Yet, for Japanese officials and entrepreneurs, the economic reasons for holding to their cautious policy on trade and investment ties with Russia remain just as compelling as before precisely because of Russia's cloudy political future. The outlook for economic reform in Russia has become progressively more uncertain, particularly after the 1995 parliamentary elections, in which the Communist party and other antireform parties took the largest share of seats. The testy relationship between Moscow and the provinces makes Japanese firms uncertain about what the rules of the game will be and who will define them, while Russia's $1.1 billion debt to Japan and the corruption, red tape, and sheer criminality that pervades its economy makes them downright leery. On the political front, the danger of instability has increased with the war in Chechnya and the uncertainty surrounding Yeltsin's health.

These concerns have not been countered by a vigorous Japanese debate on Russia in which proponents for a change in policy have made a compelling economic and strategic case for expanding economic ties; nor are there powerful economic interests capable of lobbying for a change in policy. The result, whatever sporadic delegations and their hopeful statements may suggest, has been a bloodless economic relationship. A cursory look at the data on Russian-Japanese trade from 1991 reveals, not an ascending curve, but a zigzag pattern involving paltry sums.[11] Japanese investment in the Russian economy is also meager. At the end of the first quarter of 1995, it amounted to $8 million—3.5 percent of all foreign investment in Russia. The United States, Belgium, Austria, Germany, Switzerland, Britain, and Turkey had larger investments, and Japan's foreign direct investments in Russia represented 0.1 percent of its investments worldwide.[12] While some Japanese regions (Niigata Prefecture, which faces the Russian Far East) and companies (the Toyo Engineering Corp., a supplier of refinery equipment to Russia) stand to gain from a change in Russo-Japanese economic relations, trade with Russia lacks a national constituency, amounting as it did to a mere 0.6 percent of all Japanese trade in 1992.[13]

A territorial settlement cannot, like some magic key, unlock the potential of Russo-Japanese economic relations; but it would certainly improve their prospects while also creating a better context for cooperation on regional security. Several solutions are possible.[14] One involves resuscitating the 1956 Khrushchev proposal and deferring agreement on the status of Kunashiri and Etorofu—the larger islands—for an interim period (say five years), using the hiatus to sign a peace treaty and to expand economic and cultural links. The calculation would be that the political-psychological climate would change sufficiently by then to make leaders and the public in both countries more open to a grand compromise on the remaining islands. Another hypothetical solution would be to modify the January 1991 plan offered by Yeltsin—while president of the Russian republic — for a multistage solution to be implemented over some twenty years.[15] Russia was to begin the process by acknowledging that there is indeed a territorial dispute. The follow-up phase would feature demilitarization, joint economic development of the islands, and a peace treaty. The trickier issues — acknowledging Japanese sovereignty and agreeing on which territories were to be handed back — would be deferred until the final phase. For Japan, the plan had two fatal flaws: the process was protracted, and it was unclear which islands would in fact be gained in the end. A third approach would be an embellished Yeltsin plan. The starting point would be Russia's acknowledgment of Japanese sovereignty over all the islands, followed immediately by a joint statement on upgrading economic ties (including a generous commitment of aid from Japan), the creation of a forum for regular talks on security issues, and the periodic exchange of high-level visits to prevent the process from petering out. Movement on these fronts would set the stage for a peace treaty. After a two-year interval, the territorial settlement would be implemented, beginning with the return of Habomais and Shikotan in exchange for a guarantee of demilitarization. The next phase would commence three years later and involve the joint administration of Etorofu and Kunashiri, which would also be demilitarized. Two years later, they would be transferred to Japan with the understanding that Russians would have unhindered access, the right to own property, and preferential access to fishing grounds in the surrounding waters. Japan would help relocate islanders who choose to move to Russia (or elsewhere) and pledge that those who stay would have comprehensive guarantees against discrimination and the option of dual (Russian-Japanese) citizenship.

Developing innovative models for a settlement is essential, but the hard part is translating them into concrete accords that leaders will sign and can take home and live with. Any of the solutions just proposed would require uncharacteristic daring from Russian and Japanese leaders, something not to be expected in the foreseeable future. The Japanese are hemmed in by the symbolism surrounding the "Northern Territories." They cannot accede to an agreement that does not, at a minimum, acknowledge Japan's sovereignty over all the disputed islands up front and transfers at least some of them quickly. Yeltsin's political weakness makes it impossible for him to offer such terms, especially as he campaigns for reelection in June 1996. Handing Russian territory over to Japan would make him easy prey for the likes of Alexander Lebed, Vladimir Zhirinovsky, and Gennady Zyuganov. Yeltsin is also constrained by the Frankenstein effect of the democratization that he, more than any other Russian leader, helped set in motion. A deal with Japan involving a loss of Russian territory would have to be approved by the parliament and would be open to scrutiny in the media and to challenge in the courts by the authorities of Sakhalin *oblast,* which has administrative jurisdiction over the disputed islands. Had Yeltsin lost the 1996 presidential elections—or withdrawn from the race—his successor would almost certainly have been someone even more identified with the theme of restoring Russia's great power status. Beholden to ultranationalist constituencies, preoccupied with consolidating power while trapped in the quagmire in Chechnya, and besieged by economic problems, this individual would be in no position to yield Russian land, even were he so inclined.

The cancellation of Yeltsin's September 1992 visit to Japan at the eleventh hour demonstrates how powerful domestic political constraints can be. The trip was called off because Yeltsin could not address the territorial dispute in a way that was simultaneously defensible at home and acceptable to the Japanese government, which, at a minimum, wanted a recognition of Japanese sovereignty over all the contested islands and the return within a short period of Habomais and Shikotan. Yeltsin could not accept such terms without grave political risks. And Japan did not offer any substantial economic benefits up front to make those risks less formidable and a deal more defensible at home. Indeed, in the negotiations prior to the scheduled visit, Japan would not go beyond agreeing to supply $825 million in previously committed aid.[16] Yeltsin chose wisely to avoid an explosive controversy in Russia that could not have been quieted by pointing to substantial economic gains that justified the sacrifice. And there was no doubt that opposition at home would have been fierce. Prior to the planned visit, opponents of compromise with Japan—the military, civilian hypernationalists, Yeltsin's foes in the Russian parliament, the captains of state industry, and the Sakhalin *oblast* authorities—had waged a raucous campaign aimed at making concessions to Japan all but impossible.[17]

In response, the Russian position hardened even before Yeltsin's scheduled visit, and the trend continued once it was called off. This was exemplified by some economic decisions with respect to the disputed islands. In June 1992, Russia granted South Korea fishing rights off the islands; soon after Yeltsin's trip was aborted, a Hong Kong company received rights to build a casino on Shikotan; in December, the Russian government announced the creation of special economic zones on the islands with long-term leases to entice foreign investors.[18] All three acts, ostensibly purely economic, drew protests from Japan because they were also assertions that Russia would continue exercising sovereign control over the islands notwithstanding Japanese claims. Japanese leaders understood that domestic pressures accounted for these decisions and the cancellation of Yeltsin's visit. But that did not diminish their resentment.

After calling off a trip planned for May 1993, Yeltsin finally appeared in Japan in October, but it was clear from the outset that he would do nothing to provide his ultranationalist critics with political ammunition. (The circumstances were remarkably similar to those surrounding Gorbachev's April 1991 visit.) The framework agreed on at the end of the visit for dealing with the territorial dispute included positions long emphasized by the Soviet Union and Russia.[19] It specified that neither side would be expected to make unilateral concessions and that a settlement would take account of previous bilateral treaties as well as the ways in which the two countries had dealt with each other. The latter caveat is an especially important point in the light of the Soviet/Russian contention that the 1855 Treaty of Shimoda (which placed the disputed territories under Japanese sovereignty) and the 1875 Treaty of St. Petersburg (which transferred the entire Kuril Island chain to Japan) had been nullified by Japanese aggression against Russia in 1904–5, 1918, and 1939. Yeltsin did acknowledge the existence of a territorial dispute, reaffirm the Russian government's acceptance of the 1956 Soviet-Japanese two-island formula, and announce that the withdrawal of combat aircraft from the islands (which had been completed) would be followed by the removal of all troops and weapons, a process that was already under way. But the first two statements did not involve any loss of Russian territory, and, given Russia's economic predicament, the third may have been necessity masquerading as virtue.

Prerequisites for a Territorial Settlement

It should be clear by now that several conditions must converge for a territorial settlement. Japan must cease making it a precondition for substantive cooperation with Russia in the economic and security realms, and this must not remain a mere declarative position. Stated differently, its Russian policy must not be a mere by-product of passion for the "Northern Territories." It is much more likely, albeit by no means certain, that promoting mutually beneficial economic and security transactions — to build economic interdependence, promote trust, and lessen the historical legacy of suspicion — will create a political climate that eventually enables Russian leaders to sell a controversial territorial compromise at home. Japan's strategy of making benefits to Russia conditional on a territorial settlement is understandable given the depth of its commitment to regaining the islands and the apparent leverage provided by Russia's dire economic problems. But the linkage strategy has demonstrably failed, and there is no reason whatever to believe that it stands a better chance of succeeding in the future. Russian leaders may want the economic benefits of expanded trade with, and investment from, Japan; but they will not commit political suicide to obtain them.

In April 1993, Japan did officially change its policy of linking the growth of economic and political ties with Russia to progress on the territorial dispute.[20] But the impetus for this shift was not an epiphany that the old strategy had failed; it was provided by the fear of isolation within the G-7 on the issue of assistance to Russia.[21] Until 1992, the United States shared Japan's skepticism about large-scale economic aid to the Soviet Union, and this enabled Tokyo to appeal for support on its territorial dispute with Russia during G-7 summits, to deflect West European (especially German) criticism of its doggedness on linkage. The Soviet collapse destroyed the viability of that strategy. The United States changed its position and became a proponent of multilateral aid to post-Communist Russia, thereby making Japanese adamancy on linkage a recipe for isolation. In response, not only did Japan drop linkage in favor of a "balanced" development of all facets of Russo-Japanese relations, but in April 1994 it pledged $1.8 billion in aid to Russia at a G-7 meeting held to prepare for the summit scheduled for July.[22]

But Japan's jettisoning of linkage in favor of a "balanced" development of economic *and* political ties is not as consequential as it might appear. Russia and Japan continue to differ about whether economics (trade, investment, and credits) or politics (the territorial dispute and the signing of a peace treaty) should be the pacesetter in their relationship. As was apparent during the visits to Japan by First Deputy Prime Minister Oleg Soskovets (November–December 1994) and parliamentary speaker Ivan Rybkin (April 1995) and from the remarks made in February 1995 by Foreign Minister Andrei Kozyrev (prior to his departure for Japan) and in January 1996 by his newly appointed successor, Yevgeny Primakov, Russian officials stress the expansion of economic ties. By contrast, their Japanese counterparts, explicitly invoking linkage, emphasize the need for progress on political issues.[23]

Another condition for resolving the territorial dispute is that citizens must come to see compromise, not as a betrayal, but as sensible, equitable, and beneficial. For this, a settlement must include demonstrable benefits so that leaders can counter the rhetoric of nationalist opponents by demonstrating to people that the settlement has provisions designed to increase their economic well-being and safeguard their security. There are, as I suggest in the last section, ways to do this.

The prospects for a solution will also improve if Japan reconsiders its all-or-nothing approach, which rests on the false assumption that sheer economic desperation will ultimately force Moscow to settle on Japanese terms. In fact, economic hardship will weaken democratic forces in Russia, and they are the only ones apt to compromise on the territorial dispute. A corollary is that economic crises will increase the power of ultranationalists (whether of the Left or the Right) — the people least likely to yield. While it may be impossible for Japan to accept a settlement limited to the 1956 formula, it should consider a 1956-plus variant in which a peace treaty with Russia and the acquisition of Habomais and Shikotan are supplemented by an unorthodox arrangement for Etorofu and Kunashiri combining demilitarization in perpetuity and joint administration.

Stable domestic conditions within each country are also essential. The frequent turnover in Japanese prime ministers (which marked the Gorbachev years) and fragile coalition governments (the pattern since 1993) are hardly conducive to compromise on an emotionally laden dispute. The same observation applies to Russia, characterized by the weakness of its president (which his bluster should not obscure), the fragmentation of its state, deep divisions in its society, the cacophony of conflicting positions on the territorial dispute (the prime minister contradicting the president; the military high command sniping at the Foreign Ministry; the Security Council setting terms for a settlement that, in effect, rule it out),[24] and the eagerness of political elites to use red-blooded nationalism for infighting.

Why Russo-Japanese Relations Matter

With the end of the cold war, the concept of a cooperative regional security system in the Asia-Pacific region has gained attention. The existing security arrangement, which lingers by default and seems increasingly obsolete, is based on explicit and tacit alliances created by the United States to contain the Soviet Union. While regional elites understand that the creation of a full-blown security structure is premature, they are now discussing the need for initial efforts. This is true not only in the United States and Russia but also in Japan, where the traditional skepticism about regional security has been reconsidered since mid-1991. The new Japanese perspective is reflected in the writings of leading scholars, the statements of ranking officials, and the initiation in 1993 in Tokyo of a dialogue on North Pacific security among Japanese, Russian, and American officials and specialists.[25]

Among the conditions that will affect the feasibility of a new security order in Northeast Asia is Russia's post-Soviet transition.[26] A strong, united, democratic Russia is the most desirable outcome. While developments within Russia will be the most important in determining whether it is possible, foreign trade, investment, and the external security environment—in short, the nature of Russia's relations with important countries like Japan—will shape the nature of domestic politics: a deteriorating economy and an obsession with national security will inevitably strengthen forces that oppose democracy, reform, and arms control. Should Russia's democratic experiment fail, one possible denouement is an authoritarian hypernationalist regime that rejects a cooperative regional security order and even acts as a spoiler. This would make multilateral solutions to such future security problems as runaway arms transfers, ecological crises, transnational criminal networks, and the security of nuclear installations and fissile material far more difficult because Russia's role matters in each instance. Another possible scenario is the progressive weakening of Russia or its fragmentation owing to internal conflict. In either case, it will lack the power to derail an emerging regional security regime as a spoiler. But neither will it be a robust contributor; indeed, a Russia in upheaval will aggravate all the security problems just noted.

The nature of Russo-Japanese relations also matters for effective regional responses to a potentially hegemonic China. Given China's immense potential power, its determination to upgrade its now-limited power projection forces, the troubled history of Sino-Japanese relations, doubts about the staying power of the United States, and the Sino-Japanese territorial dispute over the Senkaku/Diaoyutai Islands, the specter of a belligerent China is now very much on the minds of Japanese officials and experts on security.[27] The apprehension about China exists in Russia as well despite the delimitation of the Sino-Russian border, major arms sales, the implementation of various CBMs, and rising trade. Some of Russia's most insightful foreign policy specialists worry that a weak Russia, estranged from Japan, uninvolved in regional security structures, and enamored of the short-term gains from arms sales to China, could be vulnerable as it becomes increasingly powerful and nationalistic. To avert this scenario, they argue specifically for improved relations with Japan (including the resolution of the territorial dispute) and participation in regional security initiatives.[28]

Should China shun cooperative regional security and challenge the East Asian status quo by threatening to use, or actually using, force, regional states will have two options, collective deterrence (balancing) or appeasement. An authoritarian Russia, itself alienated from the region, will not participate in a balancing strategy; if it is mired in economic difficulty, it may well abet a hegemonic China by selling it weapons. And a Russia torn by internal upheaval will be too weak to contribute to balancing and may resort to appeasement. Without Russian cooperation, restraining China will be problematic, especially if the American military presence in Northeast Asia is eroded by declining public support for far-flung commitments, the pressure of growing economic and social problems, declining support in Japan and South Korea—of which there are signs[29]—for permanent U.S. deployments, strains in U.S.-Japanese relations, and Korean reunification.

U.S. forces in the region have been reduced since 1990.[30] Should the trend continue, Japan cannot simply fill the void unilaterally given the array of (well-known) regional, domestic political, and constitutional barriers. To be acceptable in the region and at home, a Japanese strategy of balancing China must be anchored in a coalition. South Korea—or even perhaps a united Korea—could be a partner, but the power added may not be sufficient to offset China's, and the deeply rooted tensions between the two countries will lead South Korea to seek additional partners to forestall Japanese domination. Russia is a natural candidate, but its willingness to join will depend on the nature of its relationship with Japan—if Russian-Japanese relations are worse than Sino-Russian relations, Russia will abstain or, worse, tilt toward China. As for a Russia weakened by internal upheaval, its most likely response to a hegemonic China—to whose power its remote, thinly populated Far Eastern region will be directly exposed—will be appeasement or neutrality; either would increase a rogue China's freedom of action by freeing its northern flank.

What Is to Be Done?

There are no signs that a transformation of Russo-Japanese relations is in the offing. The territorial problem remains intractable, and political conditions in Japan and Russia rule out bold moves by either side. To be sure, this situation is not uncommon, and the United States has helped disputants overcome it by greasing the wheels of diplomacy. But Russia's reaction to any prospective U.S. mediation will be colored by the legacy of the cold war, the American alliance with Japan, and Washington's support for Japan's claim to the islands. The public reiteration of this support by the U.S. ambassador to Russia in December 1995 was seen as a diplomatic solecism and produced a torrent of indignation.[31] Thus, Russia is unlikely to accept the United States as a neutral party. Even if it were to, the United States could provoke a nationalist backlash in Russia while simultaneously raising doubts in Japan about the steadfastness of its support by mediating a dispute that can be settled only through large sacrifices by each side.

That said, the United States can improve the context for a solution by reducing the security risks that Russia will have to assume in transferring territory to Japan. These risks exist because the contested islands, together with the other Kurils, enclose the Sea of Okhotsk, a deployment zone for Soviet (now Russian) strategic subsurface ballistic nuclear submarines (SSBNS). The Russian military, like its Soviet predecessor, believes that the islands should not therefore be yielded to a historic adversary allied to the world's remaining superpower.[32] True, while the strategic importance of the Sea of Okhotsk is noted routinely,[33] it could diminish with the end of the cold war. If Russia implements the START II treaty, it is expected to reduce its submarine-launched ballistic missiles (SLBMS) from 3,700 (the number it had in 1991) to 1,360.[34] With the closure and deterioration of facilities that service and support Pacific Fleet submarines, the smaller SLBM force may be deployed with the Northern Fleet—which has always controlled most of the Soviet/Russian SLBM force—and defended within the Barents Sea by air and naval forces capable of thwarting Western antisubmarine warfare operations. And those not protected in this way could be sent on open ocean patrol, an option that will become more feasible as the Russian navy's far more quiet *Severodvinsk*-class SSBNS, scheduled to undergo trials during 1996–98, become operational.[35] That is one possibility. Another is that, even with the implementation of START II, Russia—for reasons that are strategic (reducing SSBN vulnerability by not relying on a single deployment zone) and bureaucratic (rivalry between the Northern and Pacific Fleets)—continues using the Sea of Okhotsk as a secondary SSBN deployment zone. If the latter scenario materializes, it could be argued that, from a purely military standpoint, the United States has a continuing rationale for retaining the capabilities to reconnoiter and penetrate the Sea of Okhotsk. Yet doctrinal formulations, operational plans, and threat assessments abstracted from political realities are meaningless.[36] What matters is not the array of weapons that states deploy but the political relationship among them; the United States does not, for instance, worry about British and French nuclear missiles. With the post-Soviet political changes in Russia and its armed forces weakened by draft evasion, shoddy maintenance, budget cuts, and plummeting morale, the utility to the United States of operations in the Sea of Okhotsk — a facet of its 1980s "maritime strategy" — is dubious.[37] Washington can now contribute to a territorial settlement by engaging Russia and Japan in developing a system of verifiable air and naval CBMs in the North Pacific, including provisions that prohibit using the Northern Territories/southern Kurils for military purposes.[38] This will help civilian leaders in Moscow counter militarily based criticisms of a territorial settlement in two ways: generally, by altering the lingering remnants of the cold war security environment in Northeast Asia and, specifically, by enabling them to demonstrate that relinquishing the islands will not endanger SLBMs that Russia chooses to deploy in the Sea of Okhotsk even after START II is implemented.

But it is myopic to dwell solely on the territorial issue; Russia's political future is far more significant for Northeast Asian security. While neither Japan nor the United States can ensure that Russia becomes a market economy and democratic polity, both can do more jointly than they have so far to increase its chances — especially given the solemn statements about the continuing relevance of their security alignment, the end of the cold war notwithstanding. The United States and Japan (joined by South Korea) could increase lending to Russia, enact measures that spur private investment, assist in converting defense industries to nonmilitary production, and create a contingency fund to alleviate politically explosive shortages — and they could do so cooperatively through a division of labor guided by a long-term strategic vision that can withstand the detours and setbacks inevitable in Russia. This may be the best way to prevent the dreaded scenario of an authoritarian, ultranationalist regime rising from the wreckage of Russian reform and reducing both the chances for resolving the Russo-Japanese territorial dispute and the security of Northeast Asia. The United States and Japan unquestionably face severe economic limitations, but a joint, long-term program of aid to Russia does not require the mobilization of additional resources if it is financed by redirecting some of the military expenditures made unnecessary by the end of the cold war. If done bilaterally or multilaterally (with South Korea), it will reduce national burdens through collective action while also increasing Moscow's incentives to cooperate on matters important to Japan, such as arms sales to China, the dumping of nuclear waste in the Sea of Japan, access to the waters surrounding the disputed islands for Japanese trawlers, and the territorial problem itself.

The fly in the ointment is that U.S. and Japanese perceptions of the Russian problem diverge. Japan believes that to initiate a long-term policy of aid before settling the territorial dispute is to reverse the proper sequence (although this logic has not been applied to South Korea, which has received Japanese aid despite the dispute over Takdo and Takeshima Islands). There is no instant remedy for this variance in perceptions and priorities, and the direction of Russia's economic and political change since 1993 is hardly conducive to altering Japanese views. The results of the December 1995 parliamentary elections in Russia, the removal of reformers (such as Kozyrev and Anatoly Chubais) from top-level positions in the government, the resignation of Yeltsin's liberal advisers (such as Sergei Kovalev and Yegor Gaidar), the war in Chechnya, and the likelihood that the 1996 Russian presidential elections will further complicate reform (by bringing to power a Communist or an ultranationalist president or extending the term of a Yeltsin without the physical stamina and political strength to revive the momentum for reform) have made Japan's pessimistic prognosis for Russia persuasive. But Russia's fate matters to Japan and the United States individually and to Northeast Asian security, and slothfulness must not be rationalized by determinism disguised as realism. Russia's post-Soviet transition will not be decided by specific parliamentary and presidential elections; rather, it will be a protracted process punctuated by periods of stagnation and regression. Nothing less should be expected given that powerful elites are waging a high-stakes battle to decide what kind of country Russia should be. Accordingly, as they define the purpose of their strategic partnership for the post–cold war era, the United States and Japan should take a long-term view and seek a common policy toward Russia aimed at fostering economic reform and democracy. This common policy must rest on some fundamental and explicitly stated assumptions lest it oscillate between euphoria and despair: there is no quick solution to the epochal task of creating a democratic polity and market economy in Russia given that country's history; the course of reform will be lengthy and fraught with setbacks; citizens in the West must be given a realistic picture of these complexities if the required level of public support for assistance to Russia is to be maintained; the scale and scope of Western assistance must be calibrated to the ebb and flow of the reform process and the shifts in the balance of political forces within Russia; while Russia's fate is ultimately in the hands of its people, Western policies can make a difference; the future of Russia is important enough to the global balance of power to make a policy of persistence and patience worthwhile despite the uncertainties involved.

The balance of political forces in Russia—specifically, the appeal of Russia's ultranationalists, who oppose reductions in military spending and deployments on the grounds that they would make the country more vulnerable to U.S. and Japanese power—can also be influenced by a new U.S.-Japanese approach to security in Northeast Asia. Russian apprehensions regarding Japan should not be dismissed. Russia and Japan have fought several wars in this century, they have a territorial dispute, and they are not united by cooperative ties strong enough to offset the psychological weight of this legacy. Despite significant deficiencies, the Japanese Self-Defense Forces possess state-of-the-art armaments, and Japan's military budget is the world's fifth largest.[39] To a Russia in decline—and aware that its status as a great power may be a thing of the past and hence fearful of the future—Japan's military potential must be both impressive and worrisome. Japan's $4.2 trillion economy is the world's second largest, compared to Russia's, which ranks eighth at $777 billion;[40] it has developed (or perfected) many technologies that have revolutionized late twentieth-century warfare; and, since the early 1980s, the share of research and development in its defense budget has increased, as have the efforts of its corporations in research and development with military applications. Against these realities, pious reassurances notwithstanding, the U.S.-Japanese security alignment may not look harmless to Russia.[41]

The existing U.S.-Japan security treaty, a product of the cold war, requires a new rationale now. Transforming it from a Russia-centered bilateral mechanism, which it remains by default, to one that focuses on emerging security problems in Northeast Asia—through institutionalized consultations with other regional states—would be wise in five respects.[42] First, the treaty would become relevant to new regional security challenges—among them, nuclear proliferation and safety, environmental mishaps, the drug trade, destabilizing arms sales, and conflicts over maritime resources. Second, a reconfigured treaty would constitute the first step toward a multilateral regional security regime (for which conditions do not exist at present) that involves the United States, thus allaying fears that Japan will beef up its military power as China rises and the United States retrenches. Third, it would create a regional environment in which reform-minded Russian leaders are politically more able to reduce military expenditures, defend their actions before critics at home, and embrace the idea of regional security. Fourth, Washington's efforts to encourage a larger Japanese role in regional security in the name of burden sharing would be more acceptable not only in Russia (and China and the Korean states) but also in Japan itself if it takes place in the context of multilateral, inclusive security. Finally, if China rejects the model of inclusive security and becomes a revisionist power, the cooperative efforts that had enabled that model could be tapped for a balancing strategy. Of course, the prospects for these suggestions (aid for Russia's economic reform, CBMs in the North Pacific, inclusive regional security) depend not just on creative thinking in Washington, Tokyo, and Moscow but on Russia's future. Outsiders can influence that to a degree. But it is beyond their power to determine.

Notes

An earlier version of this essay appeared in the Summer 1996 issue of *Survival* published by Oxford University Press on behalf of the International Institute for Strategic Studies.

1 Rajan Menon, "Gorbachev's Japan Policy," *Survival* 33, no. 2 (March–April 1991): 158–72.

2 For details, see Rajan Menon, "New Thinking and Northeast Asia," *Problems of Communism* 38, nos. 2–3 (March–June 1989): 1–29.

3 On the history of the Soviet/Russian-Japanese territorial dispute over the islands of Habomais, Shikotan, Etorofu, and Kunashiri (the Soviet/Russian designation for them is "southern Kurils," and they are considered part of the main Kuril chain; to the Japanese, they are the "Northern Territories," or "Hoppo Ryodo," and are not part of the Kurils), located northeast of the Japanese island of Hokkaido at the southern end of the Kuril archipelago, see, among others, Fuji Kamiya, "The Northern Territories: 130 Years of Japanese Talks with Czarist Russia and the Soviet Union," in *Soviet Policy in East Asia,* ed. Donald S. Zagoria (New Haven, Conn.: Yale University Press, 1982), 121–52; and David Rees, *The Soviet Seizure of the Kuriles* (New York: Praeger, 1985).

4 Harry Gelman, *Russo-Japanese Relations and the Future of the US-Japanese Alliance* (Santa Monica, Calif.: Rand, 1993), 44–55.
5 I do not accept the view that the territorial dispute is but "a convenient excuse" used by Japan for not deepening economic ties because it grossly underestimates how strongly Japanese feel about the islands and overestimates their need for an excuse (Sergei Chugrov, "Russia and Japan: Drifting in Opposite Directions," *Transitions* 1, no. 17 [22 September 1995]: 14).
6 See Menon, "Gorbachev's Japan Policy," 165–66.
7 See Gilbert Rozman, *Japan's Response to the Gorbachev Era, 1985–1991: A Rising Superpower Views a Declining One* (Princeton, N.J.: Princeton University Press, 1992).
8 Menon, "Gorbachev's Japan Policy," 159.
9 The Soviet offer to return Habomais and Shikotan was contained in the Soviet-Japan Joint Declaration of October 1956 (which preceded the reestablishment of full diplomatic relations) and was conditional on the signing of a peace treaty between Japan and the Soviet Union. The Japanese later decided to reject such a settlement, and the Soviets withdrew the offer after the United States and Japan signed a revised security treaty in 1960. The question of whether the agreement binds Japan to accept the return of Habomais and Shikotan as the basis for a final settlement and obligates Russia, as the successor state of the Soviet Union, to honor the 1956 commitment remains disputed. Also disputed is whether in 1956 the Soviets communicated in letters to the Japanese that the agreement to return Habomais and Shikotan and to conclude a peace treaty would lead to further negotiations to settle the status of Etorofu and Kunashiri before the actual signing of a peace treaty (see Gelman, *Russo-Japanese Relations,* 16; and also n. 25 below).
10 This project envisages cooperation among Japan, South Korea, North Korea, Russia's Maritime provinces (Khabarovsk, Primorski, Sakhalin, and Amur), and China's northern provinces (Heilongjiang, Jilin, and Liaoning) to create a zone of economic growth featuring a division of labor involving Chinese labor, Russian natural resources, and Japanese and South Korean capital and technology (Valery K. Zaitsev, "Problems of Russian Economic Reforms and Prospects for Economic Cooperation between the Russian Far East and Northwest Pacific Countries," *Journal of Northeast Asian Studies* 10, no. 4 [Winter 1991–92]: 38–39).
11 "OECD Trade with the Former Soviet Union," in *1995 Economist Intelligence Unit: Country Report* (29 May 1995). The following were the monthly averages, in millions of U.S. dollars, for Japanese exports to the entire former Soviet Union: 1991, 176.3; 1992, 99.4; 1993, 138.5; and 1994, 112.4. The average monthly imports were as follows: 1991, 27.6; 1992, 208.6; 1993, 248.3; and 1994, 305.3.
12 "Foreign Trade and Payments: Foreign Direct Investment Remains Low," *1995 Economist Intelligence Unit,* (15 August 1995). The figure for Japan's in-

vestment in Russia as a percentage of its total investments worldwide is from Chugrov, "Russia and Japan," 16.

13 Reuters, 26 April 1993.

14 For a range of solutions, see Graham Allison, Hiroshi Kimura, and Konstantin Sarkisov, *Beyond the Cold War to Trilateral Cooperation in the Asia-Pacific Region: Scenarios for New Relationships between Japan, Russia, and the United States* (Cambridge, Mass.: Harvard University Strengthening Democratic Institutions Project, n.d.), 29–37.

15 Vladimir Ovsyannikov, "USSR-Japan," *New Times* (Moscow), no. 6 (February 1990): 20–21.

16 This sum consisted of the $100 million in humanitarian aid pledged in December 1990, a $700 million loan for the purchase of Japanese equipment for Russia's gas industry, and $25 million for increasing the safety of Russian nuclear reactors (Gelman, *Russo-Japanese Relations,* 72–74).

17 Ibid., 63–68.

18 Robert F. Miller, "Russian Policy toward Japan," in *Russian Foreign Policy since 1990,* ed. Peter Shearman (Boulder, Colo.: Westview, 1995), 147–48. Miller notes that the Hong Kong company withdrew once Japan threatened to nullify the concession on acquiring Shikotan.

19 *East European Markets,* 29 October 1993.

20 *Nikkei Weekly,* 19 April 1993.

21 This is covered superbly by Gelman, *Russo-Japanese Relations,* 40–63.

22 At the July summit, Japanese Prime Minister Kiichi Miyazawa reaffirmed the abandonment of linkage in a meeting with Yeltsin. Japan also contributed to the $3 billion in aid, much of it accounted for by funds previously allocated, offered Russia during the summit (*New York Times,* 9 July 1993).

23 See "Russia Asks Japan to Join Free Economic Zone on Isles," *Kyodo,* 12 October 1994; "Rybkin, Kono at Odds over Boosting Bilateral Ties," *Japan Economic Newswire,* 27 April 1995; "Kozyrev Says Peace Treaty with Japan Still Difficult," *Japan Economic Newswire,* 28 February 1995; "Russia Hopes to Up Economic Ties with Japan," Jiji Press Ticker Service, 28 April 1995; ITAR-TASS, 17 January 1996, reprinted in *Foreign Broadcast Information Service, Central Eurasia* (hereafter *FBIS/SOV*), 17 January 1996, 12. The last source quoted Primakov as saying at a press conference that Japan should "leave the settling of the territorial problem for future generations and, meanwhile, develop relations in order to create the most favorable situation for settling it in the future." In response, a Japanese foreign ministry official said that Primakov's suggestion was "unacceptable." The priority that Japan continues to accord to a territorial settlement was evident in a speech to the Diet by the new prime minister, Ryutaro Hashimoto. The reaction of Russian Deputy Foreign Minister Aleksandr Panov underscored Russia's emphasis on prior improvements in overall relations (Interfax, reprinted in *FBIS/SOV,* 24 January 1996, 17).

24 Details in Chugrov, "Russia and Japan," 14–16.

25 Eugene Brown, "Japanese Security Policy in the Post–Cold War World: Threat Perceptions and Strategic Options," *Journal of East Asian Studies* 8, no. 2 (Summer–Fall 1994): 349–56; Tsuneo Akaha, "Russia in Asia in 1994," *Asian Survey* 35, no. 1 (January 1995): 105–6. Other developments under way could also help the movement toward regional security. Russia and Japan are working on regular contacts between defense officials, there are yearly meetings between Russian and Japanese naval officers, meetings are being planned between security experts from each country, and a visit to Russia by the head of Japan's defense agency is being planned for 1997 (ITAR-TASS, 19 January 1996, reprinted in *FBIS/SOV,* 22 January 1996, 35–36).

26 Mikhail Titarenko, *Rossiia i Vostochnaia Aziia: Voprosy mezhdunaordnyky i mezhtsivilizationnyky otonoshenii* (Moscow: Kuchkovo Pole, 1994), 108.

27 Brown, "Japanese Security Policy," 337–40.

28 Alexei Arbatov, "Rossiia: Natsional'naia bezopasnost, v 90-e gody," *Mirovaia ekonomika i mezhdunarodnye otnosheniia,* nos. 8–9 (1994): 14. Arbatov notes, however, that conservative opposition to concession on the islands and enthusiasm for arms sales to China could block the measures he favors.

29 Nicholas Kristoff, "Welcome Mat Is Wearing Thin for GI's in Asia," *New York Times,* 2 December 1995, 14.

30 It is estimated that the reductions in the U.S. military presence in East Asia begun under the Bush administration and continued by President Clinton will cut the number of troops on land and at sea from 135,000 in 1990 to 102,000 by the end of 1995. For future contingencies, U.S. strategy emphasizes rapid deployment to the area and a greater military role by allies (William T. Tow, "Changing US Forces Levels and Regional Security," in *Post–Cold War Security Issues in the Asia-Pacific Region,* ed. Colin McInnes and Mark G. Rollins [Ilford: Frank Cass, 1994], 12–18, esp. table 1).

31 The U.S. position was restated by ambassador Thomas Pickering—in response to a question at a press conference—a week before the December 1995 Russian parliamentary elections while visiting Sakhalin. For critical reactions by Russian officials and scholars, see *Nezavisimaya gazeta,* 10 December 1995, 1; and *Komsomolskaya pravda,* 10 December 1995, 1, translated in *FBIS/SOV,* 11 December 1995, 25–26; Konstantin Sarkisov, "Political Earthquake Hits the Kurile Islands," *Moscow News,* no. 49, 15–21 December 1995, 4.

32 A forceful statement of this position is Captain Boris N. Makeev, "Kuril'skaia problems: Voennyi aspekt," *Mirovaia ekonomika i mezhdunarodnye otnosheniia,* no. 1 (1993): 56–57. Makeev provides a detailed account of why the islands claimed by Japan have a special military significance for the passage of Russian submarines and the placement of radar systems.

33 See, e.g., Iu. Lilin, "VMS SShA: Starye postulaty novoi morskoi strategii," *Morskoi sbornik,* no. 2 (February 1989): 66–70; Gerald Segal, *The Soviet Union and the Pacific* (Boston: Unwin Hyman, 1990), 100–101.

34 See the figure in *Strategic Assessment 1995* (Washington, D.C.: National De-

fense University Press, 1995), 117, on the effect that START II will have on the Russian (and American) strategic nuclear force structure.

35 Alexei Zagorsky, "The Post–Cold War Security Agenda of Russia: Implications for Northeast Asia," *Pacific Review* 8, no. 1 (1995): 93–94. The deterioration of the Pacific Fleet and its infrastructure is discussed in Douglas L. Clarke, "A Hollow Russian Military Force in Asia?" *Transition* 1, no. 17 (22 September 1995): 26–27. On the Russian navy's new, quieter submarines (the *Aklua* II hunter-killer and the *Severodvinsk*-class SSBN), see James Adams, "New Russian Subs Outsmart Royal Navy," *Sunday Times* (London), 18 February 1996.

36 Alexander Wendt, "Constructing International Politics," *International Security* 20, no. 1 (Summer 1995): 73–74.

37 The objective of the "maritime strategy" as applied to the Soviet Far East was to raise the costs to Moscow of waging war in Europe by opening up a second front against its remote eastern seaboard, using land- and carrier-based air forces, Tomahawk missiles, surface ships, and attack submarines to put Soviet shore-based installations (ports, airfields, and air defenses) and SSBN deployments in the Sea of Okhotsk at risk (James R. Kurth, "The US and the North Pacific," in *Security and Arms Control in the North Pacific,* ed. Andrew Mack and Paul Keal [Sydney: Allen & Unwin, 1988], 27–49).

38 Arbatov, "Rossiia," 15. The argument that North Pacific CBMs would facilitate a territorial settlement is also made by Captain Boris Makeev, despite his emphasis on the military importance of the islands. He argues that Russian concessions would be possible if CBMs created a situation in which Japan and the United States were no longer regarded as Russia's hypothetical adversaries in Northeast Asia (Makeev, "Kuril'skaia problems," 58).

39 Reinhard Drifte, *Japan's Foreign Policy* (New York: Royal Institute of International Affairs and the Council on Foreign Relations, 1990), 35; David Arase, "New Directions in Japanese Security Policy," in *Post–Cold War Security Issues,* 48.

40 U.S. Arms Control and Disarmament Agency, *World Military Expenditures and Arms Transfers, 1993–1994* (Washington, D.C.: U.S. Government Printing Office, 1995), 32.

41 Titarenko, *Rossiia i Vostochnaia Aziia,* 156.

42 For a detailed argument, see Rajan Menon, "Revitalizing the United States–Japanese Alliance," *Pacific Review* 7, no. 2 (1994): 183–94.

The Korean Peninsula

ALVIN Z. RUBINSTEIN

Russia's Relations with North Korea

Perhaps nothing symbolizes the changing position of Russia in Asia more than the end of the military-political relationship between Moscow and Pyongyang. A relationship that began after the defeat of Japan in 1945, that congealed during the Stalin and Khrushchev periods, and that remained firmly entrenched during the final years of Soviet power was spasmodically shaken and finally destroyed during the post-Soviet seesaw Yeltsin years. On 7 September 1995, the Russian Ministry of Foreign Affairs (MFA) announced that Moscow had officially proposed to terminate the 1961 Soviet–North Korean defense treaty.[1] The North Koreans apparently had no objections, observing: "We considered it to be insignificant and as good as nullified after the collapse of the Soviet Union and informed the Russian Federation of our position. Since then we have paid no attention to the treaty."[2] In accordance with the provisions of article 6 of the treaty signed on 6 July 1961, the treaty will officially terminate on 10 September 1996.

When the Soviet Union collapsed in December 1991 and transferred to Russia responsibility for dealing with the nations of Northeast Asia, a period of political ambiguity was ushered in between Moscow and the Democratic People's Republic of Korea (DPRK), more commonly called North Korea. From a Russian point of view, North Korea was a dubious, even expendable, client; from North Korea's, Yeltsin's reformist, pro-Western bent differed only in degree, not substance, from the foreign policy of the last and unlamented Soviet leader, Mikhail Gorbachev, a possibility Kim Il-sung had correctly anticipated.

While Russia groped for a reconceptualized national interest, North Korea looked to its own survival. Moscow's distinctly unfriendly policy was merely part of the strong aftershock of the political-strategic changes that had undermined the former Soviet system and that had so profoundly and unpredictably affected its institutions, political processes, military considerations, and foreign policy priorities. Moreover, its relationship with North Korea was affected not only by Russia's domestic upheaval but also by its courtship of South Korea and the United States.

Perspective on the Soviet Era

Stalin's aims on the Korean peninsula were as imperialistic as those of the most expansion minded of Czars, who had recognized the strategic importance of the peninsula's warm-water ports and location in relation to China and Japan. The rapid Soviet occupation in August 1945 surprised the Americans and strongly suggests that control of Korea was a key Soviet objective. Stalin envisaged "domination of the entire country as a base for the extension and strengthening of Soviet power in the Far East." Anxious not to alarm Washington, he agreed on 15 August 1945, immediately after Japan's surrender, to a U.S. proposal to have the thirty-eighth parallel serve as a temporary line of demarcation between Soviet and American forces; but this also prompted him "to concentrate on a short-term goal, the establishment of a firm base in northern Korea. For that purpose the Soviet occupation forces moved rapidly to seal off northern Korea by setting up a fortified border along the 38th parallel."[3]

By 1948–49, Soviet "advisers" of Korean origin, who had been trained in the Soviet Union, permeated and controlled key North Korean institutions, including the party, the military, industry, culture, and propaganda.[4] Ironically, Kim Il-sung, who was not a member of the Soviet-Korean "faction" but part of a Korean-Chinese guerrilla detachment operating against the Japanese in Manchuria along the border with Korea, was selected by Stalin himself for the role of figurehead leader, a choice future Soviet rulers were to rue.[5]

The responsibility for the Korean War (1950–53) was Stalin's—wherever one comes out in the debate on whether it was Kim Il-sung who persuaded Stalin to give the go-ahead or Stalin who manipulated Kim to do his bidding.[6] For certain, one legacy of the Stalin era has been a divided Korea. Throughout the Korean War and immediately thereafter, Moscow's hegemonic position was unchallenged in Pyongyang. But by 1956 and the aftermath of the twentieth congress of the Communist party of the Soviet Union (CPSU), de-Stalinization in the Soviet Union gave Kim Il-sung the opportunity to purge the party and government of most of "the Russian men," the "so-called Soviet Koreans," and to build a political network of his own.

From the late 1950s on, Kim Il-sung exploited the emerging Sino-Soviet rift, gaining for himself a growing independence, as Moscow and Beijing tried to offset the other's influence in North Korea with generous economic and military assistance. For a time, Kim sided with Mao against Khrushchev, then tilted toward Moscow in the late 1960s, during the years of Mao's destructive isolationist Cultural Revolution. Thereafter, he adapted adroitly to his two patrons, whose enmity continued through the 1970s and most of the 1980s. Moscow's aims were to keep Pyongyang from slipping too close to China and ensure that it did not start a new war to reunify Korea.

The Soviets had few illusions about their "friendship" with North Korea. Writing in the mid-1980s, two Rand Corporation analysts observed:

> The Soviets [i.e., Russians] are aware that although the warmth of Sino-Korean relations has varied, Pyongyang has rarely been truly neutral, and has *never* shown preference for Moscow except for those four aberrant years of the late 1960s, when it was in effect driven away by the Maoists. It seems clear that over the past twenty-five years, Soviet diplomatic representatives in Pyongyang have become accustomed to finding themselves severely isolated in a cold and rather hostile environment; and over most of that period, Chinese dealings with the North Koreans have been at least somewhat less constrained. In sum, looking back over the panorama of the past, the Soviet leaders are likely to believe that they labor under a permanent, built-in disadvantage in geopolitical competition with the PRC for predominant influence in Korea.[7]

This shrewd commentary on the Soviet–North Korean condition in the period 1950–85 needed some modification in the 1990s because of the Russian and Chinese competitive interest in South Korea, the changed strategic environment for North Korea, and possible reassessments of which powers have the most to lose from Korean unification and which the least.

Like a consumptive, the Soviet–North Korean relationship took on an appearance of renewed health and vigor in the mid-1980s, even as it was entering a period of terminal decline. Kim Il-sung visited Moscow in May 1984, for the first time since 1967, in an international environment of high tension between the Soviet Union and the United States. Particularly worrisome to both Moscow and Pyongyang was the improving relationship between China and the United States. This prompted Moscow's hard-line leadership, headed by the infirm Konstantin Chernenko, to court Kim and reward his unrelenting anti-Americanism. Moscow's aid package was substantial: economically, extensive credits and deferral of North Korea's debt; militarily, advanced equipment to upgrade North Korea's air force and air defense capability; and, technologically, the provision of Soviet technicians to help with the transfer of new technology and signed agreements pertaining to conventional and nuclear power generation.[8]

Kim again visited Moscow in October 1986 to meet Gorbachev, Chernenko's successor, and obtain reassurances of Moscow's commitment to the May 1984 agreements. Not only did Gorbachev satisfy Kim on this, but in addition he "promised 30 MiG-29 advanced air-superiority fighters, and an unknown number of Su-25 fighters and SAM-5 missiles. Moscow also promised Kim the *Tin Shield* advanced radar system for early warning, ground control and target acquisition. Deliveries of the MiG-23s [called for under the 1984 agreements] began in 1985 and of the MiG-29 in 1988."[9] In return, Pyongyang permitted Moscow to use North Korean airspace for military flights to and from Vietnam and agreed to greater naval cooperation, including joint naval operations in the Sea of Japan and Soviet access to the port of Wonsan. The high level of military consultations and exchanges introduced after Kim's 1984 visit were continued all through the Gorbachev period.

However, at the political level, Soviet–North Korean relations started deteriorating in 1988, in the wake of Gorbachev's decisions to participate in the Olympic games, which were held in Seoul in August–September, and to establish trade relations with South Korea. Despite Moscow's reassurances to the contrary, Pyongyang expected that diplomatic recognition would follow trade links.[10] Kim Il-sung believed that Gorbachev's "New Thinking," his growing détente with the United States, and his courtship of South Korea were threats to his regime. As a result, he accelerated the country's nuclear program, notwithstanding his having signed the nuclear nonproliferation treaty (NPT) in 1985, at Moscow's behest.

In 1989, North Korea watched the gradual normalization of Soviet–South Korean relations unfold. Consular relations were established; permanent trade offices opened in each other's capital; a direct sea link was inaugurated between Vladivostok and Pusan; the Soviet press wrote positively on South Korea's economic accomplishments and prospects; trade expanded; and Kim Young-sam, coleader of the Democratic Liberal party, visited Moscow, where he explored possibilities for full political normalization.

During Gorbachev's visit to the United States in June 1990, he met in San Francisco with South Korean President Roh Tae Woo and agreed to establish full diplomatic relations, although no timetable was given. As in his approach to West Germany, Gorbachev's policy toward South Korea was driven by great expectations of assistance for the troubled Soviet economy.

On 30 September 1990, disregarding its previous assurances to North Korea, and a scant two months after agreeing to German reunification, Moscow established formal diplomatic relations with South Korea. To encourage Moscow's process of disengagement from Pyongyang—and doubtless as part of the price for rapid recognition—Seoul established a $3 billion aid package for the Soviet Union a month after South Korean president Roh made his first official visit to Moscow. Relations between Moscow and Seoul warmed quickly, and, on 20 April 1991, President Roh hosted Gorbachev on the island resort of Cheju. Gorbachev's proposal to negotiate a treaty of friendship and cooperation surprised the South Koreans and stimulated speculation regarding the suddenly ambiguous status of the 1961 Soviet–North Korean treaty.

Meanwhile, a paradoxical situation was developing between Moscow and Pyongyang: at the same time that their military cooperation was peaking as a result of the flow of Soviet weapons and equipment promised in the 1984 and 1986 agreements, Moscow was manifesting displeasure over North Korea's nuclear intentions. With the improvement in U.S.-Soviet relations, Washington provided Moscow with information obtained by its spy satellites suggesting that North Korea was trying to develop a "potential for developing nuclear weapons": "With the passage of time, the anxiety had grown even more since the United States obtained photographs which showed what was considered to be a nuclear fuel reprocessing plant and a site for A-bomb testing. . . . The growing anxiety over the problem induced Moscow to seek direct discussions with Pyongyang on the complex of non-proliferation issues. In 1989, working-level consultations on the question between the foreign offices of the two countries took place for the first time."[11] During his last visit to North Korea in September 1990, Soviet foreign minister Eduard Shevardnadze tried to persuade Pyongyang to permit inspections of its nuclear facilities by the International Atomic Energy Agency (IAEA), at the same time reaffirming Moscow's continued support for Pyongyang's "idea on setting up a nuclear-free zone on the Korean peninsula" and its intention of raising "the question of American nuclear presence in its contacts with the United States."[12] But his efforts failed to allay Pyongyang's security concerns.

Sensing the unreliability of the Soviet Union and his own worsening diplomatic isolation, Kim Il-sung applied for UN membership in May 1991. This marked a major retreat from his long-standing position that the two Koreas should occupy a single seat in the United Nations. In September, the two Koreas were admitted to the world organization. For Kim, membership was a kind of political guarantee of his sovereign independence; at the same time, he considered acceleration of his nuclear effort the key to North Korea's security doctrine for survival. His timing was excellent. In August 1991, although Gorbachev's opponents in the Politburo bungled their attempt to oust him, Gorbachev proved incapable of adapting to the new circumstances that he himself had helped create. By late December, the Soviet Union was no more, a victim of its leaders.

Russia's Strategic Situation under Yeltsin

The demise of the Soviet Union transformed Russia's strategic environment in Northeast Asia to one that differs markedly from that known to any previous Russian leader during the past three centuries. First, in contrast to its immediate neighbors—China, Japan, and the two Koreas—Russia finds itself at the beginning of the post–cold war period in a state of precipitous socioeconomic, political, and military decline. Even in 1905, when defeated by Japan, to which it remained militarily inferior until the late 1930s, Russia was a major power to be contended with by a China that was underdeveloped, headed by incompetent, corrupt leaderships, and heavily dependent on foreign powers and also by a Korea that was a colonial possession of Japan's until 1945.

Second, unlike Gorbachev, Yeltsin lacks political clout or respect in the region, if only because of a severely diminished military capability.[13] For example, the Pacific Fleet, which was the largest of the four fleets in the Soviet navy, deploying the most surface ships, is aging and rusting from lack of funds to operate. In November 1994, Moscow agreed to sell to South Korea, for scrap metal, two of its thirty-seven-thousand-ton Kiev-call VTOL (vertical takeoff and landing) aircraft carriers—the *Minsk* and the *Novorossiysk,* which started operating in 1979 and 1984, respectively.[14] Under normal circumstances, such ships would have an additional fifteen to twenty years of active service.

A third change from the Gorbachev era is that Moscow is no longer a major player in the game of nations in the region. The erosion of Russia's power ended the significance of Moscow's alliances with North Korea and Vietnam. Moreover, absent the Russian threat, Beijing has been left without a strong card to use in its dealings with Washington, even as it and the United States begin to loom larger in each other's strategic and security calculations. Although it is too early perhaps to talk with confidence about the implications of the decline of Russia for U.S.-Chinese relations, the preliminary evidence suggests the advent of difficulties ahead with China over its territorial claims in the East China and South China Seas, missile and nuclear technology transfers to Iran and Pakistan, trade issues, human rights, and naval and air power projection capabilities particularly as they relate to the future of Taiwan.

Fourth, as regards North Korea, even if Russia desires to continue its role as great power patron-protector, its ability to do so is much reduced. It lacks the wherewithal to service North Korea's dependence on imports of energy and heavy industrial equipment. This factor alone is sufficient to account for Moscow's withered influence in Pyongyang.

Finally, Moscow can look forward with equanimity to a unified Korea. Of the involved powers—China, Japan, the United States—Russia has the least to lose politically, militarily, or economically from unification. In an acentric world, balance-of-power considerations suggest that a unified Korea would be a better defender of freedom of the seas than a weak and divided Korea dominated by China or Japan, that its historic animosity toward Japan and suspicion of China would prompt it to cultivate closer relations with Russia, and that as a major industrial producer it would find a natural complementarity in Russia's markets, energy, and raw materials.

These changes between the Gorbachev and the Yeltsin eras help define Moscow's aims and dilemmas in relations with North Korea. But, before turning to the key issues in their relationship, we need to keep in mind the continuities in Soviet and Russian policy, which cannot but influence Moscow's policy choices, irrespective of the leadership in the Kremlin.

Geographic contiguity is a permanent focuser of a country's diplomacy. No matter what are the political, military, economic, or ideological disagreements, a shared border usually means a common stake in good relations. During the Gorbachev period, Moscow and Pyongyang settled outstanding border issues: agreements were signed on their eleven-mile boundary that starts at the three-country (China, North Korea, and the Soviet Union/Russia) junction in the Tumen River and extends to its estuary, on their "sea boundary beginning at the estuary to the outer limit of their 12-mile territorial seas in the Sea of Japan" for a length of 12.5 miles, and on their boundary delimiting their continental shelf and exclusive economic zone.[15] That these boundaries have not been challenged by either party in the Yeltsin era is a sign of essential stability.

Russia has nothing to gain from a new conflict on the Korean peninsula. It favors a peaceful unification of the two Koreas, a denuclearized peninsula, effective IAEA safeguards on power-generating nuclear reactors, and a decrease in tensions between North and South Korea. With the United States and Russia no longer major adversaries, Russia may also not be opposed to a continued, albeit low-key, U.S. military presence as a counter to growing Chinese inroads and ambitions, although in the long term it prefers the withdrawal of all great powers from the Korean peninsula.

Most of Moscow's old ties with North Korea remain, but they are either stretched thin and barely sustainable or in need of repair. Moscow's diplomatic recognition of South Korea, courtship of Seoul, reluctance to help Pyongyang cope with economic and military weaknesses, and market-oriented reforms and democratization have combined to reinforce Pyongyang's hostility and suspicion and complicate the Russian–North Korea interaction on the key issues in their relationship.

Issues

Yeltsin's approach to North Korea — to call it a policy would be to exaggerate its coherence — has been bedeviled by irreconcilable difficulties. Russia officially espouses reform, openness, and a market-oriented economy, whereas North Korea is highly centralized and totalitarian; Russia upholds the NPT and IAEA inspections, but North Korea questions their validity as a matter of political strategy; Russia retains residual economic and military connections, hoping they can be used to exercise influence in the future, but North Korea could, by reducing them, deprive Moscow of one of its last diplomatic assets in the region; and, not withstanding the elaborate network of dependencies dating from the Soviet period, Moscow finds itself virtually an outsider in Pyongyang, whereas the North Koreans lobby actively in Moscow among the ultranationalists who favor better relations between the two countries.

The Russian–North Korean relationship comprises issues that are closely interconnected and very complex. Throughout the Yeltsin period, the relative importance of each has varied, the whole being very much a function of Yeltsin's difficulty devising a policy for East Asia, the ups and downs in the Russian–South Korean relationship, and the turmoil in Russian domestic politics. Of key importance are the fate of the 1961 treaty, North Korea's nuclear challenge, military ties, economic relations, and domestic determinants.

The 1961 Treaty

Over the years, Yeltsin's policy toward North Korea underwent sharp and often sudden turnabouts. Soon after Russia inherited the former Soviet Union's sovereign attributes and international commitments,

Yeltsin sent a personal envoy, the veteran diplomat Deputy Foreign Minister Igor Rogachev, to Pyongyang to explain Russia's policy and to probe North Korea's. According to Andrei Bouchkin, research analyst with the Russian Institute of International Economics and International Relations, Rogachev found that the North Koreans considered the 1961 treaty of friendship and cooperation "outdated." Not only did they not object to its being terminated, but they dismissed Rogachev's reassurances that the Russian nuclear umbrella still covered North Korea, implying that they had revised their concept of national security and no longer relied on Russian guarantees.[16] Evidently, both Moscow and Pyongyang placed little stock in the treaty. This suited Yeltsin's approach. In this matter, he relied on the tack taken by Gorbachev, namely, looking to Seoul for the economic assistance that would generate a further redefining of Moscow's priorities on the Korean peninsula.

In March 1992, when Foreign Minister Andrei Kozyrev went to China, Japan, and South Korea, the omission of North Korea from the itinerary was deliberate, a signal of Moscow's intention to look to the south rather than the north for comprehensive diplomatic-economic ties. As if to reinforce this message, on 30 June 1992, Yeltsin told the visiting South Korean foreign minister that the 1961 treaty "has lost its effectiveness and exists in name only" and that Moscow was no longer providing military or economic assistance to Pyongyang.[17]

In November 1992, during his visit to Seoul, Yeltsin "quite spontaneously declared, entirely upon his own initiative, in a way so typical of him, that it was necessary to terminate the treaty with the DPRK," a pronouncement that came as a total surprise to Russia's Ministry of Foreign Affairs.[18] By signing, on 20 November, the Treaty on the Basic Principles of Relations between the Russian Federation and the Republic of Korea, and by pledging to end military assistance to North Korea and turn over documents on the Korean War, he further conveyed his preference for close relations with South Korea.

To improve the worsening relationship with North Korea and exchange views on various issues, including the status of the 1961 treaty, in January 1993, Deputy Foreign Minister Georgy Kunadze (currently Russia's ambassador to South Korea) flew to Pyongyang. This time, in contrast to what Bouchkin and others had reported a year earlier, both parties affirmed the importance of the treaty, although they could not agree on specifics. The Russian aim was an interpretation that could be achieved in an exchange of letters at the governmental level rather than a change in the treaty's text. Pyongyang was noncommittal, preferring to "study" the proposals. Increasingly, throughout 1993, as in 1992, North Korean criticisms of Russia's "unfriendly behavior" took on the aspect of political warfare. Nothing was done directly about the treaty. In other matters, Pyongyang's accusations that the rights of North Koreans working in Russian logging camps were being violated, that the Russian media was hostile to North Korea, that Moscow was preventing Russian scientists from working in North Korea, and that the supply of military spare parts had been disrupted reflected its deep mistrust of Yeltsin's Russia.[19]

The deteriorating Russian–North Korean relationship led to the belief, especially in South Korea, that the Soviet–North Korean Treaty of Friendship, Cooperation, and Mutual Assistance signed in Moscow on 6 July 1961 would not be renewed. The treaty had come into force on 10 September 1961 for a ten-year period, had been renewed every five years thereafter until September 1995, when Moscow decided not to renew, and therefore will expire in September 1996. The treaty's demise was triggered by Moscow's insistence that any renewal exclude the key defense clause in article 1, which stipulates: "Should either of the Contracting Parties suffer armed attack by any State or coalition of States and thus find itself in a state of war, the other Contracting Party shall immediately extend military and other assistance with all means at its disposal."

Yeltsin's utterances in 1992, 1993, and early 1994 had suggested that Moscow viewed the treaty as an anachronism. But a series of developments seemed to give the treaty a new lease on life: the shift to the right in Russian domestic politics that followed the emergence to prominence of ultranationalists and conservatives in the December 1993 elections; North Korea's nuclear challenge; South Korea's coolness — even disdain — toward Moscow; and Washington's virtual exclusion of Moscow from efforts to manage regional security. Suddenly, in the months preceding September 1995, it appeared that the treaty's future gave Moscow a bargaining chip to play in the ongoing diplomatic game in Northeast Asia.

That the Russian leadership was divided on the treaty was suggested by the Panov incident. On 29 March 1994, amid rising tensions between the United States and North Korea over Pyongyang's refusal to permit IAEA inspectors to implement safeguards inspections of its nuclear facilities, Deputy Foreign Minister Aleksandr Panov (a career diplomat and East Asian specialist with previous postings in Japan [1983–88] and South Korea [1992–93] said that Russia would render military aid to North Korea in accordance with the 1961 defense treaty in the event of an unprovoked aggression.[20] The following day, however, the Washington-based South Korean correspondent Chin Chang-uk was told something quite different by a Russian diplomat in Washington. According to Chin, he was informed that, "if North Korea is found to have a nuclear weapon, the Russian Government will not help North Korea militarily even if a Western country, such as the United States were to take military action, such as preventive bombing, against North Korea," because Russia would regard "confirmation that North Korea has developed nuclear weapons as provocation"; furthermore, if it turned out that North Korea was developing nuclear weapons, "Russia will not give assistance to North Korea even if North Korea is attacked militarily because such an attack on North Korea will not fall under the provisions" of the 1961 treaty of alliance, which, although "still valid with Russia's succession to the Soviet Union," does not obligate Russia to act when it is North Korea that provokes a war.[21]

A week later, in a discussion designed for wide coverage on Moscow Ostankino Television First Channel Network, Panov modified his own earlier position and also sought to soften the impact on Pyongyang of the unusually critical views expressed by the anonymous Russian diplomat in Washington. He noted that Moscow favored the convening of a conference that, among other things, would ensure "the unconditional and full return of the DPRK to the Nuclear Nonproliferation Treaty and inspection by the International Atomic Energy Agency, . . . the denuclearization of the Korean peninsula," and guarantees to North Korea against intervention in its internal affairs. Backing away from his earlier assurances, Panov reinterpreted Moscow's position on the treaty: "As the legal successor of the Soviet Union, Russia continues to fulfill the commitments of the treaty," but "the situation has changed," and therefore Russia has informed North Korea that "we interpret the article that stipulates assistance and support . . . in the event of an emergency situation [to mean that] assistance would be given only in the event of an *unsanctioned* aggression against the DPRK": "We ourselves will analyze the situation on the basis of our sources of information and how the problems are dealt with. We will assess the degree of threat, the degree of aggression and its character, and we will operate within our legislation and our Constitution, and we will certainly take into account Russia's international obligations—for instance those under the International Atomic Energy Treaty and the UN Charter."[22] In effect, Panov signaled Pyongyang that, although qualifying the military provisions, Moscow was not rejecting the treaty itself.

However, on 2 June 1994, during a state visit by South Korean president Kim Young-sam, Russian president Boris Yeltsin seemed to drive the final nail into the 1961 treaty, with his statement at a press conference that "there is no strict provision envisaging that we help and side with the DPRK."[23] South Korean sources gave the details. According to Chung Jong-uk, the South Korean president's chief foreign policy adviser, Yeltsin had said during the discussions "that Article One of the treaty stipulating Moscow's military intervention can be regarded as dead now."[24] This was virtually a repetition of the remarks he made during his visit to Seoul in November 1992, surprising at the time not only his hosts but his own advisers. The statement did not receive the attention it apparently warranted, until the flare-up of the North Korean nuclear crisis, this time underscoring Moscow's focus on improved relations with Seoul. Yeltsin arranged with President Young-sam "to install a hot line between their offices at Chong Wa Dae and the Kremlin."[25] As regards the treaty itself, judging by the joint declaration issued on 2 June, Yeltsin did not clarify his position.[26] But, the following day, President Young-sam stated that Yeltsin "had promised that Moscow will not conclude any pacts of alliance with Pyongyang after the Russia–North Korea Friendship, Cooperation and Mutual Assistance Treaty expires."[27] Seoul believed that it had a firm commitment from Yeltsin on the issue. This was the high-water mark of Yeltsin's off-the-cuff pro-Seoul statements that did not take into consideration the views of his MFA specialists. And indeed, on 17 June, Foreign Minister Kozyrev strongly denied that Russia would not "prolong the treaty," insisting that the matter would be raised, presumably with the Duma, in the fall of 1995. "A more updated interpretation of the treaty, including Article One, with due account of today's realities is being discussed," he added.[28]

By the fall of 1994, in the months after Kim Il-sung's death, attempts at a balanced policy could be gleaned from Moscow's moves. For example, in early September, on the occasion of the Democratic People's Republic's forty-sixth anniversary, Valentin Moiseyev, head of the MFA's Korean section, noted that Moscow was interested "in developing relations in all areas—politics, the economy, culture—all the more so because our traditions of cooperation go back a long way. . . . The decline of our bilateral relations is unnatural, and is not in keeping with the interests of the peoples of Russia and the DPRK."[29] In late September, Deputy Foreign Minister Panov went to Pyongyang, in part to signal Moscow's support for Kim Jong-Il and explore ways of jump-starting economic and political talks, but in Moscow it was announced that he intended to discuss the treaty.[30]

In the spring of 1995, Yeltsin's position on the treaty seemed more equivocal. In mid-May, on the eve of Russian Defense Minister Pavel Grachev's visit, South Korean newspapers reported that he was bringing word that Yeltsin had decided not to renew the treaty; however, as things turned out, Grachev was said to have conveyed Moscow's desire to have a treaty with North Korea similar to the 1992 treaty with South Korea, that is, with no defense provision. A thoughtful evaluation, critical of the incoherence in Yeltsin's policy, appeared in *Pravda* in late June. After reviewing Yeltsin's choices—to renounce, to revise, or to renew—Yurii Vanin urged renewal of the Russian–North Korean treaty, arguing that it would help preserve peace on the Korean peninsula and promote the national interests of Russia.[31]

According to two Russian analysts, Eugene Bazhanov and Natasha Bazhanov, the Russian foreign ministry argued as far back as mid-1992 "that Moscow should seek balanced relations with both South and North Korea, and that it was important for Russians and Americans to maintain their security arrangements on the peninsula to ensure stability."[32] The case for a policy of balance was incongruously enhanced by Pyongyang's failure to hold security consultations with Russia as provided for by the 1961 treaty, on the one hand, and Seoul's repeated deflating of Moscow's "euphoric and unreasonable expectations in relations," on the other.[33]

We do not know the considerations that eventually prompted Yeltsin's preference for nonrenewal / renunciation. Failing health, absorption with the bungled and protracted Chechnya quagmire, difficulty with an increasingly hostile parliament, accession to Kozyrev's wishes, a desire to help South Korea's president in the hope of some reciprocal gesture on the economic front — the list of possible explanations is long. Only time will tell whether the end of Moscow's treaty relationship with North Korea is a precursor of better relations with South Korea or a harbinger of ever-lessening leverage on the Korean peninsula.

North Korea's Nuclear Challenge

In February 1993, North Korea, which had signed the nuclear nonproliferation treaty in 1985 and an inspection agreement with the IAEA in April 1992, refused to permit full inspection of its facilities to determine whether it had accounted for all its weapons-grade nuclear material. A month later, Pyongyang declared its intention to withdraw from the NPT. At the last minute, amid a flurry of intense diplomatic activity and acrimonious exchanges, it announced the deferral of a final decision. The effect was to galvanize the Clinton administration. For more than two years, it kept North Korea negotiating and refraining from the production of any further plutonium. An agreement between the United States and North Korea that was concluded on 21 October 1994 and later challenged by North Korea required additional negotiations. The result was an agreement in May 1995 that, it is to be hoped, clarifies the modalities entailed in its implementation over the next ten years.

The nuclear issue has only recently been a problem between Moscow and Pyongyang. During the Soviet period, starting with a research reactor in 1965, Moscow was instrumental in providing the expertise and material that enabled Pyongyang to develop its nuclear facilities at Yongbyon. Rich in natural uranium deposits, North Korea pushed ahead with a comprehensive extraction, production, and reprocessing program. Its five-megawatt experimental reactor at Yongbyon became operational in October 1987. Estimates are that four to seven kilograms of plutonium a year can be reprocessed from the reactor's spent fuel rods. In addition, fifty-megawatt and two-hundred-megawatt graphite-type nuclear reactors were close to completion when Pyongyang denied the IAEA permission to carry out inspections. Since all three North Korean reactors are geared "to operating on the basis of natural uranium and graphite moderation—a technology which, although not advantageous for the energy industry or for safety technology—is well-suited for plutonium production," and since the five-megawatt reactor is not connected to the electricity grid, the suspicion is strong "that the primary function is to produce plutonium."[34]

When the crisis broke between Pyongyang and the IAEA, Moscow unequivocally aligned itself with the agency, thereby demonstrating its commitment to the NPT. Yeltsin signed an executive order freezing a project, valued at $4 billion, plans for which had been concluded in the last year of the Soviet regime. Moscow was to build three light-water nuclear reactors at Sinpo, on North Korea's east coast: "It was," a Russian diplomat was quoted as saying, "a hard decision for us to swallow, but we cooperated" with the IAEA.[35] Although finding little support for its own proposal for an international conference to negotiate an end to the North Korean nuclear threat, Moscow upheld UN and U.S. efforts in that direction. It supported denuclearization of the Korean peninsula, "including the abstention from attempts, production, possession, importation, and involvement in the distribution of nuclear weapons," as Deputy Foreign Minister Panov reaffirmed in a press interview on 23 June 1994.[36]

The absence of accurate information on the current status of North Korea's nuclear capability has given rise to disagreements among the Russians. The government no longer has privileged access to North Korean sources, and elements in the Russian military and intelligence community may well be concealing information from the government and trying to maintain secret links to their North Korean counterparts, out of mistrust of Kozyrev and the MFA and from a belief in the alliance.

A furor epitomizing such uncertainty erupted in late January 1994 with the publication in the Japanese weekly *Shukan Bunshun* of an alleged top secret document from the Russian General Staff linking it to covert assistance for North Korea's nuclear weapons and missile delivery programs. On 27 January 1994, *Izvestia* analyzed the document's assessments, concluding, as persuasive and probably accurate, the following: that Pyongyang accelerated its nuclear and missile programs "in the second half of the eighties with active Russian participation"; that "almost 160 Russian nuclear scientists and missile specialists have passed through North Korean laboratories and specialized centers since then"; that some specialists continue to work in North Korea on an "unofficial" basis, outside the normal framework of bilateral cooperation; that the Korean Nodong-1 intermediate range missile was successfully completed with the assistance of "Russian brains"; that "North Korea has accumulated a sufficient stock of enriched nuclear raw materials"; and that it "already possesses one or two nuclear warheads."[37] The following day, a spokesman for the Russian General Staff categorically dismissed the articles in *Shukan Bunshun* and *Izvestia* as based "on a gross and obvious forgery."[38] Perhaps the document in question was a forgery, but other evidence of Russia's complicity over the years in North Korea's nuclear-missile buildup is finding increasing acceptance.[39] For example, at various times, Russian nuclear and missile scientists have been prevented from going to North Korea, and others who had gone as "tourists" were persuaded to return. In both kinds of situation, Moscow acted to quash North Korean recruitment attempts on grounds of suspected violations of the NPT.

On 9 June 1994, in an interview with Interfax, Deputy Foreign Minister Panov said that "no one confirms yet that North Korea has a nuclear bomb"; nor has the IAEA concluded that Pyongyang even has the necessary plutonium.[40] Shortly thereafter, on 21 June 1994, Kozyrev said, "North Korea has no nuclear bomb at present," but he went on to add that it may soon create one because to do so "is no problem for a centralized economy which has a plutonium-producing nuclear reactor." Coincidentally or purposefully, a similar assessment came on the very same day from the head of the Russian Ministry for Nuclear Power Engineering, who reported that his staff had concluded that "North Korea does not have nuclear arms."[41]

But, three days later, *Izvestia* printed another explosive story that reverberated throughout the military-intelligence community. This time the document in question, dated 2 February 1990, was a KGB memorandum, approved by Vladimir Kryuchkov, who headed the agency at the time.[42] Citing "a reliable source," the memorandum stated that North Korea was "actively" developing nuclear weapons, that the program was operating under the personal supervision of Kim Il-sung's son, Kim Jong-Il, and that "the first nuclear device had been completed," the aim being to gain "military superiority over South Korea." The document appears authentic. It was obtained by the journalist Yevgenia Albats when she was a member of a Russian government commission in the fall of 1991, looking into the role of the KGB in the planning of the August 1991 coup against President Mikhail Gorbachev. Still more fuel for the heated debate over North Korea's capability was the contention of a North Korea defector, "identified as the son-in-law of North Korean Prime Minister Kang Song San," who told a news conference in Seoul on 27 July 1994 "that the North possesses five nuclear weapons and is trying to develop five more while it stretches out negotiations with the United States."[43] The unresolved controversy over whether North Korea has a nuclear bomb is as much semantic as substantive. Is a *nuclear device* a *nuclear bomb,* or does a device need to be deliverable to be considered a bomb?

Whatever its prevailing view, the Russian government has not been prepared to support economic sanctions against the North in the interest of pressuring it into compliance with IAEA safeguards and inspection. This suggests that it does not believe that all diplomatic alternatives have as yet been exploited; or it is not convinced that North Korea can be considered a nuclear-weapon state under the terms of the NPT; or it seeks to maintain some semblance of the old special relationship with North Korea that it enjoyed on nuclear and nuclear-related issues in the past.

Military Relations

The strained Russian–North Korean military relationship is a consequence of the courtship of South Korea by Gorbachev and Yeltsin and of the greatly diminished economic circumstances that have made Moscow less a patron than an insistent debt collector. The once shared antipathy to the United States and South Korea and Moscow's readiness to supply bargain-priced military equipment and installations on generous terms have been superseded by limited cooperation and wary coexistence. One Russian scholar who has studied the issue carefully believes that the military relationship has been damaged beyond reconstruction and that continuation of minimalist low-level military contacts is due to the desire of "Russia's power structure" to preserve "an effective channel of influencing Pyongyang" and to keep a foothold in the North Korean market.[44]

Notwithstanding the tensions of the 1990s, Russia is still providing North Korea with some arms, albeit primarily of a defensive character, and some spare parts. It is true that Yeltsin categorically stated during his November 1992 summit in Seoul that "military cooperation with the DPRK has been stopped." This was accurate only insofar as *cooperation* is identified with *aid*.[45] Bouchkin maintains that deliveries of nonoffensive arms have occurred, and previous contracts to build more than thirty military-industrial installations are being fulfilled.

Indeed, one important change in Moscow's foreign policy in the post-Soviet period is the pursuit of arms sales for commercial purposes—to earn hard currency or buy needed equipment and expertise. Future arms sales are restrained in the case of North Korea by Moscow's demand for payment in hard currency. Approximately 70 percent of North Korea's estimated $4 billion debt to Russia can be accounted for by unpaid-for weapons. Moscow understands that the changed Russian–North Korean relationship has heightened Pyongyang's apprehensiveness and sense of isolation, but it is not prepared, or able, to resume the old-style system of doing business or transferring military hardware. For the time being, it can do little about Pyongyang's expressions of animosity—its refusal to permit friendship calls by Russian naval vessels on Wonsan, the periodic expulsion of Russian diplomats, and the imposition of severe restrictions on the movements of Russians in North Korea—but it is hoping for incremental moves toward normalizing relations with Kim Jong-Il.

Economic Relations

In the last year of the Soviet era, Soviet–North Korean trade fell by a calamitous 70 percent, from about 60 percent of North Korea's total foreign trade to less than 20 percent. The decline stemmed from an agreement imperiously imposed by Gorbachev on 2 November 1990, stipulating that henceforth the basis of foreign trade would be mutual settlements in hard currency at world market prices. No longer able to pay for its imports of petroleum and petroleum products at substantial discounts and in local currency, North Korea turned to China, which in 1992 became its main trading partner.

Although from 1993 on there has been a gradual improvement in the attitude of Russia and North Korea toward their overall economic relationship, trade levels remain low, falling in 1994 to an all-time low, about $100 million.[46]

After a vice-ministerial meeting in Moscow in August 1993, a number of modest steps were taken to move the economic relationship back to a semblance of normalcy, with particular attention to agriculture, fishing, and forestry.[47] For example, in December 1993, an understanding was reached in Pyongyang on fishing quotas; and, in the fall of 1994, the two parties agreed to reactivate the joint intergovernmental commission for trade and economic, scientific, and technical cooperation for the first time since the demise of the Soviet Union.[48] In February 1995, an agreement on timber production—an area of longtime Russian–North Korean cooperation—was signed in Pyongyang. Worth about $57 million a year to Russia, it sets forth terms of payment for the seven thousand North Korean guest workers and, in a major concession from Pyongyang, includes a provision allowing each North Korean "the right to free exit from the Russia Federation to any state."[49] While positive steps, they are far from indicative of any imminent major turnabout in the economic relationship. North Korea's indebtedness effectively limits bilateral trade to barter arrangements. Russia simply does not have the resources to finance purchases on long-term credit.

Domestic Determinants

Like Humpty-Dumpty, Russia and North Korea have had a great fall, and nothing can put together again their former "special relationship." But there is, as Foreign Minister Kozyrev has acknowledged, "a pro–North Korea lobby" in the Duma. Drawn from factions of Communists, agrarians, and liberal democrats and led by the ultranationalist Vladimir Zhirinovsky, this group is united in its belief that Russia's future lies in full engagement with all nations of the Asia-Pacific region; that as its closest neighbor North Korea has "substantial potential for cooperation" with Russia; that the government has shown insufficient concern for promoting "normal inter-state relations" with the leaders of North Korea; and that it has been too quick to follow the U.S. lead in dealing with North Korea's nuclear challenge and too neglectful of Russia's national interests.[50] Most, but not all, of its adherents manifest suspicion, if not outright hostility, toward U.S. policy: both Vladimir Lukin, chairman of the Duma's Foreign Affairs Committee, and Ivan Rybkin, speaker of the Duma, have actively pushed for government accountability as regards its North Korean policy. The pro–North Korea group favored extension of the 1961 friendship treaty. Early on in the emerging "debate" over its renewal, Lukin had called the Ministry of Foreign Affairs misguided in its statement that "Russia is ready to fully or partially annul the treaty of friendship and cooperation with North Korea two years before the expiration of its term."[51] But the most extreme position is Zhirinovsky's. In late June 1994, at the height of the nuclear crisis and shortly before Kim Il-sung's death, he sent a letter of solidarity to North Korea in which he, in effect, upheld North Korea's right to develop and deploy nuclear weapons: "We, who are Russians, regard that as a sovereign state, the DPRK has a complete right to conduct voluntary science and research work to safeguard its people's welfare and interest."[52]

In persisting in his early position to disengage from too close a link to North Korea, Yeltsin appears to have acted in opposition to the lobbying of three groups that taken together represent a potentially important coalition on foreign policy issues: his Ministry of Foreign Affairs; the "stabilizers" and neoconservatives who advocate greater support for domestic industries; and the military. The emergence in the late summer of 1992 of a view in the MFA recommending balanced relations with the two Koreas was predicated on the assumptions that Russia had to regain influence and prestige throughout Korea "and show its flag wherever possible," that Moscow had created the North Korean regime "and spent much time and money nourishing it," and that, "while leaders come and go, people's memories and friendship endure."[53] In this position, balance-of-power calculations rather than ideological predispositions predominated.

The "party of stabilizers," typified by First Deputy Premier Oleg Soskovets, argued that one way to support domestic industries that are in deep economic trouble is by opening former markets for the competent but not internationally competitive goods of today's Russian industries.[54] He proposed that relations with North Korea "should not be sacrificed for the sake of development of relations with South Korea" and stressed the benefits to be derived by fulfilling the needs of factories and infrastructure in North Korea built by the former Soviet Union for Russian machinery, spare parts, and the expansion of existing installations. The rationale behind the policies of the "stabilizers" is primarily economic.

The final constituency whose views Yeltsin appears to have slighted was the military. According to Stephen Blank, "Russian generals discount Pyongyang's possession of nuclear weapons as having little serious strategic significance for Russia." Their main concern is a nuclear Japan, "either within the umbrella of the U.S. security treaty or, if that breaks down, on its own." Favoring arms sales as a way of saving Russia's defense industries, they support "renewed sales, even if only spares, to Pyongyang."[55] Presumably, too, the Russian military would like to retain as many as possible of its former links to its North Korean counterparts in order not only to promote security and stability with a neighbor but also to enhance the importance of the military as an institution. Viewed from this perspective, Yeltsin's decision not to renew the treaty or even try seriously to renegotiate a new one may further erode his support among groups who have been in his camp in the past.

Fallout for the U.S.-Russian Relationship

When Presidents Yeltsin and Clinton met in Moscow in January 1994, their joint statement signaled an underlying parallelism of aims with respect to North Korea:

They agreed that nuclear weapons on the Korean peninsula would represent a grave threat to regional and international security, and decided that their countries would consult with each other on ways to eliminate this danger. They called upon the DPRK to honor fully its obligations under the Treaty on the non-proliferation of nuclear weapons and its safeguards agreement with the IAEA in connection with the treaty, and to resolve the problems of safeguards implementation, inter alia, through dialogue between IAEA and the DPRK. They also urged full and speedy implementation of the joint declaration of the ROK and the DPRK on denuclearization of the Korean peninsula.

However, by the latter part of 1995, political dissonances were evident. Moscow was increasingly bitter over what it regarded as U.S. (and South Korean) indifference to Russia's interests and status as a regional great power. Yeltsin had believed that Russia would be included in the diplomatic efforts to promote regional security. This was undermined by a series of developments relating to the negotiation of the U.S.–North Korean general framework agreement of 21 October 1994 and the subsequent clarifications and elaboration in the May 1995 accords. Moscow expected more from Washington for its support of international pressure to compel Pyongyang's adherence to the NPT and of the U.S. initiative to obtain Pyongyang's agreement to a complicated arrangement that could, if fully implemented over the next five to ten years, greatly minimize the long-term nuclear threat on the Korean peninsula. But all it received was a mixture of indifference and disdain.

For instance, during the spring of 1994, when North Korea and the United States appeared to be on a collision course over IAEA inspections, Moscow proposed the convening of an international conference on the security and nuclear status of the Korean peninsula, with a broad agenda and representation that would include the two Koreas, Japan, China, the United States, Russia, and the IAEA. The proposal never attracted any support. Moscow felt that it had been given the cold shoulder and was peeved enough to state in mid-June 1994 that it would oppose a U.S. resolution in the UN Security Council calling for the imposition of sanctions on North Korea. According to Foreign Minister Kozyrev, the resolution contradicted an agreement between the United States and Russia "to act jointly, to work out a draft resolution jointly and not to put forward unilateral initiatives" and to include "both the idea of sanctions and specific ideas on an international conference."[56]

A second issue that proved more serious was Washington's lack of interest in having Russia provide one of the two light-water reactors that are to replace North Korea's current graphite, plutonium-capable reactors. Moscow eagerly sought such consideration, probably more for commercial than political reasons, and it had reason to rue Yeltsin's abrupt decision in 1993 to suspend the 1991 contract to supply light-water reactors of its own to North Korea. From mid-1994 until the official announcement on 13 June 1995 that South Korea would provide the two reactors under the aegis of an international consortium operating through the Korean Energy Development Organization (KEDO), which was created specifically for this purpose, Moscow lobbied hard in Washington, Pyongyang, and Seoul.[57] Shortly after returning from Pyongyang in late September 1994, Deputy Foreign Minister Panov had reported that "North Korea is interested in obtaining Russian reactors," noting the advantage that North Korea was already well acquainted with Russian reactor technology. He acknowledged the existence of "financial problems and the position of the U.S., which would like North Korea to use South Korean reactors built by American license which must be taken into account."[58] If Panov's insistence that in his meetings neither the 1961 treaty nor military assistance were discussed is true, then Pyongyang's lukewarm interest in Russian reactors becomes clearer.

When the U.S.–North Korean framework agreement of October 1994 seemed in jeopardy, Foreign Minister Kozyrev tried to interject a Russian presence: "Russia believes that it is she who should supply light-water nuclear reactors to North Korea within the framework of an international program designed to solve the problems of the DPRK's nuclear program, which is suspected by the international community of secretly developing nuclear weapons."[59] Shortly afterward, according to the *Wall Street Journal,* Kozyrev offered to cancel the $800 million contract for the construction of a light-water nuclear reactor and power plant that Moscow had signed with Iran earlier in the year, in return "for $200 million in alternative nuclear work," that is, for "a piece of a new deal to give nuclear-power equipment to North Korea."[60] Secretary of State Warren Christopher never considered the offer seriously. Nor, in all likelihood, did North Korea. With an economy in even worse condition than Russia's, North Korea had excellent reasons to craft a settlement of the nuclear issue with the United States and open the way for economic assistance from the United States, South Korea, and Japan—however it chooses to explain such transactions. Thus, with food in short supply, in June 1995, North Korea signed an agreement with South Korea in Beijing, which was unreported in the North Korean press, accepting 150,000 tons of emergency rice supplies.[61]

Sergei Agafonov of *Izvestia* put it well. Writing on Washington's success in striking a deal with North Korea in October 1994, he provided a perspective that purportedly describes how the Japanese see the unfolding reality but that sheds light on Moscow's outlook as well:

> Pyongyang has acquired clear freedom of maneuver and has quickly shifted from a position of "pariah" to a position of a partner in dialogue with the Americans, who will henceforth have a monopoly on initiatives where North Korea is concerned; South Korea unexpectedly finds itself bound by the results of talks held without its participation and will have to bear this "cross" without any particular right to revise those results; and Japan, which had tried to pursue a kind of independent policy in contacts with Pyongyang and had laid claim to special rights as a mediator, has again been put in the position of reluctant financier, providing credits for others' diplomatic wishes. As for Russia, its situation is the most regrettable. Not only have its efforts to "lend a hand" been disregarded; in addition, it will have to scrap both its initiative for conducting a six-way forum on the North Korean question and its hopes to help modernize the North Korean nuclear energy complex, a prospect Russia was very much counting on.[62]

Agafonov's colleague Leonid Mlechin was more bitter—and probably even more accurate—in describing the mood of Moscow's foreign policy establishment and its critics: "Now it turns out that Russia, which has strictly observed its international commitments, is essentially being squeezed out of the nuclear market. . . . In the opinion of Moscow experts, the agreement between Washington and Pyongyang undermines the nuclear nonproliferation regime and sets a bad precedent: Dictators see that blackmail can be successful and that it isn't hard to win major political and economic concessions in exchange for nothing more than a promise to meet their own international commitments."[63]

Many in Moscow initially viewed the North Korean nuclear crisis as providentially rescuing Russia from marginalization and thrusting it once again into the center of the region's diplomatic game. Subsequent developments have exacerbated the humiliation and rancor they feel at how far Russia has fallen as a power. No regional actor is more peripheral or less esteemed. For the first time in its history as an East Asian country, Russia has no discernible role to play in shaping outcomes or fashioning security in the region. How distant seems Yeltsin's heady address to the South Korean National Assembly on 19 November 1992, when he proposed "creating a body for mediating international military disputes and a center for regional strategic research in the region" and making "the Korean Peninsula a zone free from weapons of mass destruction under the guarantee of Russia and other regional powers: Russians feel responsible for the fate of the Asia-Pacific region and are willing to contribute to strengthening mutual confidence among countries in the region."[64]

Moscow has been outplayed on the Korean peninsula, not only by North and South Korea but by the United States as well. Alternatively, one could say that Moscow played its diplomatic hand poorly. North Korea has opened direct links to the United States, which now has a stake in closer ties, without sacrificing any of the advantages that it derives from a residual Russian connection. For its part, South Korea has treated Russia shabbily: not only refusing to reschedule the debt Russia incurred from Seoul's extension of a $3 billion credit in 1991 but also failing to resolve the disposition of the former Soviet embassy compound, which was nationalized in 1970, without compensation. Moscow now refuses to accept an offer that it considers a totally inadequate amount.[65] U.S. policy toward Russia in Northeast Asia is one of "indifferent neglect." All the regional actors assume that Russia is unlikely to count for much in the region for the foreseeable future, given its preoccupation with internal divisions and dilemmas.

Notes

1 *Foreign Broadcast Information Service, Central Eurasia, Russia International Affairs* (hereafter *FBIS/SOV/Russia*), 7 September 1995, 26.

2 As cited from Reuters, 8 September 1995.

3 Robert M. Slusser, "Soviet Far Eastern Policy, 1945–1950: Stalin's Goals in Korea," in *The Origins of the Cold War in Asia,* ed. Yonosuke Nagai and Akira Iriye (New York: Columbia University Press, 1977), 127, 136–38. A new study sheds additional light on Soviet policy during this period: Sergei Goncharov, John W.

Lewis, and Xue Lital, *Uncertain Partners: Stalin, Mao and the Korean War* (Stanford, Calif.: Stanford University Press, 1994).

4 See Chong-sik Lee and Ki-Wan Oh, "The Russian Faction in North Korea," *Asian Survey* 8, no. 4 (April 1968): 270–88.

5 See Leonid Vasin, "Historical Details on DPRK's Kim Il-sung," *Nezavisimaya gazeta,* 29 September 1993, 5, translated in *FBIS/SOV/Russia,* 2 February 1994, 31–37. Vasin, who worked for the Soviet army's special propaganda section dealing with Korean affairs, says that Kim Il-sung was "created . . . from scratch" by the CPSU and KGB authorities, that he had no major role in the liberation of Korea from Japanese forces, and that, far from being a brilliant leader for years, in 1945 "he was unable to put together decent notes for a speech at the political classes, despite the program's demands for the study of Russian, and had not in three years mastered the basics of Marxism-Leninism. . . . What, in fact, is the point of reproaching Kim Il-sung and gauging the parameters of his honor and conscience? He is, after all, copied from us. He is as we used to be. We had the same military commanders and theorists. We extolled him and praised him in such a way that he in actual fact decided that he was great. It is hard now to persuade him that he with his mumbo-jumbo—Chuche philosophy—is an ignoramus. . . . So who is he? Not, of course, a military commander, not a theorist, and not a philosopher, and a leader in the broad meaning of this word even less" (pp. 36–37). Vasin's derisory political portrait may help explain Kim Il-sung's attachment to the Stalinist model of society he was nurtured on.

6 According to one authority on Korea, given "the DPRK's continuing dependence on the Soviet Union for its economy and defense, the Koreans could not help but to defer to Soviet advice and suggestions. It was years before the DPRK leaders openly aired their pent up emotions against Soviet arrogance and haughtiness" (Chong-sik Lee, "The Origins of the Korean War: A Reflection" [typescript], 8). Kathryn Weathersby, a scholar at the University of Florida who has been able to work in the Soviet archives on issues relating to the Korean War and the cold war, cites documents suggesting that it was Kim who came up with the plan for the invasion, which Stalin approved, for reasons relating to his relations with Mao ("From the Russian Archives: New Findings on the Korean War," *Cold War International History Project Bulletin,* no. 3 [Fall 1993]: 14). Her assessment that the initiative for the war came from Pyongyang, not Moscow, is dismissed by Adam Ulam of Harvard University, who questions "the notion that in 1950 Kim, or any other Communist leader, was in a position to pressure—compel or shame—the Soviets into doing something they had not planned in the first place, or that the North Koreans have invaded without Soviet permission/command." Ulam notes that the document that Weathersby cites was produced in 1966—the height of the Sino-Soviet conflict—when "there would have been a strong inclination to dilute Soviet responsibility for the invasion" (*Cold War International History Project Bulletin* no. 4 [Fall 1994]: 21). The availability of new material has thus far not resolved the issue. For additional comments and documents, see

Kathryn Weathersby, "Korea, 1949–50: To Attack, or Not to Attack? Stalin, Kim Il-sung, and the Prelude to War," *Cold War International History Project Bulletin,* no. 5 (Spring 1995): 1–9.

7 Harry Gelman and Norman D. Levin, *The Future of Soviet–North Korean Relations* (Santa Monica, Calif.: Rand, October 1984), 15.

8 Daniel Abele, "Soviet–North Korean Relations on the Upswing," RL 356187 (Radio Free Europe/Radio Liberty, 24 August 1987), 2.

9 David Rees, *Moscow's Changing Policy toward the Two Koreas* (Washington, D.C.: International Security Council, August 1991), 6–7.

10 For a Soviet account of the considerations that motivated Moscow and of the difficulties between Moscow and Pyongyang, see Georgy F. Kunadze, "USSR-ROK: Agenda for the Future," *Korea and World Affairs* 15, no. 2 (Summer 1991): 197–210. At the time, Kunadze was a senior researcher and head of the Department for Political Problems Concerned with Japan and Korea at the Soviet Academy of Sciences Institute for World Economy and International Relations. At present, he is Russia's ambassador in Seoul.

11 This account was written by a Russian diplomat while first secretary at the Russian embassy in Seoul (Oleg V. Davidov, "Russia's Position towards North Korea's Development as a Nuclear Power," in *Russia in the Far East and Pacific Region,* ed. Il Yung Chung and Eunsook Chung [Seoul: Sejong Institute, 1994]) 360–61).

12 Ibid., 362.

13 For an overview of this issue, see Benjamin S. Lambeth, "Russia's Wounded Military," *Foreign Affairs* 74, no. 2 (March–April 1995): 86–98.

14 *FBIS/SOV/Russia,* 14 November 1994, 14.

15 Choon-ho Park, "River and Maritime Boundary Problems between North Korea and Russia in the Tumen River and the Sea of Japan," *Korean Journal of Defense Analysis* 5, no. 2 (Winter 1993): 65–66.

16 Andrew A. Bouchkin, "North Korea and Russia: A Blind Alley?" in *Foreign Relations of North Korea during Kim Il Sung's Last Days,* ed. Doug Joong Kim (Seoul: Sejong Institute, 1994), 314–15.

17 *Current Digest of the Post-Soviet Press* (hereafter *CDPP*), 44, no. 31 (1992): 17.

18 Bouchkin, "North Korea and Russia," 315.

19 Georgi D. Boulychev, "Moscow and North Korea: The 1961 Treaty and After," in *Russia in the Far East and Pacific Region,* 109–14.

20 *Foreign Broadcast Information Service, East Asia* (hereafter *FBIS/EAS*), 1 April 1994, 11. See also "Russia Will Aid N. Korea If It's Attacked, Envoy Says," *Baltimore Sun,* 9 April 1994, 4.

21 "Russian Diplomat Cited on DPRK Nuclear Issue," *Seoul Chungang Ilbo,* 31 March 1994, 1, translated in *FBIS/EAS/Northeast Asia,* 31 March 1994, 26.

22 "Panov Calls for Multilateral Conference on Korean Crisis," *FBIS/SOV/Russia,* 8 April 1994, 1 (emphasis added).

23 "Yeltsin Warns DPRK of Sanctions," ITAR-TASS, 2 June 1994, reprinted in *FBIS/SOV/Russia,* 2 June 1994, 7.
24 "Yeltsin Pledges Pressure on N.K.," *Newsreview,* 4 June 1994, 4.
25 Ibid.
26 *FBIS/SOV/Russia,* 3 June 1994, 3–8.
27 Ibid.
28 *FBIS/SOV/Russia,* 20 June 1994, 6.
29 *FBIS/SOV/Russia,* 12 September 1994, 14–15.
30 *FBIS/SOV/Russia,* 21 September 1994, 13.
31 Yurii Vanin, "Zemlya Korei—ona riadom s nami," *Pravda,* 28 June 1995, 6.
32 Eugene Bazhanov and Natasha Bazhanov, "The Evolution of Russian-Korean Relations: External and Internal Factors," *Asian Survey* 34, no. 9 (September 1994): 793.
33 Mikhail L. Titarenko, "Korean Peninsula in the System of Russia's National Interests," *Sino-Soviet Affairs* (Seoul) 18, no. 4 (Winter 1994/1995): 66.
34 Hanns W. Maull, "North Korea's Nuclear Weapons Programme: Genesis, Motives, Implications," *Aussenpolitik* 45, no. 4 (1994): 355.
35 Shim Jae Hoon, "Silent Partner," *Far East Economic Review,* 29 December 1994, 5 January 1995, 14–15.
36 "Russia and the North Korean Problem," *Diplomaticheskii vestnik,* nos. 13–14 (July 1994): 38–41.
37 Sergei Agafonov, "160 Russian Nuclear and Missile Specialists Helped North Korea to Create a Nuclear Bomb," *Izvestia,* 27 January 1994, 1, 4.
38 Aleksandr Golts, "'General Staff Secret Report' . . . in Fact Blatant Forgery," *Krasnaia zvezda,* 28 January 1994, 1, in *FBIS/SOV/Russia,* 28 January 1994, 7–8.
39 For example, Valerii Vladislavlev, "Russia and DPRK Nuclear Problem," *Nezavisimaya gazeta,* 29 April 1994.
40 A. Panov, Interfax, 9 June 1994, in *FBIS/SOV/Russia,* 9 June 1994, 10–11.
41 *FBIS/SOV/Russia,* 22 June 1994, 8.
42 See Yevgenia Albats, in *Izvestia,* 24 June 1994, 4, translated in *FBIS/SOV/Russia,* 24 June 1994, 11–12.
43 Byung-joon Ahn, "The Man Who Would Be Kim," *Foreign Affairs* 73, no. 6 (November–December 1994): 103; James Sterngold, "Defector Says North Korea Has 5 A-Bombs and May Make More," *New York Times,* 28 July 1994, A7.
44 Bouchkin, "North Korea and Russia," 327.
45 Ibid., 322–23.
46 ITAR-TASS, 22 September 1994, translated in *FBIS/SOV/Russia,* 23 September 1994, 14.
47 See, e.g., *FBIS/SOV/Russia,* 2 February 1995, 5.
48 ITAR-TASS, 21 September 1994, translated in *FBIS/SOV/Russia,* 22 September 1994, 15–16.
49 See V. Yakubovsky, "Economic Relations between Russia and DPRK: Prob-

lems and Perspectives" (paper presented at the Institute for Sino-Soviet Studies, Hanyang University, Seoul, 1995).

50 Aleksandr Chudodeyev, *Segodnya,* 8 September 1994, 5, in *FBIS/SOV/Russia,* 9 September 1994, 16.

51 Pavel Kuznetsov, ITAR-TASS, 10 June 1994, in *FBIS/SOV/Russia,* 13 June 1994, 4.

52 *FBIS/SOV/Northeast Asia,* 27 June 1994, 27.

53 Bazhanov and Bazhanov, "The Evolution of Russian-Korean Relations," 793–95.

54 Yakubovsky, "Economic Relations between Russia and DPRK."

55 Stephen J. Blank, *Russian Policy and the Korean Crisis* (Carlisle Barracks, Pa.: U.S. Army Strategic Studies Institute, 1994), 9.

56 Alessandra Stanley, "Moscow Miffed by U.S. Draft on Korea," *New York Times,* 17 June 1994; see also *FBIS/SOV/Russia,* 16 June 1994, 4–5.

57 See, e.g., Hoon, "Silent Partner," 14–15; *FBIS/SOV/Russia,* 21 February 1995, 11.

58 Interfax, 27 September 1994, in *FBIS/SOV/Russia,* 28 September 1994, 9. See also Aleksandr Platkovskii, *Izvestia,* 28 September 1994, 3; and *FBIS/SOV/Russia,* 7 November 1994, 8.

59 *FBIS/SOV/Russia,* 6 March 1995, 10.

60 Carla Anne Robbins, *Wall Street Journal,* 5 May 1995, 14.

61 *Economist,* 24 June 1995, 6.

62 *CDPP* 46, no. 42 (1994): 21–22.

63 Leonid Mlechin, *Izvestia,* 29 October 1994, 3.

64 Quoted in Alexander N. Panov, "The Problem of Regional Stability and Security in the Asia-Pacific Region," in *Russia in the Far East and Pacific Region,* 169.

65 See *FBIS/SOV/Russia,* 2 June 1994, 68–69.

HONGCHAN CHUN AND CHARLES E. ZIEGLER

The Russian Federation and South Korea

Russian foreign policy in the post-Soviet period is a foreign policy in transition. Many defining elements of Soviet foreign policy were transformed late in the Gorbachev era, and much of the Soviet Union's raw power disappeared with its collapse. While crafting a new Russian foreign policy in a radically changed international environment has proved difficult, we can discern certain patterns that emerged during the first four years of the Yeltsin administration. A case study of Russian relations with South Korea in this period provides insight into the broader forces shaping the formative stages of Russia's international behavior.

In the interests of preserving a comparative framework, we have organized this study of Russian–South Korean relations to cover the following topics. First, we discuss the effect of the Soviet Union's demise and Russia's emergence on the Russian–South Korean relationship. Next, we examine changes in the Russian Federation's approach toward South Korea in comparison with that of the Soviet regime under Gorbachev. Third, we analyze the key political, security, and economic issues in Russian–South Korean bilateral relations. In the fourth section, we discuss the implications of Russian–South Korean relations for U.S. interests and policy options. We then conclude with some observations about Russian–South Korean relations and the general directions of Russian foreign policy.

The Soviet Demise and Russian-Korean Relations

As was the case with all other countries of the world, the dissolution of the Soviet Union was shocking to South Korea. The event was a sobering occasion for the South Korean government, which had pursued diplomatic normalization with the Communist powers ("northern policy," or *Nordpolitik*) as one of its most important foreign policy goals in the late 1980s. The euphoria was certainly evident when South Korea finally succeeded in establishing diplomatic relations with the Soviet Union on 30 September 1990. South Korean firms were optimistic that normalized relations would open a new market of huge potential in the Soviet Union. Most significantly, the South Korean government regarded, and publicized, the event as a security breakthrough, given Moscow's presumed influence over North Korea.

South Korea's euphoria and sense of achievement, however, began to falter with the disintegration of the Soviet Union. The uncertain future of the former Soviet republics cast doubt on the wisdom of Seoul's erstwhile approach to Moscow. Disenchantment with the Communist superpower had emerged in South Korea as early as June 1991. The election of Boris Yeltsin that month as the first democratically chosen president of Russia, the failed coup attempt against Gorbachev in August, and the dissolution of the Communist party of the Soviet Union (CPSU) immediately afterward all indicated that Moscow was losing control of the internal empire. Indeed, when the Soviet Union finally disappeared in December 1991, President Roh's Soviet policy came under attack. The decision to provide $3 billion in credits to an unstable government was subject to particularly harsh criticism.

In spite of the uncertainty and turmoil, the series of events since the summer of 1991 have on balance had a positive effect from South Korea's standpoint. Above all, the failure of the military coup, the critical factor that expedited the collapse of the Soviet system, contributed to decreasing the influence of the conservatives and strengthening that of Yeltsin and reformist leaders in Moscow. In Moscow's Korean policy, this change meant closer ties with South Korea and further distance from the North. Indeed, the Soviet foreign ministry excluded the North Korean ambassador from a postcoup briefing it held for foreign ambassadors. Gorbachev himself sent President Roh a letter thanking him for his support during the coup.[1]

Moscow's Korean policy shifted toward greater emphasis on South Korea as the Russian Federation assumed the Soviet Union's international obligations. As early as December 1991, Russian officials suggested revising the Soviet–North Korean Treaty on Friendship, Cooperation, and Mutual Assistance, concluded in 1961.[2] President Yeltsin chose to visit South Korea in November 1992, which further strained Russia's relations with the North. At that time, he publicly confirmed the Russian Federation's critical attitude toward the treaty by promising to pursue its revision.[3] Therefore, the process that led to the collapse of the Soviet Union and the assumption of power by Yeltsin and his reformist leaders helped consolidate Moscow-Seoul ties.

These developments were, from Seoul's perspective, not entirely favorable to South Korea. A further cooling of Moscow's relations with Pyongyang eliminated Moscow's residual influence with North Korea. In other words, for Seoul, the strategic value of the Russian Federation, at least initially, was less than that of the Soviet Union. Furthermore, the extensive domestic problems that consumed the Russian Federation after independence reinforced Russia's image as a power in decline. These factors made the new democratic Russia somewhat less attractive a partner in comparison with the former Soviet Union.

In order to understand the utility of this relationship for both Moscow and Seoul, it is worth briefly reviewing the process by which Mikhail Gorbachev reversed four decades of Soviet policy toward the Korean peninsula.

Gorbachev's South Korea Policy

As a close ally of the United States, South Korea was subject to unrelenting Soviet hostility throughout the postwar era. Moscow supported the Democratic People's Republic of Korea, concluded the Treaty of Mutual Friendship and Support with Pyongyang in 1961, and refused to extend diplomatic recognition to the South. However, Pyongyang's stubborn adherence to a policy of self-reliant independence (*juche*) and close ties with the People's Republic of China constrained relations with the Soviet Union. Moscow provided subsidized oil and other goods on concessionary terms to the North, frequently without Pyongyang's acknowledgment. However, the Sino-Soviet dispute and Moscow's decision to expand its Pacific presence during the Brezhnev period conferred on North Korea the status of a key ally in Northeast Asia.

There was no indication of any significant change in Soviet policy toward the Korean peninsula during the first three years of Gorbachev's administration. Kim Il-sung made his second state visit in three years to Moscow in 1986 and received Soviet promises to deliver advanced jet fighters, thus fulfilling a deal negotiated in 1984. By 1988, however, it was clear that a reassessment of Soviet Korean policy was under way, prompted by the reformers' recognition that economic clout, not military force, was the key to prominence in Asian-Pacific affairs.

Acting on this new perspective, Moscow expanded trade links with South Korea and resisted Pyongyang's pressure to boycott the Seoul Olympic games. Gorbachev's meetings with President Roh Tae Woo in San Francisco and then in Cheju Island were followed by the establishment of diplomatic relations on 30 September 1990, a move that elicited bitter protests from the North Koreans.

These abrupt changes in Soviet policy toward the two Koreas were strongly influenced by a parallel transformation of Sino-Soviet relations, combined with a relaxation of U.S.-Soviet tensions in the Pacific. Over a three-year period starting in 1987, Moscow acceded to China's preconditions for improved ties, and normalized government and party links were realized with Gorbachev's May 1989 visit to Beijing.[4] Gorbachev's 1988 announcement of major troop reductions in both Asia and Europe accelerated the pace of superpower reconciliation, leading the United States to reassess its force posture in the Pacific. President George Bush unilaterally withdrew American nuclear weapons from South Korea in 1991 and announced the removal of all nuclear cruise missiles from U.S. warships in the Pacific.

As East Asia's strategic environment changed, North Korea lost much of its utility for Soviet East Asia policy. Competition between Moscow and Beijing for influence with North Korea was now largely irrelevant. Access to North Korean ports and overflight rights were no longer needed as the Soviet military reduced its forces in Vietnam's Cam Ranh Bay and abandoned the goal of power projection into the Pacific. Nor could North Korea aid Gorbachev's goals of economic reform and integration into the Asian regional economy. Pyongyang had been a drain on the Soviet treasury, yet the leadership insisted on maintaining the country's autarkic and inefficient centrally planned economy.

With North Korea's utility as a friend and ally of the Soviet Union declining, South Korea's position in Moscow's Asia policy grew rapidly.

South Korea's dynamic economy made it a far more attractive economic partner than North Korea; Gorbachev hoped to attract South Korean investment and technology as part of his strategy for developing the Soviet Far East. Overtures toward Seoul were also part of Moscow's effort to extract concessions from the Japanese. Soviet officials clearly were signaling that, if Tokyo refused to cooperate fully on trade and territorial issues, Moscow had an equally valuable partner in South Korea.

The New Russian Federation and South Korea

The major shifts in Northeast Asia's political and strategic environment that occurred in the late 1980s and early 1990s have not been reversed with the collapse of the Soviet Union and the emergence of the Russian Federation as its successor state. After the collapse of the Soviet Union, however, the Russian Federation found itself in a changed geostrategic environment, which resulted from the loss of the western and the southern republics of the former Soviet Union.

The disintegration of the Soviet internal empire into a number of smaller independent states shifted the new Russian Federation eastward. First of all, the loss of numerous economic resources in Ukraine, Belarus, the Baltic states, Central Asia, and the Transcaucasian republics has made Siberia and the Russian Far East more important. As major former Soviet ports in the Baltic and the Black Sea became foreign holdings, Russia's Pacific ports grew in importance. This shift of geostrategic center also partially reorients Russia's external economic relations in the direction of Northeast Asia. The Asia-Pacific region's dynamic economic trends reinforce Russian interest in Asia. Finally, Russia's move to the east has revived early twentieth-century discussions about the Russian nation's cultural identity—the Eurasianist/Eurocentrism debate.

In defense matters, many Russian foreign policy makers remain sensitive to the security environment of Northeast Asia. Central Asia and the Caucasus are the primary security concerns for Russia. However, in Northeast Asia, Russia shares an immense border with China and is still in the process of sorting out its regional ties to Japan, the Koreas, and the United States. Russia has pursued improved relations with all Asian-

Pacific nations, but China and Washington's two closest allies, Japan and South Korea, rank highest on Moscow's priority list.

In coping with this new security environment, Russia is in one sense better equipped and has more options than the former Soviet Union. Moscow's policy makers are no longer constrained by the socialist ideological blinders through which Northeast Asian policies were conceived. In the past, as far as Korean affairs were concerned, the Soviet leadership found itself locked into supporting Kim Il-sung's unpredictable and not very pliable regime. The payoffs from Moscow's substantial investment were not very high, but the Soviet leadership could not find any "reasonable" alternatives. Now, with the abandonment of the Communist world outlook in the new Russia, Moscow has been able not only to deal more directly with Seoul but in general to undertake more flexible approaches toward the peninsula. At the same time, Moscow's initiatives are not automatically opposed by Washington and Beijing, as in the past.

In another sense, however, Moscow's options in the region are limited by a substantial reduction in military capabilities. Signs of the military decay in the Far East were first noticed toward the end of the Soviet period. These difficulties accelerated with the collapse of the Soviet Union.

The implosion of the Soviet empire led to the loss of nearly half the population base and many critical military installations. Russian forces suffer from chronic shortages of manpower—demographic factors, the poor health and low morale of conscripts, and pervasive draft evasion, all contribute to lowered levels of combat preparedness. Stories of corruption and hazing, abysmal living conditions, and repeated violations of military discipline are common throughout Russia.[5]

The situation was particularly serious in the inhospitable Far East. As early as July 1992, the Pacific Fleet had no more than half the requisite personnel.[6] Given these conditions, the Yeltsin government's troop reductions in the Far East, including the 30 percent reduction on the Kuril Islands, did little more than formalize an existing situation. The supportive infrastructure of Russia's Far Eastern forces was disrupted with the breakup of the Soviet Union. For example, the Pacific Fleet lost the services of the Nikolaevsk Ship Repair Association on the Black Sea, formerly the main dock for the maintenance and repair of Soviet navy ships, when these facilities were turned over to Ukraine. Since the Dalzavod repair center was not equipped to handle major, high-tech ships, the Pacific Fleet retired the *Minsk* and *Novorossiisk* carriers.

In addition to its reduced military capability, the virtual abandonment of the Russian Far East following the breakup of the Soviet Union also contributed to Russia's weak position in Northeast Asia. Little progress has been made in the Russian Far East in developing economic links to East Asian states. Moscow's politicians, who during the Soviet period granted a wide range of privileges to the inhabitants of this strategic outpost, are now preoccupied with issues centered around the capital and largely ignore the Far East.[7]

Declining military preparedness and the deteriorating economic situation in its Far East have seriously constrained the Russian Federation's foreign policy toward Northeast Asian countries. Of course, even before the breakup, Soviet policy under Gorbachev had rejected the Brezhnev-era, power-based security policy in favor of a more accommodative, economics-based approach toward East Asia. Under Yeltsin, Moscow has continued to push an economic agenda, albeit with minimal success, and has sporadically tried to strengthen its bilateral ties with East Asian nations, supplementing these links with calls for multilateral forums in which Russia would play a prominent role befitting its putative great power status.

This approach is reflected in Russia's approach toward South Korea. Moscow has proposed increased bilateral security cooperation with Seoul while also actively promoting the idea of a multilateral security system for all Northeast Asia. For instance, in April 1994, when the South Korean defense minister visited Moscow, his Russian counterpart, Pavel Grachev, presented the idea of a multilateral security system in Northeast Asia and asked for South Korea's cooperation.[8] A similar proposal was repeated again when Grachev visited South Korea in May 1995, according to a source in the Korean defense ministry.

The Yeltsin administration's initial approach toward the Korean peninsula leaned heavily toward the South. Soviet policy in the later Gorbachev years made great efforts not to alienate the North, even as relations with South Korea were developing rapidly. For example, Moscow honored its deal to deliver advanced weapons—MiG-29s and SU-25s—to North Korea.[9] As a goodwill gesture, Moscow postponed for a year implementation of its decision to shift Soviet–North Korean bilateral trade to a hard-currency basis.[10] And the Gorbachev government decided in 1991 to renew the Soviet Union–North Korea treaty for another five years, against the express wishes of the South Korean government.

Normal relations with both Koreas, which other great powers lacked, would have given the Soviet Union unique diplomatic leverage on and influence in Korean affairs. Yeltsin's visit to Seoul in late 1992 provided a clear signal that, unlike its predecessor, the Russian Federation was no longer straddling the fence in dealing with the two Koreas. Critics of the Yeltsin administration's tilt toward Seoul complained that Moscow was squandering an opportunity to serve as a major power broker on the peninsula.

With his November 1992 trip to Seoul, Boris Yeltsin had become the first Soviet or Russian president to visit the South Korean capital. The summit demonstrated Russia's willingness to develop a partnership with South Korea beyond the level of normalized diplomatic relations. These provisions included an agreement on the principles of bilateral relations, trade and economic cooperation, and a memorandum of understanding on military exchanges. While the former delineated principles and areas of cooperation in broad and general terms, the latter was more noteworthy in that it served as the basis for security cooperation between the two former adversaries. Yeltsin announced in Seoul that the Russian Federation would stop providing weapons to North Korea and that the 1961 defense treaty between the Soviet Union and North Korea would be overhauled since Russia did not plan to honor the military assistance provisions.

By 1993, nationalist and conservative criticisms of the Yeltsin-Kozyrev foreign policy moved Russian foreign policy in a less Eurocentric direction. As part of the shift in Russian foreign policy, the Yeltsin government attempted to reinvigorate relations with North Korea while preserving and expanding ties with the South. By the spring of 1994, there was no dispute that Moscow's foreign policy was significantly more confrontational and assertive than two years earlier. Instead of playing the role of junior partner to the United States, the Yeltsin government sought to craft foreign policies on the basis of Russia's national interest. This more nationalistic approach occasionally brought Moscow into confrontation with the West on international issues.

This change of mood was perceived in South Korea as well, in the way Moscow treated issues relating to North Korea. As a consequence, some government officials and analysts in South Korea detected a shift in Moscow's Korean policy toward restoring closer relations with Pyongyang; others believed that Russia was simply pursuing equidistance in its relations with the two Koreas. It is apparent that Russia is trying to strengthen ties with Pyongyang in order to regain superpower status on the peninsula.[11] The Yeltsin administration has reacted to criticism that its Korean policy neglected Russia's economic interests in the North, accepted a diminished Russian presence on the peninsula, and ceded influence to an American-dominated "new world order" by seeking to restore some measure of influence with Pyongyang.[12]

The trend toward a more balanced Russian approach in dealing with the two Koreas was apparent by the spring of 1994. This revised Korea policy is evident when the key issues of Russian–South Korean relations are brought into focus.

Key Issues in Russian–South Korean Relations

Nuclear Proliferation and Security

The shift toward a more assertive Russian stance in foreign policy has meant renewed efforts to have Moscow included in negotiations to control North Korea's nuclear-weapons program. The Yeltsin government had made clear its opposition to North Korean possession of nuclear weapons; the denuclearization of the peninsula is clearly in Russia's national interest. However, Moscow was for the most part excluded from negotiations between the United States and North Korea and the subsequent formation of the Korean Energy Development Organization (KEDO). Seoul is not opposed to Moscow's constructive participation in KEDO but has been dismayed by the Yeltsin government's insistence that Russian reactors be considered as part of the deal.

KEDO is a central component of the U.S.–North Korean agreement concluded in Geneva in October 1994. North Korea agreed to phase out its current nuclear program, which produces nuclear-weapons-grade fuel, in exchange for supplies of crude oil and assistance in building two light-water reactors (LWRS) with a total capacity of approximately two thousand megawatts. Seoul has agreed to pay most of the construction costs for the project, as long as the reactors will be of South Korean manufacture.

Pyongyang initially refused to accept South Korean reactors, claiming safety concerns, but the real reason was a matter of wounded national pride. At various times, North Korea suggested that Russian reactors would be appropriate, given the past record of cooperation between the two countries.[13] Russian officials have repeatedly suggested that Moscow would be willing to supply one or both of the reactors or provide some components for the project. The Soviet government had conducted a feasibility study on installing LWRs at Sinpo on the east coast, and a deal to deliver three 660 megawatt units was signed in 1991. However, Yeltsin suspended the project in 1993 after Pyongyang threatened to withdraw from the nuclear nonproliferation treaty (NPT).[14]

At the very least, Moscow preferred to be more directly involved in this process. As might be expected, South Korea was not eager to foot the bill for Russian equipment. However, South Korean authorities did not oppose Russian participation in KEDO in principle and asked both Russia and China to use their influence with Pyongyang to persuade North Korea to adopt a more accommodative stance.

Both South Korea and Russia were critical of Washington's dealings with North Korea. Seoul officials were suspicious that, in its naïveté, the Clinton administration might grant concessions harmful to South Korean interests. In trying to reassert a great power role for Russia in East Asia, Russian officials pointed out that Russia was an Asian country and had significant national interests in developments on the peninsula. Deputy Foreign Minister Aleksandr Panov openly asserted that Russia wanted to play a leading role in reforming the North Korean nuclear program and would not settle for secondary status.[15] On several occasions, Moscow proposed convening a multilateral conference, composed of Russia, the United States, Japan, China, and the two Koreas, to resolve the issue, but to no avail. In short, both countries were largely excluded from the process by the United States.

Moscow's handling of the revision of the 1961 mutual security treaty has been characterized by confusion and mixed signals over Russian intentions. Yeltsin's critical 1992 comment on the treaty was contradicted in March 1994 by Russia's deputy foreign minister Aleksandr Panov, who hinted that Russia might uphold the treaty. Speaking in the context of Pyongyang's refusal to allow IAEA on-site inspections, Panov claimed that Russia would come to the aid of North Korea in accordance with the defense treaty were North Korea attacked without provocation.[16] When this statement, interpreted as an expression of support for Kim Il-sung's government, caused an international sensation, the Russian foreign ministry and Panov personally issued corrective explanations.[17]

In May 1994, the Russian government invited a North Korean diplomatic delegation (at the deputy foreign minister level) to Moscow and sent Deputy Foreign Minister Panov to Pyongyang to restore cooperative relations.[18] On the forty-sixth anniversary of the establishment of Soviet–North Korean diplomatic relations, a spokesman for the Russian foreign ministry said that the Russian Federation was seeking a new relationship free of ideology with North Korea and that Moscow wished to promote cooperative relations with Pyongyang in all areas.[19]

When Grachev visited Seoul in May 1995, the outlines of Moscow's position on the treaty became clearer. Grachev suggested that a consensus had been achieved within the Russian foreign policy and security communities to scrap the treaty, replacing it with one similar to that concluded between the Russian Federation and South Korea in November 1992.[20] The Russian foreign ministry sent a revised draft agreement to Pyongyang in August 1995 and officially announced its position in early September. While Moscow's efforts to renegotiate the treaty suggested a genuine attempt to be evenhanded, Pyongyang was obviously insulted by the offer. The North Korean government agreed to study the draft but insisted that the treaty was essentially defunct.[21]

Trade and Economic Cooperation

The Asia-Pacific region has posted the world's fastest growth rates in recent years and is by some accounts projected to account for half the world's GDP by the beginning of the next century. With annual growth rates averaging 9 percent, major high-tech industries, an educated and hardworking labor force, surplus investment capital, and a GDP of $380 billion in 1994, South Korea is one of the most attractive economic partners in the region. Although the Russian and South Korean economies are naturally complementary, the process of expanding economic cooperation has proved slow and difficult.

Economic contact between the Soviet Union and South Korea was minimal prior to the 1988 Olympics; by contrast, Moscow assisted North Korea extensively by providing fuel and machinery at heavily subsidized prices. When in 1991 the Soviet Union required Pyongyang to start paying for oil in hard currency, at world price levels, trade plummeted. Russian–North Korean trade was up a marginal 13 percent in 1992, at $600 million, but dropped again in 1993. Trade with Russia in 1994 declined 77.1 percent over the previous year, according to Korea's National Unification Board.[22] North Korea now cannot pay for the food, fuel, and machinery that it needs to import and has little of value to export.[23] By contrast, trade between South Korea and the Soviet Union/ the Russian Federation expanded dramatically from 1988, with the two sides exchanging commodities indirectly through companies of third countries. Direct trade was established in 1989 with the opening of chambers of commerce and industry in Moscow and Seoul, respectively, and the signing of the "Bank Corres" agreement.[24] By the time of the Soviet collapse, bilateral trade had reached $1.2 billion, which was fifteen times greater than in 1986. This dramatic increase was facilitated by the establishment of diplomatic relations in 1990 and the $3 billion South Korean credit to Moscow.

Toward the end of the Soviet era, enormous interest and expectations mounted on both sides regarding the potential for economic cooperation, given the apparent complementarity of the two economies. The Soviet Union was one of the world's richest countries in natural resources, together with strong capabilities in some sectors of science and technology. By employing South Korean investment capital and light-industry technologies, the Soviet Union hoped to develop unexploited resources and consumer industries and bring its ailing economy back to life.

For its part, South Korea was heavily dependent on foreign natural resources and faced substantial difficulties in acquiring advanced technology from Japan and Western countries, which had begun to perceive South Korean firms as serious competitors. South Korean businessmen expected to diversify their foreign market portfolio with new access to the Soviet market of 280 million and to the East European socialist countries.

The collapse of the Soviet Union was accompanied by a 28.5 percent decrease in trade for 1992, to $860 million. Especially hard hit were South Korean exports, which declined by 41.7 percent. Many factors affected the overall trade decline at this time: political instability after the military coup and the breakup of the Soviet Union; the general decline of the Russian economy; Russia's inconsistent application of exchange rates to trade; and arbitrary restrictions on exporting natural resources.[25] But the biggest factor affecting the decline was Seoul's suspension of the promised $3 billion export credit to the Soviet Union when it collapsed. This credit issue has since become a major issue between Moscow and Seoul and is treated separately below.

Notwithstanding these difficulties, Russian–South Korean trade expanded to $1.57 billion in 1993 and then to $2.2 billion in 1994. Russia exports primarily raw materials to South Korea (metals, timber, seafood, coal, oil, and chemical products), while Korean businesses sell electronic goods, footwear, textiles, and furniture to Russia.[26] Korea's huge *chaebol*—Daewoo, LG, Samsung, and Hyundai—are making serious efforts to establish a foothold in the emerging Russian market. Korean firms have aided Russian factories in the difficult process of defense conversion, and cooperation in fishing is expanding. Russian traders (*chelnoki,* or "shuttlers") are a common sight in Pusan—some 100,000 visited the southern port city in 1994.[27] This upswing in trade is particularly remarkable given the fact that the South Korean government is no longer providing export credits for its companies. Therefore, the trend indicates that trade between the two countries is being established on a firm commercial basis.

The steady expansion of trade has not been accompanied by a commensurate growth in direct investment in Russia. Only thirty-three Korean-Russian joint ventures had been established in all Russia by late 1995. Overall, Korean direct investment in Russia is still very modest—between $27 and $50 million. This compares with total Korean investment of some $1.225 billion in China.[28] Russia's oppressive and complicated tax codes, conflicting national and local laws, and environmental considerations have made it difficult for South Korean investors attempting to do business in that country.[29]

There are a number of major projects in various stages of planning that could greatly expand economic cooperation between Russia and

South Korea. Most of these projects involve Korean assistance in exploiting Russian natural resources in Siberia and the Far East. A number of Korean businesses have contracted with Russian firms to trade with or operate in the Nakhodka free economic zone (FEZ). In March 1995, an agreement was signed granting the Korea Land Development Corporation, a government company, the rights to develop an eight-hundred-acre tract in the Nakhodka FEZ. The company is expecting to attract electronics, textile, furniture, and other light-industrial firms to the region.[30] Russian and South Korean business concerns are also exploring the feasibility of jointly developing natural gas fields near Irkutsk.[31]

One of the most ambitious joint projects under discussion is the construction of a natural gas pipeline from the Sakha Republic to South Korea. First proposed during Yeltsin's 1992 visit to Seoul, an economic cooperation agreement between the Sakha Republic and South Korea focusing on energy and natural resource development was concluded early in 1995.[32] During his September 1995 visit to Seoul, Prime Minister Viktor Chernomyrdin discussed the Sakha and Irkutsk projects extensively and in addition proposed the joint development of Buriat and Yakut coal fields. The Russian premier also proposed formation of a trilateral economic cooperation model including North Korea.[33] Pyongyang's participation in such an arrangement could make the gas pipelines feasible.

Both Russia and South Korea are participating in the Tumen River Area Development Project (TRADP). This proposal has generated great hopes, especially among Koreans, Chinese, and regional officials on Japan's west coast. The concept is to transform an area adjoining North Korea, southern Primorskii Krai, and China's Jilin Province into a major commercial hub and trade zone in Northeast Asia. Officials in Tokyo, however, are distinctly unenthusiastic about the project and are not willing to devote the financial resources necessary to make it viable. Japan was conspicuously absent when the other five nations initialed a formal agreement for the Tumen project in May 1995.

For North Korea, the Tumen project is an opportunity to stimulate its moribund economy and to enhance its international standing through participation in a regional organization. To demonstrate its commitment to the project, Pyongyang established the Rajin-Sonbong free economic and trade zone in 1991. North Korea is extremely reluctant, however, to allow "corrupting" foreign influences into its closed economy.[34]

South Korea is expecting this project, like KEDO, to act as a wedge, prying open North Korea to personnel and technology from other countries. Over time, the hope is that economic liberalization will produce results in North Korea similar to the transformation that has taken place in China.[35]

Russia's participation in the TRADP is less than enthusiastic. Moscow welcomes the idea of developing a vibrant economic hub in the region but at present lacks the political commitment and the financial resources to follow through. Local officials are more wary of the project—they are concerned that zone development could lure potential business away from the Vladivostok-Nakhodka region and might accelerate the influx of Chinese nationals into Russia. Ecology groups have misgivings about the possible environmental consequences. Finally, the dispute between Moscow and Primorskii Krai over transferring border territory to China and governor Yevgeny Nazdratenko's decision to allow armed Cossack settlements in the disputed region complicate the situation.[36]

Russia's difficulties repaying loans incurred late in the Soviet era have slowed the development of economic cooperation. Seoul's $3 billion aid package to Moscow was concluded when the two sides established diplomatic relations in 1990, but Seoul suspended the loan package in 1991, after disbursing $1.47 billion, when Moscow defaulted on repayment of the principal and interest. The Russian Federation inherited this debt and has had difficulty repaying it according to schedule. Russia was $450.7 million in arrears in principal and interest by the end of 1993. After a series of intermittent negotiations, the two sides came to an agreement in April 1995 on the method and schedule of Moscow's repayment of this portion of debt. Russia agreed to pay back the debt in kind with commodities (50 percent), helicopters (5 percent), and defense equipment (45 percent).[37]

What is notable about this deal is the fact that for the first time South Korea will acquire Russian military equipment, worth $208.81 million. Items covered include an unknown number of T-80U main battle tanks, BMP-3 infantry combat vehicles, AT-7 "Saxhorn" antitank guided missiles, and SA-16 "Gimlet" low-altitude surface-to-air missiles. These will be delivered over a three-year period from 1995 to 1998, supplemented with spare parts and ammunition.[38] This deal will enable South Korea to analyze the weapons systems that North Korea deploys and to acquire Russia's state-of-art military technologies. During Chernomyrdin's September 1995 visit, the two sides discussed cooperation in the development of military technologies and the production of high-tech weaponry.

The potential for Russian–South Korean economic cooperation has proved disappointing. Russia's murky legal structure, pervasive organized crime gangs, unsettled political situation, and weak infrastructure make doing business there extremely difficult. While South Korean investors are reputedly more willing to take risks than their cautious Japanese counterparts, there are many better investment opportunities than Russia. Substantial progress in economic cooperation is not likely to be realized until Moscow gets its political and economic systems in order.

Military Cooperation

In a dramatic departure from the Soviet era, the Russian Federation has cautiously expanded military contacts with South Korea as one component of its drive to increase bilateral security cooperation with neighbors in Northeast Asia. It is true that during the Gorbachev period the Soviet government also made great efforts to improve relations with other countries in the region. By comparison, however, under Yeltsin the Russian Federation initiated bilateral contacts for security cooperation with military units. This change seems to reflect the unsuccessful experience of Gorbachev's proposals for a multilateral security system embracing the whole Asia-Pacific region. Yeltsin's government revised this approach: while it narrowed the target area to the subregion of Northeast Asia, at the same time it also started vigorous efforts to improve security cooperation with its Northeast Asian neighbors on a bilateral basis.

There are two implications of Moscow's efforts at strengthening bilateral cooperation. First, developing security cooperation with these countries, most of which were Moscow's adversaries during the cold war, would presumably help stabilize the security environment in and around the Russian Far East. Second, from a long-term perspective, it could also provide the necessary groundwork to encourage regional actors to accept a multilateral security system for Northeast Asia.

Following several high-level military exchanges, a formal memorandum of understanding (MOU) on military exchanges was signed at the time of Yeltsin's 1992 visit. This MOU's six articles stipulated the exchange of military personnel, visits by the naval vessels of each country, and sending observers to each other's military exercises, and it served as the basis for subsequent security cooperation measures between the two countries.[39] During the South Korean defense minister's visit to Moscow in April 1994, which occurred amid rising tensions over North Korea's nuclear program, Moscow announced that it was ready "to set up full-scale military cooperation" with Seoul.[40] A high-ranking Russian military delegation led by Grachev in May 1995 further advanced security cooperation with two additional sets of agreements: one for the protection of military secrets, the other for mutual cooperation in the research and development of military supplies and possible joint production.[41] The agreement reached in the previous month to provide Russian arms to South Korea as part of its debt repayment plan was officially signed at this meeting.[42]

The South Korean government values these exchanges very highly and would like to expand military cooperation further. Russian military contacts with South Korea are more frequent and are conducted at a higher level than those with North Korea. Reportedly, only about ninety Russian military personnel remain in North Korea, and port visits and overflights have been substantially reduced.[43] This is immensely reassuring to South Korean security planners.

Through closer military cooperation, access to Russia's modern technologies, and joint production, South Korean firms can expand into the world market for high-tech military hardware. Seoul stands a better chance of enlisting Russia's support on the nuclear issue since close military cooperation will undoubtedly drive a wedge deeper between Moscow and Pyongyang. Finally, South Korea gains additional leverage with Washington by diversifying its sources of military hardware and technology.

The U.S. Factor in Russian–South Korean Relations

The turnaround in Soviet/Russian policy toward the Korean peninsula has been a welcome development for U.S. foreign policy. By the late 1980s, a more benign regional environment led the United States to reassess the status of its military forces in the Asia-Pacific region. The resulting changes in U.S. force structure in the western Pacific were formalized in the East Asia Strategy Initiatives of 1989 and 1992, which envisioned the possibility of significant reductions. However, the continuing threat from an unpredictable North Korea, reflected in Pyongyang's 1993 threatened withdrawal from the NPT, caused Washington to suspend plans to reduce forces deployed in South Korea.

Although the Pentagon's February 1995 East Asia Strategy Report does not devote much attention to Russia, it does note that Russia has contributed toward international peace efforts in North Korea and Cambodia. Furthermore, Russia is praised for cooperating with China to demilitarize the Sino-Russian border. The report concludes that "Russia has a significant role to play in preventing the emergence of future security problems in the Pacific."[44]

It is worth noting that, unlike the Sino-Soviet split, Soviet hostility toward South Korea did not work to the advantage of the United States. While Sino-Soviet (and later Sino-Russian) rapprochement has caused some apprehension in Washington, for the most part the United States welcomes closer ties between Seoul and Moscow. Although the Korean War demonstrated reluctance on Moscow's part to intervene directly in support of Pyongyang, according to the 1961 treaty Moscow was legally obligated to assist the North. The normalization of relations with South Korea and repeated assurances that Moscow will not support aggressive action by Pyongyang are reassuring to U.S. policy makers.

The United States and Russia now share a number of interests on the Korean peninsula. For the United States, South Korea is a major trading partner. In fact, it is the one Northeast Asian country with which the United States is running a trade surplus. South Korea is relatively less important for Russia's economy, but it accounts for over 10 percent of Russia's Asian trade. As noted above, there is great potential for expanded economic cooperation. Instability on the peninsula, therefore, could threaten the economic interests of both Russia and the United States.

Washington and Moscow both favor the peaceful transformation of North Korea from a totalitarian dictatorship toward a more democratic system and the gradual reunification of the peninsula. North Korea's repressive, unpredictable regime is the key factor in the continuing instability on the peninsula. Russia and the United States are both committed to a Korea free from nuclear weapons, but for slightly different reasons.

The United States is obligated to protect its close ally but clearly would prefer not to be drawn into any conflict on the peninsula involving the use of nuclear weapons. Combined U.S.–South Korean forces could likely deal with a conventional attack, but the use of nuclear weapons on the crowded South would be devastating, both to the thirty-six thousand U.S. troops stationed there and to South Korea's armed forces and society. The United States is also wary of North Korea's potential for nuclear terrorism, given its past record. Finally, North Korea seems determined to assist other radical, anti-American regimes, such as those in Libya and Iran, in acquiring weapons of mass destruction. For these reasons, U.S. policy has concentrated on eliminating North Korea's potential for developing and spreading nuclear weapons.

Russia, too, is interested in limiting the proliferation of nuclear weapons. However, unlike the United States, the Russian Federation shares a border with North Korea. Much of the population of Primorskii Krai is concentrated within a few hundred kilometers of this border. Any use of nuclear weapons on the Korean peninsula would contaminate significant areas of the Russian Far East. In addition, any serious conflict—nuclear or conventional—could produce a flood of refugees across Russia's now porous borders. Finally, although China is not likely to support North Korea as it did forty-five years ago, a new Korean conflict could exacerbate differences between Moscow and Beijing over how to deal with the crisis and thus could jeopardize Russia's ties to East Asia's dominant power.

Russia and the United States also differ over KEDO. Moscow would prefer to be included as a full participant in KEDO since this would enhance Russia's international prestige and provide an opportunity to earn additional income by supplying one or both of the LWRs or at least some of the equipment to be used in the project. The three major participants in KEDO—the United States, South Korea, and Japan—have made significant financial commitments to support the process. Russia, however, cannot afford to be included as a full participant. Moscow's strategy also includes drawing a parallel between its LWR deal with Iran and the U.S. arrangement with North Korea. Russia's cooperative stance on the KEDO process and its frequently reiterated claim that the two situations are comparable undermine America's opposition to the Iran deal.

On several occasions, Russia has proposed a multinational conference to deal with the North Korean nuclear problem, a conference that would replace U.S.–North Korean bilateral negotiations.[45] The United States is not in principle opposed to Russian participation, but it does not want the process complicated by expanding the number of participating countries. China, in particular, might side with North Korea against Washington, given recent tensions in U.S.–Chinese relations. The United States also does not want to strengthen Pyongyang's position by giving it the option of taking Russian reactors in place of South Korean equipment.

For the most part, however, Russia has cooperated with the United States and South Korea on the nuclear issue because eliminating North Korea's nuclear potential is in Russia's national interest. The presence of nuclear weapons on the peninsula threatens the Russian Far East, as noted above. Moreover, the presence of nuclear weapons in Korea raises the possibility, however remote, that Japan might develop a nuclear device to balance a perceived asymmetry. Several states in Asia either possess nuclear weapons or could readily develop them, including China, Kazakhstan, Pakistan, and India. Russian officials fear the establishment of a nuclear belt along Russia's eastern and southern boundaries and would prefer the dismantling of these states' nuclear capabilities.[46]

Russian–South Korean Ties and Russian Foreign Policy

There are many uncertainties that will continue to affect Russian–South Korean relations. The evolution of the relationship depends partly on what happens inside Russia and partly on developments on the Korean peninsula.

First, we may expect that Russia will remain in a state of political turmoil for the near future and possibly into the next century as well. Although the economic decline seems to have bottomed out and modest growth may be achieved over the next few years, Russia does not seem poised to record the growth rates experienced by China or other dynamic Asian economies. Even if economic growth in European Russia takes off, the Russian Far East will probably be left behind. And, since influence in East Asia will increasingly depend on a nation's economic strength, Russia seems consigned to play a marginal role at best over the next decade.[47]

Russia's position in world politics and its relative weight in East Asia could be enhanced if efforts to reintegrate some of the former Soviet republics through the Commonwealth of Independent States succeed. Russia is cooperating more closely with the Slavic and Central Asian states on economic and security issues, and further "integration" may be expected in these areas. But, with the possible exception of Belarus, all these states would strongly resist attempts at reincorporation into a single Russian-dominated polity. Such a move could provoke violent confrontations in Ukraine and Kazakhstan, which would prove far worse than the Chechnya fiasco.

Nonetheless, some foreign policy elites in Seoul are concerned about a possible Russian resurgence through the mechanism of CIS integration. Reintegration, it is assumed, would augment Russia's economic potential, thereby enhancing its political influence in the region. From Seoul's perspective, a strong Russian presence in East Asia would diminish South Korea's relative influence, complicating the nuclear issue and North-South reunification. A weak Russia preserves the expanded foreign policy options that South Korea has enjoyed since the end of the cold war.

East Asia in general and the Republic of Korea in particular will remain important in Russian foreign policy, regardless of what political forces control the government. Russia has significant interests on the Korean peninsula, stemming from its shared border with North Korea, the proximity of major population centers in the Russian Far East, growing trade relations and military contacts with the Republic of Korea, and uncertainty over possible Chinese expansionary goals. Some of the more extreme nationalist politicians lament the "abandonment" of North Korea, but the South now has strong supporters across the Russian political spectrum.

Having decided not to renew the military assistance provisions of the Soviet–North Korean treaty, Moscow's foreign policy establishment is in agreement on the need to prevent North Korea from developing or utilizing nuclear weapons. Virtually all political forces in Russia, aside from perhaps the fringe right wing, favor a gradual transition in North Korea from totalitarianism toward a reformist system. Most assume that reunification under a democratic regime is simply a matter of time, given the record of other former Communist systems. Moscow's leaders share the Seoul government's preference for a peaceful and gradual reunification of South and North. Overall, there are many areas in which Moscow and Seoul find themselves in agreement.

Russia has lost much ground with North Korea since the collapse of the Soviet Union. Moscow is now attempting to redress the excessive imbalance in favor of the South in its ties with the two Koreas by reestablishing normal relations with Pyongyang while preserving links to South Korea. This is a delicate balancing act, however, and Russia's options are circumscribed by its weak economic position and various internal crises.

Moscow's Korean policy reflects broader trends currently influencing Russian foreign policy. Russia is clearly not returning to a Soviet-style brand of power politics—the country does not have the military capability for such policies. But, more important, Russian officials realize that not much would be gained by a heavy-handed approach in East Asia. The best strategy seems to be a more flexible combination of political and economic instruments while maintaining sufficient military strength to preserve control of Russia's historical frontier regions.

Russian policy also has evolved beyond the rather simplistic and, to many, demeaning reliance on the United States and Western democracies toward a more balanced approach to nations regardless of political coloration. This adjustment is designed to restore Russia's "rightful" position as a respected world power, a demand voiced by many segments of Russia's political elite. Moscow's Korea policy—characterized by efforts to restore ties with North Korea while expanding links to the

South — indicates a strong desire to be accepted as a major power in East Asian affairs.

Russia's "national interests" are claimed to be driving foreign policy decision making. Although these national interests are not clearly stated and perhaps not thoroughly understood by many in Moscow, they represent the outlines of a third route between the old Soviet foreign policy and that preferred by Washington. Pride in Russian distinctiveness, as neither European nor Asian but somehow superior to both, seems to have emerged as a central element of Russian foreign policy. This concept of a unique Russia is rooted in Russian history and underlies current debates on Russia's national identity. If this analysis is correct, students of Russian foreign policy would be well advised to acquire a more thorough understanding of Russia's cultural trends and domestic political developments.

Notes

Research for this project was carried out while Charles Ziegler was a Fulbright Lecture / Research Scholar at Pusan National University. Additional support was provided by a Graduate Research Grant from the University of Louisville. Their support is gratefully acknowledged.

1 The North Korean government adopted an implicitly supportive attitude toward the coup in progress by reporting the coup leaders' statements in detail in its mass media. Nothing was said about the measures taken by the Russian reformist leaders, including Yeltsin. When the putsch ended in failure, Pyongyang's media kept silent for twenty hours before reporting the result at noon on 22 August (*Newwoe Tongshin,* no. 758, 23 August 1991, and no. 759, 30 August 1991).

2 It was Russia's ambassador to Seoul, Oleg Sokolov, who first raised this possibility on 26 December 1991 (*Chosun Ilbo,* 27 December 1991, 4).

3 *Chosun Ilbo,* 21 November 1992, 1.

4 For a more extended discussion, see Charles E. Ziegler, *Foreign Policy and East Asia: Learning and Adaptation in the Gorbachev Era* (Cambridge: Cambridge University Press, 1993).

5 Draft evasion, e.g., is reputedly 75 percent. For a succinct discussion of the Russian military's problems, see Benjamin Lambeth, "Russia's Wounded Military," *Foreign Affairs* 74, no. 2 (March / April 1995): 86–98.

6 ITAR-TASS, 5 July 1992, in *Foreign Broadcast Information Service, Central Eurasia* (hereafter *FBIS/SOV*), 8 July 1992), 30.

7 In a recent plea, Far Eastern authorities claimed that the situation was desperate, adopting a resolution urging Moscow to help the region. Sakhalin officials threatened to appeal directly to Japan for relief assistance if the center refused to respond (*Izvestia,* 3 February 1995, 1). Early in 1995, Catholic Relief Services assessed conditions in the Russian Far East as extremely serious, citing hyperinflation, massive unemployment, the collapse of the military-industrial complex, the inability of the federal authorities to fund regional budgets, delayed wage payments, and decreased agricultural production as factors contributing to a crisis situation (Catholic Relief Services/Russia, letter to U.S. Ambassador Thomas R. Pickering, 1995).

8 Yonhap, 14 May 1994, in *Foreign Broadcast Information Service, East Asia* (hereafter *FBIS/EAS*), 16 May 1994, 29.

9 *SIPRI Yearbook 1989* (Stockholm: SIPRI, 1989), 256–57.

10 Yonhap, 17 April 1991, in *FBIS/EAS,* 18 April 1991, 32.

11 *Seoul Sinmun,* 13 February 1995, in *FBIS/EAS,* 14 February 1995, 53–54.

12 One example of such criticism in Yevgeny Aleksandrov, "Immoral Position: Russia and Nuclear Security in Korea," *Pravda,* 7 May 1993, in *Current Digest of the Post-Soviet Press* (hereafter *CDPP*), 2 June 1993, 21–22. Some deputies to Russia's state Duma, including Viktor Ilyukhin, Sergei Baburin, and Aleksandr Navzorov, expressed deep concern over heightening tensions in Korea. However, they condemned, not North Korean blackmail, but rather certain American circles that they claimed supported a new world order and were making new and unfair demands on a "traditional ally"—North Korea—that could only aggravate the situation (Aleksandr Chudodeyev, "National Patriots Switch Their Sympathies to North Korean Dictator," *Segodnya,* 31 March 1994, in *CDPP,* 27 April 1994, 25).

13 North Korea developed its Yongbyon nuclear complex with Soviet assistance, and the reactors there are the accident-prone, plutonium-generating, Soviet-type graphite-moderated reactors. However, Soviet leaders did not care to see Pyongyang develop nuclear weapons—North Korea signed the nuclear nonproliferation treaty (NPT) under pressure from Moscow in December 1985.

14 *Far Eastern Economic Review,* 29 December 1994/5 January 1995, 14–15.

15 ITAR-TASS, cited in *BBC Summary of World Broadcasts,* 31 January 1995.

16 *Chosun Ilbo,* 31 March 1994, 5.

17 The gist of it was that Moscow would take into account other considerations as well and would not be mechanically bound by the treaty. In any case, the question itself was not controversial because there was no chance of unprovoked aggression occurring against North Korea (Maksim Yusin, "Moscow Doesn't Want to Quarrel with Washington and Seoul over Kim Il-sung's Nuclear Ambition," *Izvestia,* 1 April 1994, in *CDPP,* 27 April 1994, 25).

18 *Naewoe Tongshin,* no. BO9184, 19 October 1994.

19 Ibid., no. BO9175, 13 October 1994.

20 The Russian Federation has replaced the mutual assistance treaties, which

the former Soviet Union had signed with certain allies, with such new agreements.

21 *Joong-ang Ilbo,* 7 September 1995, 1–2; *Izvestia,* 8 September 1995, 3.

22 *Korea Times,* 16 March 1995, 2.

23 It is revealing that up to two-thirds of North Korea's exports to Russia are high-tech electronic products originating in third countries, possibly Japan or South Korea (G. Ia. Levchenko, "Ekonomicheskoe otnosheniia mezhdu Rossei i KNDR: nyneshniaia situatsiia i perspektivy," *Informatsionnyi bulletin Instituta Dal'nego Vostoka Akademii Nauk Rossii,* no. 8 [1994]: 79–83). The speculation about the source of the products is ours, not Levchenko's.

24 *Russia: Tuja (Investment) Guide* (Seoul: Korean Export-Import Bank, June 1994), 48.

25 The 1992 figures account for trade between South Korea and all the former Soviet republics (*Korean Statistical Yearbook* [Seoul: National Statistical Office, Republic of Korea, 1993], 300–301).

26 Data for 1992 and 1993 are from the Korean Trade Center; 1994 figures are from *Rossyskie vesti,* 7 February 1995, in *CDPP,* 8 March 1995, 29–30.

27 Approximately forty-five thousand Russian shuttlers journeyed to Seoul in 1994. Dr. Valerii Yermolov, consul general to Pusan, kindly provided this information.

28 A figure of $27.3 million is cited in Sergei Zhikharyov, "Moscow Proposes Trilateral Cooperation," *Kommersant-Daily,* 29 September 1995, in *CDPP,* 25 October 1995, 25. Two other sources suggest that the figure is closer to $50 million: Valerii Denisov, "Russia in the APR: Problems of Security and Cooperation," *International Affairs* (Moscow), nos. 4–5 (1995): 75; and conversation with Valerii Yermolov, counsel general to Pusan. On South Korean international investment, see Shim Jae Hoon, "Going Global," *Far Eastern Economic Review,* 2 November 1995, 46–50.

29 Daewoo's plans to set up a car-assembly plant in Yelabuga, Tatarstan, ran into difficulties when the Russian government refused to grant tax concessions. The biggest South Korean investment project, a $16 million Hyundai-Svetlaya timber operation in Primorskii Krai, faced an environmental lawsuit brought by a native group in 1993. As a result, Hyundai lost millions of dollars when forced to reduce operating capacity (see Yoke T. Soh, "Russian Policy toward the Two Koreas," in *Russian Foreign Policy since 1990,* ed. Peter Shearman [Boulder, Colo.: Westview, 1995], 190–93.

30 *Korea Times,* 24 March 1995, 1.

31 Ibid., 8 June 1995, 8.

32 Ibid., 28 February 1995, 8.

33 Sergei Zhikharyov, "Moscow Proposes Trilateral Cooperation," *Kommersant-Daily,* 29 September 1995, in *CDPP,* 25 October 1995, 24–25.

34 For an excellent discussion of Pyongyang's approach to the TRADP, see Hirokazy Shode, "Tumen River Area Development Programme: The North

Korean Perspective," in *Growth Triangles in Asia: A New Approach to Regional Economic Cooperation,* ed. Myo Thant, Min Tang, and Hiroshi Kakazu (Hong Kong: Oxford University Press, 1994). North Korea has fenced off the Rajin-Sonbong FEZ with barbed wire to shield its population from harmful influences.

35 Duck-Woo Nam, "Multilateral Economic Cooperation in Northeast Asia: A Korean Perspective," keynote address to the fifth conference of the Northeast Asian Economic Forum, Niigata, Japan, February 1995. It is worth noting that South Korea sent the largest delegation to this conference, with about forty participants, while North Korea refused to send any.

36 See Valerii Venevtsev and Denis Demkin, "1500 ga Russko-Kitaiskikh problem," *Vladivostok,* 25 January 1995, 6; and Gennadi Chufrin, "Border Drawn by Compromise," *Moscow News,* no. 8, 24 February–2 March 1995, 14.

37 *Maelil Kyonje Shinmun,* 22 April 1995, 5.

38 *Jane's Defence Weekly,* 13 May 1995, 3.

39 *Chosun Ilbo,* 17 November 1992, 1.

40 *International Herald Tribune,* 30 April 1994, 4.

41 *International Herald Tribune,* 22 May 1995, 4.

42 Large purchases of military hardware, however, might incur Washington's disapproval, so the focus has been on technology imports and limited equipment sales for intelligence and training purposes.

43 Interview with the Korean Ministry of Defense, Seoul, May 1995.

44 U.S. Department of Defense, "United States Security Strategy for the East Asia–Pacific Region" (Washington, D.C., February 1995).

45 Early in 1994, Moscow proposed that an international conference of eight parties—North and South Korea, Japan, China, the United States, Russia, representatives of the UN secretary general's office, and the IAEA—be convened to deal with the nuclear issue. South Korea and Japan were cool to the idea (*International Herald Tribune,* 25 March 1994, 2). Later, Russia revised the format and proposed a ten-party conference, including the United Kingdom and France.

46 Interview with Foreign Minister Andrei Kozyrev, *Izvestia,* 18 June 94, 1–2.

47 For a more complete development of this argument, see Charles E. Ziegler, "Russia in the Asia-Pacific: Major Power or Minor Participant?" *Asian Survey* 34, no. 6 (June 1994): 529–43.

Russia and the United States

HARRY GELMAN

Implications for the United States of Russia's Far East Policy

The United States and the Russian Geopolitical Heritage in East Asia

Russia's policies today in East Asia and their effect on U.S. interests are strongly conditioned by several adverse considerations inherited from the past.

During the cold war era, when the bilateral relationship was primarily adversarial, the Soviet Union's geopolitical leverage on its neighbors and ability to put pressure on U.S. interests were generally considerably weaker in East Asia than in Europe. Moreover, while the Far East was not considered unimportant, it was always a secondary priority for Moscow compared with Europe. Despite much recent talk about a geographic reorientation of Russian foreign policy since the fall of the Soviet Union, these two central constraints — Russia's relatively weak position in East Asia and the secondary priority that Russia assigns to the region — have thus far not essentially changed.

Throughout Soviet history, Soviet East Asia was a stepchild for state investment, and it is not too much to say that, traditionally, the region was tacitly regarded in Moscow as a net economic liability maintained primarily for strategic and military reasons. Today, military considerations are no longer all important in Russia's attitude toward its eastern regions, but the inherited pattern of lagging domestic investment in the region — and adverse regional terms of trade with the rest of the country — remains essentially the case in Russia today, much to the unhappiness of local inhabitants. Since the fall of the Soviet Union, the region has become more dependent than ever on trade with East Asia and on whatever investment it can obtain from external sources.[1] Over the last few years, considerable small-scale foreign entrepreneurial activity has materialized in the Russian Far East, but today, as in the Soviet past, Russian economic weakness continues to preclude significant participation in the economic boom of the East Asian capitalist states.

Because of the inadequacy of their political and economic levers, the Soviet leaders generally found their overall position in this region to be even more dependent on military strength and military relationships than was the case in Europe. In the long run, however, even on the military side Moscow got little political or economic payoff in East Asia from its immense and costly exertions. Today, all Moscow's old Communist client states in East Asia remain largely, although not entirely, oriented elsewhere. And, despite various degrees of friction with the Americans, North Korea, China, and Vietnam all have a stake in the future of their economic relations with the United States that is much larger than the stake in their relationship with Russia.

Finally, in the aftermath of the collapse of the Soviet Union, the impressive military presence that Brezhnev created in the Far East has been gradually decaying because an impoverished Russia has found it difficult to maintain. The Far East Fleet, in particular, is in very poor shape today as a result of the severe Russian budget constraints. Although this trend of local Russian military decline might eventually be reversed, that seems quite unlikely to happen very soon. As will be seen below, this fact has ongoing consequences for the U.S. relationship with Japan and for the U.S. military position in the region generally.

The Main Lines of Russian East Asia Policy Today

Given this discouraging background, Yeltsin's Russia has sought to make a fresh start in East Asia, with two aims in mind. On the economic side, the main Russian goal has been to find some way at long last to harness the dynamism of East Asia—still the most rapidly growing region of the world—to invigorate the Russian economy and assist Russia's painful transition to a market system. On the political side, Moscow's central aim in East Asia—as elsewhere—is to become an important independent factor in the regional equation and a major participant in decisions on key international issues. This imperative has grown in importance as the Russians have come to perceive, in Europe, growing conflicts of national interest with the United States and other Western states. While

Yeltsin's post-Soviet Russia sought cooperation with the United States when this was deemed consistent with Russian interests, it also sought to demonstrate that Russia is still a great Far Eastern power that must be consulted and is nobody's toady, particularly not that of the United States.

In East Asia, this impulse is reflected in, among other things, Russia's efforts to broaden its presence across the board: for example, to try to invigorate its new relationship with South Korea; to reestablish dealings with Vietnam; to participate in such gatherings as the ASEAN Regional Forum; to press for admission to the Organization for Asian-Pacific Economic Cooperation (APEC) and various other Asian multilateral bodies; to launch very vague appeals for multilateral security consultations in East Asia;[2] and, beyond this, to seek multilateralization of important negotiations in which Russia was not a direct participant but that had implications for Russia's interests (such as the North Korean nuclear talks). All this behavior has been quite natural for a state in Russia's position, and much of it should be welcome to the United States. However, some aspects of Russian efforts to shore up its relationship with East Asia—for example, the sales of advanced weapons technology to China—have more disturbing implications for the United States.

In the discussion to follow, I will review the possible consequences for the United States of the way in which these imperatives of Russian policy have expressed themselves in behavior toward Japan, toward the Korean peninsula, and, above all, toward China. I will then consider prospects for the future.

U.S. Interests and the Russo-Japanese Impasse

The Russian relationship with Japan today affects the United States for two reasons. First, since the collapse of the Soviet Union, the United States and Japan have no longer had that virtual identity of interests in policy toward Moscow that they had during the cold war. Second—as I shall discuss later—the cool and distant Russo-Japanese relationship also has indirect consequences for the United States, to the degree that it becomes a factor in Russian policy toward China.

THE "NORTHERN TERRITORIES" AND JAPANESE INVESTMENT

Russian-Japanese relations today are indeed cold and likely to remain so, even if they are no longer quite as icy as they were at the nadir of the relationship, in September 1992, when Yeltsin at the last moment abruptly canceled his first scheduled visit to Japan. Both sides have completely abandoned the unrealistic hopes for fundamental change that briefly emerged in August 1991, after Yeltsin defeated the first attempted right-wing coup in Moscow.

The Japanese, on their side, have had to give up initial hopes that the defeat of the 1991 coup and the resulting shift in the balance of Russian political power might make possible decisive Russian steps toward eventual accommodation of Japanese demands for return of the "Northern Territories," the four small islands at the bottom of the Kuril chain closest to Hokkaido that are the subject of the Japanese-Russian territorial dispute. In the years since Yeltsin took over, it has become abundantly clear that Russian nationalist passions and the political troubles generated for Yeltsin by economic hardship would for a long time make it impossible for Russia to offer more than marginal and token concessions on the territorial issue. The political pressures on Yeltsin to remain inflexible are amplified by the intransigence of the General Staff, which continues to insist publicly that it needs the islands for early warning intelligence purposes and also has traditionally feared that hostile powers possessing the islands could launch antisubmarine warfare (ASW), operations against Russian subsurface ballistic nuclear submarines (SSBNs) in the Sea of Okhotsk.

Meanwhile, during the Yeltsin years, the Russians, for their part, had to give up hopes that Japan might be induced to make a decisive difference in the Russian struggle to build a market economy. The possibility that Japan might play the leading role in helping Russia was not always as far-fetched as it seems today. On one occasion, six months before Gorbachev lost power, Japan had in fact made a concrete offer to play such a role, by spelling out a possible quid pro quo for the first and last time. A month before Gorbachev's April 1991 visit to Japan, Ichiro Ozawa, who was then secretary-general of the ruling Liberal Democratic party (LDP), had put together a shaky and very ephemeral consensus in Tokyo to offer Gorbachev informally a massive package of some $26 billion in economic benefits, in exchange for Soviet agreement to give up outright the two least important of the four Northern Territories and also to recognize Japanese "residual sovereignty" over the other two islands.[3] By this time, however, Gorbachev had become far too weak politically to accept that deal.

Japan has never repeated to Russia's Yeltsin the offer it made "under the table" to the Soviet Union's Gorbachev. The Japanese position has always been to hold out vague prospects of unspecified subsequent economic rewards in exchange for prior concrete Russian concessions on the territorial issue. Japan has never repeated the Ozawa offer for two paradoxical reasons: first, because the offer would probably never be accepted and, second, because there was always the danger, however faint, that it might be accepted.

The Japanese governing elite has seen China and other areas of Asia as far more promising recipients of both investment and assistance funds. Meanwhile, enormous Russian debts to Japan, as well as to other Western creditors, remain unpaid. Faced by the lack of Russian infrastructure in many areas, the spectacular growth of crime and corruption, the chaotic diffusion of authority, the precariousness of contractual agreements, and the great uncertainties of the political future—all adding up to what seems to be a very discouraging environment for profitable investment—many Japanese business leaders have apparently been privately relieved that the foreign ministry's recalcitrance over the territorial issue provided them with an excuse for not investing in Russia. In short, the Northern Territories are simply not deemed to be worth a massive bribe.

THE 1992 U.S. SPLIT FROM JAPAN ON AID TO YELTSIN

However, the fading chance that Japan might take the lead in rescuing the Russian economy has not meant that Japan has been able to avoid some participation in such efforts. From the moment the Soviet Union collapsed, Japan's Western partners in the G-7 were in a different position from Japan because, unlike Japan, none still had a specific national interest at stake that Russia has not satisfied. Western Europe and the United States therefore tended to see the issue of succoring democracy and moderation in Russia as more pressing than did Japan. In 1992 and

1993, Japan had to respond to severe Western pressure on this issue, particularly from the United States and Germany. Bit by bit, Japan was propelled by Western insistence—and by Tokyo's fear of becoming isolated—into reluctantly agreeing to participate in the IMF and World Bank rescue operation that eventually emerged. To the degree that Japan yielded to these demands, it was forced to cede in advance part of the economic quid pro quo that it had sought to withhold from Russia pending the return of the Northern Territories. The Japanese leaders reacted with anger and dismay. Despite its compulsory participation in international agreements to assist Russia, Japan sought at every turn to minimize that participation to the degree politically feasible—that is, to do as little as it thought consistent with not becoming isolated.

Since 1994, however, these strains between Japan and its Western partners over the issue of aiding Russia appear to have eased somewhat, for two reasons. First, the acute tension between Moscow and Tokyo diminished to some extent after Yeltsin finally visited Japan in October 1993 and made a number of small conciliatory gestures that were fairly well received, at least for the moment. Second, during the first two years after Yeltsin's visit to Japan, some Russian economic trends did create modest ground for hope about Russia's future. Particularly noteworthy was the readiness of both Yeltsin and the Russian legislature to hold down Russian military spending despite the bitter protests of the military leadership. During 1995, the government's success in lowering inflation was impressive enough to persuade the IMF, despite Western revulsion over the Chechnya war, to begin releasing to Russia large sums previously promised but long delayed. To be sure, there were still plenty of negative features on the economic horizon.[4] But, were it not for Russia's precarious political prospects, the positive aspects of the economic trends might raise hopes that Russia could eventually overcome the factors that continue to discourage large-scale foreign private investment.

However, in contrast to the signs of possible economic progress, hopes for the future of democracy in Russia and for the political stability of the country have been placed in grave jeopardy ever since Yeltsin's disastrous decision late in 1994 to begin the war in Chechnya. This event has transformed the political landscape for a long time to come, isolating Yeltsin from most moderate and reformist opinion while reinforcing reactionary trends in the polity as a whole. As Yeltsin became more dependent on the Right, he increasingly turned away from those in his administration who had favored economic reform and conciliation of the West. Certain of his new influential appointees, particularly those associated with the instruments of force, showed little enthusiasm for continuation of reform, for democracy, or for the preservation of good relations with the West. The surfacing of these attitudes within Yeltsin's camp was accompanied by a striking growth of the strength of Yeltsin's Communist and extreme nationalist opponents, vividly reflected in the results of the December 1995 parliamentary elections.

Consequently, ever since the attack on Chechnya, both the long-term stability of Russia's democratic institutions and the future of Russia's posture toward the West have been more than ever in question. Ominous precedents for Russia were posed by developments adverse to democracy in other CIS states such as Belarus. The fundamental direction that Russia would take over the next decade now hung increasingly on the results of the presidential elections scheduled for the summer of 1996.

Whatever the fate of the Russian elections, these trends in 1995 were bound to have an adverse effect on the Russian position in East Asia at least for the next few years, if only because they were likely to further complicate Japanese attitudes toward Russia for a considerable time to come. Until the Chechnya debacle, there had been some modest improvement in Japanese attitudes toward investment in Russia. Nevertheless, meaningful change in Japanese policy toward Moscow is obstructed by the overall lack of enthusiasm of Japanese business, by the instability on the Japanese political scene since the end of the long hegemony of the Liberal Democratic party in 1993, and, most fundamentally, by the general atmosphere of mutual dislike that continues to hang over the relationship even after Yeltsin's visit to Japan.[5] Strong nationalist trends in both countries periodically surface on both sides to stymie the relatively weaker efforts of those favoring conciliation.

For example, when a devastating earthquake occurred in Sakhalin in 1995, Yeltsin publicly refused Japanese assistance on the grounds that the Japanese would only take advantage of the occasion to reiterate their territorial claims.[6] Despite the promises that Yeltsin made before and during his 1993 visit to Tokyo, Russian military leaders have since made it clear that Russia has no intention of demilitarizing the Northern Territories. Moreover, like his Soviet predecessor Marshal Yazov, former defense minister Grachev repeatedly went out of his way to insist that possession of the southern Kurils is Russia's historical right, which must never be relinquished.[7] Although the Russian military leaders cannot themselves dictate foreign policy, their backing for such sentiments helps reinforce the nationalist fervor in the elite as a whole, which does indeed heavily constrain the government.[8] Moreover, the fact that Russia's borders elsewhere have also been placed in question redoubles the pressure on the Russian foreign ministry to remain adamant about the Northern Territories.[9]

RUSSIA AND THE U.S.-JAPAN ALLIANCE

Meanwhile, so long as the Russo-Japanese impasse goes on, the resulting gap between U.S. and Japanese attitudes toward Russia will continue to affect U.S. interests because it complicates the task of creating a new rationale for the U.S.-Japanese alliance.

The foundations of that alliance are gradually being eroded for a variety of reasons, including such factors as friction with the population over the U.S. base presence; the growth of economic confrontation; the new priority that the U.S. leadership has unfortunately given to the economic differences as opposed to the strategic/military dimension of the relationship; and the collapse of the hegemony over Japanese political life enjoyed by the Liberal Democratic party, the reliable Japanese defender of the relationship with the United States for four decades. Probably the most dramatic cause of the difficulties of the alliance, however, has been the disappearance of a credible Soviet threat. A momentous train of events over the last decade—Gorbachev's geopolitical retreats, the collapse of the Soviet Union, and the weakening of Russian military power—has incrementally undermined what had been the long-established, common anti-Soviet rationale for the U.S.-Japan alliance. Today, very much like NATO (although perhaps not yet to the same degree), the U.S.-Japanese strategic alliance is suffering because it still lacks a new rationale credible to the U.S. public and Congress.

To be sure, major new difficulties have emerged to cool relations between Russia and the West, and this change has somewhat reduced U.S. differences with Japan over policy toward Russia. But it has not eliminated them—a fact again demonstrated in 1995 and early 1996 by the Western governments' willingness to have the IMF approve the largest grants to the Yeltsin government to date, despite all the new Western friction with Russia, despite the war in Chechnya, and despite the advance of reactionary attitudes in the Russian polity and the growth of the influence of the Communists and extreme nationalists. Although Tokyo no longer strenuously resists such IMF decisions, it is not happy about them.

As time goes on, it seems likely that Western political conflicts with Russia will continue to emerge, particularly in the post-Yeltsin era. U.S.-Russian relations will probably settle into a pattern of some cooperation and a great deal of rivalry for a long time to come. Yet the growth of problems—even important problems—between Moscow and Washington is unlikely to rescue the U.S.-Japanese alliance even if there is a much more drastic deterioration of U.S. relations with Russia than now seems likely. Unless there is also a visible reversal of the ongoing radical decline in the *capabilities* of the Russian armed forces—and thus a restoration of a concrete Russian military threat—the Tokyo-Washington alliance is unlikely to be revitalized on an anti-Russian basis, and a gap is likely to persist between U.S. and Japanese views of the stake each has in dealings with Moscow.

Russia, the United States, and the Koreans

Meanwhile, since the demise of the Soviet Union, Russia has sought, albeit thus far with only modest results, to begin rebuilding its position in the Korean peninsula—where Russian influence today ranks a distant last compared with that of the other large interacting powers, the United States, China, and Japan. Because of the difficulties that Moscow has encountered in this effort, U.S. interests have thus far been affected only marginally by Russian policy. The chance of an eventual meaningful increase in Russian influence in the peninsula will depend mainly on the future of the Russian economy and the problematic chances of Russian political stability.

Throughout the Yeltsin years, Moscow has been trying to follow up on the fundamental shift in policy toward the peninsula set in motion by

Gorbachev in his last year. In 1990 and 1991, Gorbachev began this transformation by meeting with South Korea's leaders and formalizing relations with Seoul, at the expense of the perceived interests of North Korea and to the fury of Kim Il-sung. This overt transfer of the main weight of Soviet interest in the peninsula from north to south was one of the last triumphs of Gorbachev's pragmatism over past Soviet ideological priorities and represented tacit recognition of the enormous gap that had opened between Seoul's economic success and Pyongyang's failure.

From the American perspective, many of the consequences of this shift by Moscow have been quite useful. The pressure placed on Kim Il-sung by the Soviet rapprochement with South Korea—when amplified by the similar evolution of Chinese policy—fairly soon compelled certain North Korean diplomatic retreats long desired by the United States, including reluctant acceptance of the separate admission of North and South Korea to the United Nations.

On the other hand, while at least one indirect effect of the Soviet turn toward Seoul was hardly the fault of Moscow, it was not so benign. There is considerable evidence to suggest that this watershed event, further distancing the North Korean regime from its most powerful ally, stimulated Kim Il-sung to intensify work toward achieving nuclear-weapons capability, with consequences that will reverberate for a long time to come.

For the Russians, meanwhile, the payoff from their shift in emphasis in the peninsula has so far been rather disappointing. Trade turnover with South Korea has indeed grown substantially, but the heavy flow of investment funds anticipated has not been forthcoming. Moscow had hoped to extract huge loans and massive long-term investments from South Korea as recompense for the large political favor it was bestowing. Moreover, like Gorbachev before him, Yeltsin also hoped to extract leverage on Japan from the spectacle of large-scale South Korean interest in Russian profits. Neither result has materialized.

At the outset, Seoul did indeed offer a loan package of some $3 billion to the Soviet Union as the tacit quid pro quo for Soviet recognition, but it then delivered only half the package, suspending the second half indefinitely when the Soviet Union collapsed and Russia was unable to pay even interest on the money extended to the Soviet Union. Meanwhile, like many Japanese corporations, most Korean companies that had initially considered large investments in Russia have been discouraged by the corruption, lack of legal protection for investments, and general instability and disarray there[10] as well as by the inability to repay past debts. As one Russian writer bitterly noted, Korean investment in Uzbekistan and Vietnam has actually been more substantial.[11]

In the summer of 1995, however, an agreement was signed for Russian repayment of nearly half a billion dollars worth of its debt, with slightly more than half the total to be furnished in commodities and the remainder in weapons, including tanks, infantry fighting vehicles, antitank missiles, and air defense missiles. As this deal neared fruition, a modest quid pro quo began to emerge, as South Korean industrial leaders were said to be more seriously considering some new investment in development of Russian gas and other energy resources.[12] It remained to be seen, however, how big a change there would be in South Korean reluctance to invest in Russia.

Meanwhile, Russian hopes—blocked by South Korea and the United States—for a prominent role in supplying the new light-water nuclear reactors promised to Pyongyang under the 1994 U.S. agreement with North Korea were disappointed. Moscow of course had been eager to obtain the massive hard-currency earnings that would accrue from supplying the plants and also eager to get the guarantee of continued employment for its underemployed skilled workers that would come with such a contract. In addition, the rejection of Russian light-water plants eliminated the first possibility in years for the reassertion of a major Russian economic presence in the Korean peninsula.

To be sure, for the foreseeable future, Russia will continue to be one important factor in the geopolitical equation in both halves of the peninsula, if only because of its size and proximity. But, if the North Korean nuclear agreement with the United States survives, Russia will remain, as it is today, a considerably less important factor than China, Japan, and the United States. If the North Korean relationship with the outside world does begin to open up as a consequence of the nuclear deal, Japan in particular is likely very soon to become and remain considerably more important to North Korea than Russia will be.

There are, however, two contingencies in which radically altered strategic circumstances would make an important difference for the Russian position. The first involves the possibility that the ambiguous and still fragile nuclear arrangement with Pyongyang might some day collapse entirely, bringing about the resumption of the North Korean nuclear-weapons program and the return of even more tension than before to the peninsula. Under these circumstances, with the return of a crisis atmosphere rendered all the more acute by everything that had gone on before, Russia's reaction to the U.S. response would be more important than ever to Washington. Of course, much would depend on the internal situation in Moscow. To be sure, it is unlikely that almost any Russian government would be prepared to take military risks for the sake of the North Koreans. But a hard-line Russian regime completely estranged from the United States could prove much more openly obstructive than heretofore of any renewed U.S. efforts to bring pressure to bear on Pyongyang.

A second contingency is the possibility that the grave economic situation in North Korea may eventually bring a collapse of the Pyongyang regime and thus reunification of the Korean peninsula. This would affect Russian interests in a variety of ways, but particularly because the chain of events set in motion by reunification might well have a drastic effect on the American regional presence.

Under the new circumstances, it seems unlikely that either the Korean or the American public would long support the continued presence of U.S. forces in Korea, even if the U.S.-Korean alliance itself remained in existence. In turn, the already increasingly fragile political basis of the U.S. alliance with Japan might well suffer a severe blow. Once the United States had totally withdrawn its Korean military presence, an increasingly isolationist American public and Congress might well come to see the U.S. presence in Japan—today, the essential support base for Korean operations—as having lost its fundamental justification.[13] Should this scenario come to pass and a concrete threat arise to the continuation of the U.S. alliance with Japan, Russia, like other states in the region, is likely to become quite alarmed at the implications, notably the possibility of subsequent Japanese rearmament.

Barring such drastic changes, prospects for improvement of the Russian position in the peninsula will continue to hinge mainly on Moscow's ability to unlock South Korean investment. As suggested earlier, this, in turn, will mainly depend on South Korean perception of internal trends in Russia itself and particularly on whether a permanent stabilization of Russian political life can be brought about to backstop economic stabilization. This question remains unanswered.

The United States and the Sino-Russian Relationship

For the United States, the most sensitive aspect of Russian policy in East Asia remains today, as it has been for many years, Moscow's dealings with China. This is still the case despite the demise of the Soviet Union and the end of the global bipolar struggle.

Regardless of the international atmosphere at any given moment, none of these three powers has ever been able to regard the relationship between the other two with calm indifference, although all three have sometimes professed to do so. To be sure, it is clear that, today, the U.S. factor is no longer the biggest consideration affecting Russian and Chinese behavior toward each other, as has sometimes been the case in the past. Yet it is also true that the relationship that each has with Washington continues to be *one* important consideration. The triangular issue today is much less highly charged than it was during the cold war, when over the years each of the three in turn sought to use its dealings with one as leverage against the other.[14] But it is evident that this tendency has by no means completely disappeared. Fresh testimony in this regard was furnished in late June 1995, when Chinese Premier Li Peng, visiting Moscow during a period of heightened friction between the People's Republic and the United States, took the occasion to suggest publicly that Russia and China should stand together against alleged American bullying.[15]

In fact, despite Li Peng's angry rhetoric, both the Chinese and the Russian leaders have very mixed feelings about the prospects for their relationship with each other and the implications for their dealings with Washington. These complexities are worth examining in some detail.

On the Chinese side, Beijing desires the following from Russia, in relative order of importance:

First, of course, it requires an absence of the political and economic coercion attempted by Khrushchev and the military threat posed by Brezhnev. The Chinese are for the time being reassured on both counts, in the wake of the rapprochement inaugurated in a small way in the late

Brezhnev/Andropov era, carried much further by Gorbachev, and continued by Yeltsin. Moreover, China (like the West) is even more reassured by the decline in Soviet and Russian military capabilities over the same period as the result of economic troubles and political turmoil. Yet Chinese leaders, like some in the United States, probably remain wary about the long term because of the great uncertainties of the Russian political scene—which brings us to the next point.

Second, like the United States, China craves internal stability and predictability in Russia. Should radical change in the nature of the political leadership in Moscow occur, it could bring to power extreme nationalist forces whose behavior toward China would be difficult to foresee. China also has another reason to want domestic stability in both Russia and the Russian sphere of influence in neighboring Central Asia since instability to the north and west threatens to infect China and particularly Xinjiang.[16] For this reason, Beijing has undoubtedly been concerned over the growing Russian involvement in a war against Muslim rebels in Tajikistan, which has been sporadically spilling over into Afghanistan.

Third, China sees Russia as a fruitful source of modest-cost, high-technology weaponry. From the Chinese perspective, these weapons purchases (discussed in more detail below) have become a very valuable aspect of the relationship with the Yeltsin government. Yet by the same token they have become a source of some tension with others, including both East Asians and the United States.

Fourth, China sees Russia as a useful outlet for surplus Chinese exports and particularly for those lower-quality consumer products that are marginal hard-currency earners in the United States and the rest of the world. Yet this very practice of using Russia as such a dumping ground is a source of considerable resentment there.

Finally, to a certain limited extent, China also does indeed see its relationship with Russia as a point of potential leverage vis-à-vis the United States. This feature of the relationship is facilitated by the existence of at least a few specific foreign policy interests that are shared by China and Russia in opposition to the United States. For example, many individuals in the military and military-industrial elites of both China and Russia have a strong personal commercial interest in earning hard currency through the sale of advanced weapons abroad, even if the customers are states like Iran that the United States would like to see treated as terrorist pariahs. More broadly, some in both countries have a personal vested interest in profitable deals that threatens to transgress the worldwide constraints on the dissemination of missile technology that the United States would like to enforce. And many more share a vague, general resentment of the United States as the only remaining superpower as well as concern over the military capabilities the United States displayed during the 1991 Gulf War.

It is tempting to Beijing, when annoyed by the United States, to attempt to worry Washington with the possibility of Sino-Russian alignment against the United States, and the Chinese are now somewhat less inhibited about trying to create that impression than they were a few years ago. Yet the Chinese are well aware that, quite apart from the uncertainties and reservations of the Russians themselves on this score, the usefulness to China of the Russian connection for the exertion of pressure on Washington is limited because of the practical constraints on how far Beijing itself can easily afford to go.

In the first place, Beijing still has too many memories of the unhappy past in its dealings with Moscow to enter lightly into the kind of intimate relationship with Russia that would pose a serious threat to U.S. security interests. In the second place, Beijing has too much at stake in its quest for external trade and investment—from the United States, from Western Europe, and, above all, from Japan—readily to jeopardize those benefits by moving too far toward the kind of Russian connection that might be perceived by others (including Japan) as threatening.

This is not at all to say that such a shift is impossible. But only drastic changes in the overall strategic environment in East Asia would be likely to change this calculus of costs and benefits for Beijing. In the conclusion to this essay, I shall consider contingencies that could bring about such drastic change.

THE RUSSIAN CONUNDRUM: HOW CLOSE A CHINA CONNECTION?

The Russians also have conflicting emotions about their relationship with China, with many pros and cons that are given quite different weights by different Russian observers. A balance sheet of Russian views about the relationship might look like this:

First, and most important, many Russians would agree that China is, in principle, a heaven-sent market for Russia's growing surplus of raw materials and machinery (especially weaponry) that cannot be used by the contracting Russian economy (or the contracting Russian military machine) or that is not competitive enough to sell in sufficient quantities for hard currency in the West. The Chinese market is seen as playing a major role in helping keep workers employed in the gigantic and inefficient military-industrial complex that Russia inherited from the Soviet Union. In this respect, the assumptions of Russians about what they can get from China contrast with Russian desires regarding Japan and Korea, from whom Russia would like to get investment capital and technology to fuel development and modernization.

Second, most Russians would also agree that improving relations with China helps Russian military security in East Asia. The process of border demarcation and confidence-building measures begun by Gorbachev and continued by Yeltsin serves Russian interests because it further reduces the possibility that a security threat might return along the Russian-Chinese border in an era of profound Russian economic and military weakness.

Third, moving beyond this common ground, some Russians have expressed much broader hopes for the economic benefits that can be obtained through dealings with China. Some Russian observers appear to hope that China can make a significant contribution to the development of the Russian Far East—and even serve as a bridge for Russian integration into the booming markets of Southeast Asia.[17] Other Russians feel, as I do, that these hopes are exaggerated. Although the two economies are somewhat complementary, a central fact about this relationship is that, unlike Japan, China does not have the capability, even if it should wish to do so, to furnish either significant inputs of technology or significant capital investments to Russia. Meanwhile, as will be seen below, the small-scale entrepreneurial activity that thousands of Chinese traders have been carrying out in the Soviet Far East has itself become a significant new source of political tension.

Finally, there are many in Moscow who see the relationship with China—in principle—as a major potential geopolitical asset for Russia's dealings with the United States and the West generally. As disillusionment with the West has grown, this attitude has been voiced more frequently. In this view, the relationship with China is the most significant step that Russia has yet taken in the post-Soviet era to assert its independent geopolitical position vis-à-vis both the United States and Japan. Thus, one author sees Russia as inevitably drawn toward China "in the search for a counterweight against the West's political offensive."[18] Another considers China "the only country on which Russia can really count for the strengthening of its positions in northern Asia."[19] These sentiments tended to reinforce the perpetual carping about former Foreign Minister Kozyrev's policies as being unbalanced, too much oriented toward Europe and the United States, and insufficiently oriented toward Asia. In fact, with relations with Japan still cold and distant, the main alternative for Russia in East Asia has necessarily been China.

However, the negative aspects of Russia's present relationship with China are also considerable and have attracted increasing attention in the press—and, indeed, in official deliberations.

THE MIGRATION PROBLEM

First, perhaps the most striking and emotional problem has been that of Chinese population pressure and migration into the Russian Far East. This is a long-term issue. In the years to come, this problem could well be aggravated should the centrifugal tendencies already at work within China bring about a significant further reduction in the ability of the central Chinese government to control what are already substantial internal and external migration flows.

According to Beijing, there are now roughly 1.2 billion Chinese, and the population is increasing every few years in an amount roughly equal to the twenty-five million or so people in all of Russia east of the Urals. Today, the Russians are vividly reminded of these facts as a result of alarming experiences in recent years with uncontrolled and unmonitored Chinese migration into the thinly populated Soviet and Russian Far East. According to one authoritative official source, in 1991–93, this population flow amounted to some half a million cumulatively.[20] Although that figure is itself surprisingly large, much bigger Russian estimates—reaching to many millions—have been published regarding the scope of recent Chinese migration into Russia, and it seems likely that the Russian government in fact lacks reliable information about the size of the influx.

There is abundant evidence of genuine Russian alarm about this phenomenon in official statements and press comment. Concern over such uncontrolled Chinese immigration was the biggest single reason why Yeltsin unilaterally abolished the nonvisa regime for cross-border Russo-Chinese trade at the end of 1993[21] — a step that inflicted a major blow to previously growing trade turnover between the two countries and one from which that trade still has not fully recovered.[22] The Russians have apparently been attempting ever since to find illegal Chinese immigrants and expel them. In January 1995, the Russian federal border service declared that "an almost uncontrolled flood of Chinese had poured into Primorye and Khabarovsk Territory with the introduction of non-visa tourist exchanges between Russia and China." One border guard sweep was reported to have expelled some four hundred Chinese in a two-week period in early January. Such operations were said by the border service to be intended to "help put an end to the 'quiet expansion' of the Chinese."[23]

Unsatisfied with these efforts, local pressure on Moscow to do more apparently obtained the attention of the Yeltsin government. At a well-publicized meeting of the Russian government on 24 August 1995, the day after Russia and China signed a border-policing agreement, several members of the cabinet, eager to appeal to local anxieties with a view to the upcoming Russian election, were said to have expressed strong concern over ongoing illegal Chinese immigration in the Russian Far East. Defense Minister Pavel Grachev told a subsequent press briefing that "Chinese citizens are peacefully conquering Russia's Far East" and must be stopped.[24] The head of the Federal Migration Service, Tatyana Regent, stated that the Chinese were using "illegal immigration channels" to settle in the Russian Far East. First Deputy Prime Minister Oleg Soskovets added that the government should help local authorities by developing a more systematic program to deport illegal Chinese immigrants from the region. Regent suggested that, to offset the Chinese tide (which she did not seem to think would stop), some of the five million ethnic Russians who are expected to migrate to Russia from other areas of the former Soviet Union be resettled in the Far East. Russian television subsequently reported alleged plans to erect special housing for this purpose and to create an interdepartmental commission to oversee the resettlement.

It seems unlikely that much will come of such proposals, in view of both the financial constraints facing the Russian government and the disinclination of many Russians to move to the Far East, particularly with the high level of unemployment there. The publicity that the Yeltsin government felt obliged to give to the question, however, was testimony to the ongoing sensitivity of the issue of Chinese migration.

THE IMPLICATIONS OF CHINESE GROWTH

A second negative consideration for the Russian government in contemplating the present relationship with China is equally fundamental and also long term in nature. The Russians must ponder the ultimate political and strategic implications of continued extremely high Chinese growth rates over the next decade or two and continued very rapid modernization of industry and the military, particularly if these trends should be coupled with continued Russian economic difficulties and a perpetuation of the present gradual decay of Russian military capabilities caused by Russia's disarray.

The relative strength of the two neighboring giants is now being slowly but steadily transformed over time. Moscow is still much stronger in certain key military, industrial, and technological respects, but its overall advantage seems smaller today than it was yesterday and probably will be smaller still tomorrow.[25] This gradual, ongoing shift in the power relationship is quite likely to continue if China remains unified. Meanwhile, the gravitational weight of China is today steadily growing throughout much of Asia, increasing Chinese leverage in Southeast Asia and Myanmar, overmatching India, sustaining Japanese (and Western) readiness to invest in China—and also (particularly important for the Russians) gradually increasing over time the potential leverage that China, once more the "Middle Kingdom," may eventually be able to exert over some of the Central Asian states.

Although this latter suggestion may seem far-fetched today, the future is another matter. Thus far, the Chinese have been careful to avoid stepping on Russian toes in their dealings with the Central Asian regimes, and other foreign states, notably Turkey, Iran, Korea, and Japan, have thus far played more important roles in supplementing a generally predominant Russian influence. But, despite the progress that Russia has made to date in its efforts to reestablish hegemony over the Commonwealth of Independent States, and despite the conviction of many in Moscow that Central Asia has major strategic importance for Russia, Russia's ability to continue to dominate the region over the long term remains threatened by the fact that it simply can no longer afford to subsidize the Central Asian states on the scale they consider adequate. It is therefore conceivable that one or two decades of further extraordinary Chinese growth, coupled with continued Russian economic difficulties, could pull at least certain of those states toward the growing Chinese economic orbit and away from their traditional dependence on Russia.

THE IMPULSE TO PERSEVERE

Despite any such worries waiting over the horizon, the overriding impulse in Russian policy today is to persevere with China. Despite the misgivings it obviously has about the Chinese, the Yeltsin government has felt obliged to continue its systematic effort to enlarge the relationship with Beijing. As already suggested, the desire to expand dealings with China is greatly strengthened, indeed necessitated, by the apparently interminable Russian impasse with Japan. As Russian hopes regarding the future of their relationship with Japan have become more and more circumscribed, Moscow's felt need to do better with China, the other major Asian power, has grown proportionately.

Yeltsin's efforts to develop a profitable relationship with Beijing have therefore methodically built on the conciliatory efforts that Gorbachev began, especially after Gorbachev's landmark 1989 visit to China. In contrast to Yeltsin's abrupt refusal to come to Japan in 1992, he did make a summit visit to Beijing that year, and this was supplemented by a steady stream of high-level contacts by the foreign ministers, premiers, and, particularly, military leaders. Thus, like the Soviet government before it, the Russian government has sought through a variety of measures to overcome the points of friction inherited from the hostile past and simultaneously to extract economic benefit from political improvements.

To this end, Yeltsin continued the step-by-step effort begun by Gorbachev to settle disputes over the border with China, beginning in the eastern sector and moving methodically westward. In so doing, Yeltsin was obliged, at some political cost, to override the demagogic objections of local politicians in the Russian Far East to those small concessions made by Russia, and, even so, a few issues on the eastern border have had to be left unresolved.[26] Long-drawn-out discussions continue on the western sector of what had been the Sino-Soviet border, a sector that is now mainly the Chinese border with Tajikistan, Kyrgyzstan, and Kazakhstan. These border negotiations between China and a joint delegation of Russia and Central Asian states seem unlikely to produce decisive results for a long time,[27] yet neither side appears to feel great urgency on the matter. Meanwhile, equally protracted talks continue about a mutual force withdrawal from the vicinity of the border, a subject rendered very difficult by the existing assymetry in the geographic realities and the local disposition of forces.[28] However, Russia and China have apparently made some progress toward agreement on a mutual thinning out of forces, as distinguished from outright pullbacks.

THE ISSUE OF MILITARY SALES

While continuing these negotiations, Moscow has pursued other forms of security collaboration with considerable vigor. An intelligence agreement was reported to have been signed in 1992; its contents are unclear, but it seems to have restored at least some limited cooperation with the People's Republic.[29] As already noted, Yeltsin has sought (with varying degrees of success) to bolster foreign earnings and domestic employment by selling the Chinese a considerable variety of Russian military hardware, including, among other things, the SU-27 fighter-bomber and Kilo-class diesel submarines. Perhaps even more important to the United States in the long run, he has endeavored to restore a considerable portion (although certainly not all) of the broad cooperation on military technology that had existed between the two countries until Khrushchev destroyed it in 1960.

Thus, in the fall of 1993, a five-year military cooperation agreement was signed that was expected to broaden the transfer of military technology to China significantly. The Chinese were permitted to recruit large numbers of Russian weapons scientists to work in China, notably in research institutes under the aeronautics ministry. Others were said to be carrying out work for the Chinese in Russia. Indeed, the Russian government was said to have lost control over some weapons scientists who were offering their services to Beijing for cash even without authorization from Moscow. Meanwhile, hundreds of Chinese defense scientists are now working at Russian aerospace institutes.

In response to these phenomena, the United States was reported to have soon intervened with private démarches to Yeltsin, and Russia was said to have promised the United States not to sell China advanced-technology weapon systems with implications for "power projection," that is, weapons involving distant means of delivery. The Chinese, in turn, have privately expressed resentment at this effort to limit their acquisition of such technology.

Even beyond the issue of the U.S. reaction, however, there are some problems for the Russians involved in the sale of weapons to China. To begin with, even the economic benefit that the Russians get from arms sales to China is sometimes more limited than it seems. At least some Russian weapons plants do not, in fact, get paid in full in hard currency by the Chinese but have to accept as in-part payment Chinese goods that they sometimes have trouble reselling.

More fundamentally, it is evident that some important civilian authorities as well as some in the General Staff have had reservations about the extent of the military technology that can safely be transferred to China. In certain cases, where China has sought to buy not merely Russian weapons but the capability to make those weapons, the Russian government has hesitated, in part for obvious, although unvoiced, security reasons, and in part also because of concerns that the transfer of such manufacturing capabilities would help China compete with Russia in foreign arms export markets.

The leading such case so far was the long Russian delay in consenting to Chinese demands that Moscow follow up its initial sale of twenty-six SU-27s by agreeing to sell China the right to manufacture this plane.[30] Just as it has done in dealing with prospective Western arms sellers in the past, Beijing prefers to negotiate purchase of manufacturing capabilities rather than large numbers of the end items. While this attitude reflects a natural Chinese desire for defense self-sufficiency, it is hardly convenient for Russian weapons manufacturers. For a long time, therefore, Moscow was torn between its reluctance to sell the goose that lays the golden eggs and its urgent need for the proceeds of such a sale. Russia consequently insisted that China enhance the deal by agreeing to purchase a substantial number of additional SU-27s. In early 1966, there were reports that China had finally agreed to purchase an additional forty-eight SU-27s and that, consequently, the transfer to China of the technology to manufacture this aircraft would now take place.[31] If this deal is duly carried out, it could prove a watershed in the developing relationship.

Prospects and Contingencies for the Next Decade

Against this background, I can draw some conclusions about probabilities for Russian policy in Northeast Asia over the coming years and then finally turn to factors that could conceivably bring about changes that at the moment seems less likely.

Probabilities for the Next Few Years

Other things being equal, Russian policy in the Far East will probably not alter radically very soon, whatever the political climate in Moscow. Over the next few years, the dual pattern of Russian behavior in East Asia will probably persist, on the one hand, attempting to expand arms markets—especially in China, India, and Southeast Asia—and, on the other, seeking substitutes for and supplements to Japanese investment capital wherever possible, with a particular emphasis on South Korea.

But, although there could be some moderate improvement in investment flows from Seoul in the wake of the agreement for partial repayment of the Russian debt, the Korean alternative to Japanese investment is nevertheless likely to continue to be disappointing. Meanwhile, it is probable that Russian relations with Japan will remain cool over the next decade. Almost certainly there will be no settlement of the territorial dispute and therefore no formal peace treaty between Russia and Japan. But, more important (since economic impediments to Japanese investment in Russia are now more significant than the territorial issue), the investment climate in Russia at best will probably not have improved sufficiently over the next few years to make a real difference to the reluctant Japanese business community.

Although there will be some Japanese investment, the continued constraint in this relationship will encourage Russian leaders over the next few years to go on placing their emphasis on the relationship with China. Sales to Beijing of military technological expertise and military end items will continue, and we may also see the transfer of additional new military production capabilities. There could be some effort to increase intelligence cooperation, and the areas in which Russian and Chinese foreign policies work in tandem in opposition to U.S. wishes may gradually expand. All this will be a permanent problem for the United States, one that will probably grow as time goes on. Concern in East Asia will mount, in particular, over the implications for the region of an acceleration of Chinese acquisition of defense technology from the Russians.

However, as before, the Russian leadership—almost any Russian leadership—will probably remain ambivalent about how far to go with China, torn between the desire, on the one hand, to maximize earnings from foreign military sales and build up the relationship with China as an offset to the West[32] and concern, on the other hand, that help for Chinese military capabilities could some day produce new dangers for Russia. As insurance, the Russians are likely (to the extent their economy permits) to impose certain limits on the long-term process of reducing Russian ground and air forces opposite China. To the degree that Russia is forced to look eastward because of the loss of ports and imperial territories in the west, that will also encourage the tendency to devote scarce resources to the Asian military presence.

In sum, even if the Yeltsin regime should be replaced by (or transformed into) a hard-line Russian government completely estranged from the West, reasons for some Russian caution regarding the Chinese will still exist. But Russian restraint in dealing with China will be somewhat more likely if a regime with some stake in relations with the United States survives in Moscow over the next few years. What is at issue on the immediate horizon is thus a matter of *degree.* Other things being equal, the advent of a harder-line, overtly anti-Western regime in Moscow would make some difference, although even then most likely not a decisive difference, in how far the Russians would be prepared to take risks in selling technology to China and, more broadly, how far the Russian government would be willing to go to propitiate China. What would be required to create a more than marginal change is another matter.

What Could Revive a Moscow-Beijing Alliance?

For the United States, the most dangerous contingency for the evolution of Russian policy in East Asia over the next decade or two would be Russia's movement beyond its present cautious dalliance with China to restore the close Moscow-Beijing relationship of the 1950s. On balance, such a drastic change seems — for the time being — quite improbable, for the reasons already suggested. In addition to the various Russian interests in the West that today inhibit Russia from making so great a change in policy, we have seen that the emergence of a full-fledged Sino-Russian alliance is also impeded today by reluctance on the Chinese side. And, finally, there are the factors making for mutual suspicion already cited that will surely urge caution on both countries and particularly on Russia.

Nevertheless, the consequences for Washington if such a vast change ever did come about would be sufficiently serious to require constant watchfulness by the United States to guard against it. The reemergence of a Sino-Russian phalanx in Eurasia, forty or fifty years after it first disappeared, would be seen as menacing to the interests of many countries around the periphery of this alliance, from Europe to India to Japan. East Asians would be particularly concerned at the prospect of a sharp further boost — going well beyond what is taking place today — in Russian technological assistance to Chinese military capabilities.

What contingencies could bring about such a change? One central variable will certainly be the state of China's relationship with the United States, which at best will probably remain difficult and under some circumstances could become quite tense. The Taiwan issue — the biggest single factor in the rapid growth of U.S.-Chinese friction in 1995 — is likely to become even more neuralgic over time, simply because the political forces on Taiwan favoring Taiwanese independence (rather than the fiction that Taiwan represents China) are likely to get incrementally stronger with the continued fading of the old Kuomintang generation. The People's Republic cannot accept an independent Taiwan formally divorced from China and is very apprehensive of the U.S. response over time to Taiwan's movement in this direction. This problem will be compounded as the tendency to accept democratic norms simultaneously becomes stronger in Taiwan, in contrast to trends in China. The reaction in both U.S. political parties to these two parallel trends is fairly likely to generate renewed tension between Beijing and Washington over the next decade.

Meanwhile, any such problems between China and the United States over Taiwan are likely to be intensified by the growth of the People's Republic's economic and military strength and self-confidence as well as by a Chinese regional assertiveness born of an unvoiced conviction that China's size confers natural and legitimate geopolitical rights. Meanwhile, the Chinese military leadership, whose leverage on foreign policy has already been visibly enhanced by the Politburo succession struggle, is likely to remain very sensitive to the perception that the United States is bent on constraining, even "encircling," China.[33] In 1995, pressure on the leadership from the Chinese military played a major role in eliciting Beijing's harsh and assertive behavior toward both the United States and Taiwan in the wake of the visit of Taiwanese President Li Teng-hui to the United States. These attitudes produced considerable overt Chinese muscle flexing and threats to use force against Taiwan, which evoked a reciprocal angry reaction in the United States. Under some circumstances—particularly if a major crisis over Taiwan should in fact some day emerge—the existing hostility within the Communist Chinese regime toward the United States could grow much stronger and could increase the proportion of Chinese leaders willing to pay the high price of a more dramatic move toward Russia.

On the Russian side, there is one issue whose dynamic potential is comparable to that of Taiwan on the Chinese side. Should NATO expand eastward, not only Russian internal political dynamics but also Russian policy in the Far East, notably with regard to China, could well be affected. There is likely to continue to be some reciprocal connection between Russian policy in the east and the west. The reasons why this was the case during the Soviet era have not disappeared with the end of the cold war.

The possibility of such a major Russian "turn toward the east" would be enhanced if a rabidly nationalistic, authoritarian, and anti-Western government has already come to power in Moscow when an expansion of NATO occurs. Given both a further political advance by Russia's conservative, anti-Western forces and a concrete step by NATO to expand eastward, the craving in Russian nationalist circles for a Chinese "counterweight" to the United States — already visible to some extent in Russian policy — could, over time, become overriding.

To recapitulate, very important considerations tend to constrain both Moscow and Beijing from going beyond a certain point in broad, concerted strategic opposition to U.S. interests. Nevertheless, while such a radical evolution of policy in both capitals is less than probable, it is possible over the next decade, given two prerequisites. The first is the emergence of a leadership consensus in both places whose underlying attitude toward the United States is considerably more hostile than it has yet become. The second is the emergence of very large precipitating crises — over Taiwan, in the case of China, and over NATO expansion, in the case of Russia — in which U.S. policy appears to each to raise a concrete threat to its vital national interests.

Notes

1 One knowledgeable Russian writer has summed up the present situation by referring to "the growing economic gap between Maritime Kray / Eastern Siberia and the European portion of Russia" as well as "those regions' reorientation toward neighboring countries" and, finally, "the out-migration of the Russian population" (Sergey Rogov, *Nezavisimaya gazeta,* 31 December 1994).

2 Among Russian officials, Defense Minister Grachev has taken the lead in advocating some kind of multilateral security arrangements in East Asia, which he has never spelled out.

3 Japanese foreign ministry officials lamented at the time that there had been "a U.S. foreign policy change" that would have "a very negative effect on the negotiations between Japan and Russia." For details, see Harry Gelman, *Russo-Japanese Relations and the Future of the US-Japanese Alliance,* MR-168-AF (Santa Monica, Calif.: Rand, 1993). In early 1995, then Russian foreign minister Kozyrev published a book in which, much to the annoyance of Tokyo, he reminded the Japanese of the Ozawa 1991 offer (Kyodo news service, Tokyo, 1 February 1995).

4 Among other things, budget expenditures had been held down by the failure to pay many government bills (conspicuously including some army salaries).

5 Thus, soon after Yeltsin returned home in the fall of 1993, points of friction immediately reemerged, first over the Russian navy's practice of dumping nu-

clear waste products in ocean areas adjacent to Japan, then over the harsh Russian reaction to Japanese attempts to fish in the waters near the Northern Territories — a perennial issue in the relationship since far back in the Soviet era. Russian border guards not only have seized Japanese fishing boats near the disputed islands but have fired on them. Periodic negotiations over fishing rights continue to be protracted and bitter, as they have been for many years, since both sides are reluctant to enter into commercial agreements that might have adverse implications for the territorial claim.

6 Japanese leaders displayed a similar hidebound nationalism when they failed to accept much of the foreign assistance offered after the Kobe earthquake in 1995, but they were not so ostentatiously rude. Despite Yeltsin's statement — whose effects the embarrassed Russian foreign ministry subsequently sought to undo — Sakhalin did in fact solicit Japanese help.

7 Addressing a ceremonial meeting on the fiftieth anniversary of the end of World War II in the Pacific, Grachev said that the successful Soviet military offensive against the Japanese Kwantung army in 1945 had led to the "return to Russia of lands torn away by Japan." When asked what specific areas he had in mind, Grachev said the Kuril Islands, which he then described as "genuine Russian land" (Interfax, 29 August 1995). These gratuitous remarks evoked vigorous criticism in the Japanese press.

8 However, there have been press reports alleging that the Russian General Staff is weighing the possibility of eventually phasing out the deployment of SSBNs in the Sea of Okhotsk and henceforth basing the entire submarine-launched ballistic missile (SLBM) deterrent in the Barents Sea, the other "bastion area" north of European Russia. Should this change ever materialize, it would evidently be carried out for reasons having little to do with Japan (presumably, budgetary pressures and the new deployment choices presented by the START agreements with the United States). Yet such a strategic shift might in time have some moderating effect on Russian military opposition to relinquishing the Northern Territories since certain of the traditional military worries about giving up these islands — that this would facilitate hostile operations against Russian strategic submarines deployed in the Sea of Okhotsk — would no longer be relevant.

9 Thus, speaking to the Federation Council in July 1995, then Foreign Minister Kozyrev was asked about both Japanese claims to the southern Kurils and suggestions that Russia should demilitarize Kaliningrad. He replied, "Russia rejects everybody's territorial claims."

10 See the *Washington Post*, 4 June 1994. The practical consequences of this chronic disarray were brought home to the Koreans in May 1994, when the first meeting of a South Korea-Russia joint economic committee, scheduled to take place in Seoul in preparation for a state visit of President Kim to Moscow, was abruptly canceled by Moscow "for unspecified domestic reasons" less than twenty-four hours before it was to take place. Hours later, Moscow revised this

decision and told Seoul that it would send a delegation under a different leader. A short while later, Russia changed its mind again, saying it would not send a delegation at all (Yonhap wire service [Seoul], 20 May 1994, in *Foreign Broadcast Information Service, East Asia* (hereafter *FBIS/EAS*), 20 May 1994, 36; see also *Izvestia,* 7 July 1995). Similar behavior regarding a number of scheduled high-level meetings has contributed to Japan's antagonism toward Russia.

11 *Izvestia,* 27 May 1994. The *Izvestia* writers also complained that Seoul's trade turnover with China was "several times" more than its trade with Russia. More than a year later, this had not changed, and another *Izvestia* article complained that, despite the fact that China established diplomatic relations with Seoul two years after Moscow did, the Sino-Korean trade turnover was now four times greater than Russian-Korean trade (*Izvestia,* 7 July 1995).

12 *Korea Herald* (Seoul), 24 May 1995; Yonhap news agency, 7 June 1995.

13 For further discussion of this scenario, see Harry Gelman, "The Future of Northeast Asia: An American Perspective," *Analysis* (National Bureau of Asian Research), vol. 6, no. 2 (August 1995).

14 At the outset, when the People's Republic of China first appeared, the Soviet Union under Stalin sought to convey to the United States the impression that its new alliance with China was an immense and permanent extension of Soviet power on the world scene and also represented evidence that that power would inevitably continue to grow. A decade later, after Stalin's death, Mao Zedong sought unsuccessfully to use the alliance with the Soviet Union to serve Chinese interests in Mao's struggle with the United States, an effort that Khrushchev rejected as endangering Soviet interests. Still later, in the early 1970s, Henry Kissinger and Richard Nixon sought to encourage Chinese fears of Soviet attack and at the same time successfully used the new U.S. connection with China as a point of leverage in their dealings with Moscow.

15 Li told a press conference that "Russia and China will not allow anyone to tell us how to live and work" (ITAR-TASS, 26 June 1995).

16 In August 1995, Chinese officials in Xinjiang thus warned that "hostile forces" there were cooperating with forces from "abroad" to engage in "sabotage and trouble-making" throughout the region (Xinhua, 20 August 1995).

17 See Sergey Vostrikov, *Nezavisimaya gazeta,* 22 March 1994, in *FBIS/USSR,* 20 April 1994).

18 Viktor Gavrilov, *Nezavisimaya gazeta,* 15 April 1994, in *FBIS/USSR,* 27 April 1994.

19 Aleksey Voskresenskiy, *Nezavisimaya gazeta,* 27 May 1994.

20 October 1994 private statement to the author by a senior official of the Russian foreign ministry.

21 Russian officials have also acknowledged fears that uncontrolled cross-border trade was being used as a cover for both widespread criminal activity and considerable Chinese espionage. There also seems to have been some concern over the lack of quality control over some of the Chinese goods brought into the

Russian market through this method, as distinguished from centrally authorized channels.

22 After the nonvisa regime was abolished, Sino-Russian trade turnover dropped by one-third between 1993 and 1994 (*Segodnya,* 1 July 1995).

23 RIA Press Service (Moscow), 12 January 1995. On 1 March 1995, Interfax and AFP similarly reported that Russia had expelled more than one thousand Chinese citizens from the Russian Far East for carrying counterfeit passports or expired visas. The Chinese have resented and some have quietly protested these operations, although apparently not on an official level. The Chinese government, however, has professed a desire to cooperate and to this end signed a border-policing agreement with Russia in August 1995.

24 Interfax, 24 August 1995. Grachev further fed the tendency toward hysteria by asserting that military sources had reported that Chinese settlers in the region had organized martial arts training centers, implying that this was being done with sinister intent.

25 "In recent times, the balance of forces between Russia and China has changed drastically, and unfortunately, not in our favor" (Vladimir Lukin, interview in *Nezavisimaya gazeta,* 14 March 1995). "China has already equaled and will clearly surpass Russia in terms of GDP. The technology gap is also narrowing, thanks in part to Russian arms shipments" (Sergei Rogov, *Nezavisimaya gazeta,* 31 December 1994).

26 Notably, the status of the two small islands held by Russia but long claimed by China, at the junction of the Ussuri and Amur adjacent to Khabarovsk, collectively called Heixiazu by the Chinese. Despite the superiority of the Chinese legal claim, the strategic importance to Russia of these islands, which have been the subject of contention between the two countries for many years, makes it very unlikely that any Russian government will ever feel able to sacrifice them.

27 This is largely because the Chinese leaders have inherited from Mao an enormous claim to territory of the former Soviet Union in the Pamirs that they are certain the Russians and Tajiks will never accept but that Beijing is apparently reluctant to disavow outright, especially without territorial compensation of some sort elsewhere.

28 In May 1995, Grachev said that Chinese proposals for local mutual withdrawals were unacceptable because very few Chinese armed forces were stationed close to the border while geographic and climatic factors required Russia to position almost all its armed forces in the zone China wanted Russia to vacate (ITAR-TASS, 16 May 1995).

29 *Washington Times,* 21 October 1992.

30 *Jane's Defence Weekly,* 19 February 1994.

31 *New York Times,* 7 February 1996.

32 In May 1995, after a visit to China, Defense Minister Grachev was portrayed by some sections of the Russian and Hong Kong press as having offered Beijing a virtual military alliance, which the Chinese had supposedly rejected (see, e.g.,

Rossiyskaya gazeta, 23 May 1995). This account seems likely to have been greatly distorted. In fact, Grachev apparently sought to get the Chinese to agree to take the lead with Russia in promoting some kind of multilateral security arrangements in East Asia, a vague and ill-defined notion that Grachev had been championing for some time. Beijing apparently was not enthusiastic. It should be noted that in August 1995 the same Grachev went out of his way to denounce the threat to the Russian Far East posed by Chinese migration.

33 Some in the Chinese military also have a vested personal interest in the growth of tension with the United States and the rejection of the constraints that the United States seeks to impose on Chinese behavior. For example, some military leaders benefit personally from Chinese military shipments abroad opposed by the United States, such as the sale of missiles to Iran. Others are seeking to use the threat of American "encirclement" to influence military procurement choices.

HENRY TROFIMENKO

U.S.-Russian Relations in East Asia: A View from Moscow

One can describe U.S.-Russian relations in East Asia with brutal frankness in two words: almost nonexistent. Despite all Moscow's highfalutin declarations about a strong "Eurasian" element in Russian foreign policy, Russia, to quote the astute Russian observer of the Asian scene Sergei Agafonov, "has become an outsider in the Asian arena in recent years. . . . Moscow's unrealistic declarations claiming a special place and role in Asian affairs are at best left hanging, and at worst swept aside by pragmatic foreign partners."[1] The absence of any mention of Asia or East Asia in the documents of U.S.-Russian summits in the past few years amply confirms the validity of this observation.

Failures and Achievements of Russian Diplomacy

Russian diplomacy in the region has, regrettably, attracted the attention of the world media essentially through scandals. Russia itself generated these "scandals," starting with the notorious "gift" by President Yeltsin to the president of the Republic of Korea in November 1992 of the "black box" (a flight recorder) from the tragic KAL 007 flight shot down by a Soviet fighter plane on 1 September 1983 over Sakhalin. When opened by the South Korean authorities, the box appeared to be empty of the relevant tapes! A long series of further scandals then ensued. These were the scandals connected with the postponements of President Yeltsin's visit to Japan, the dumping by the Russian navy of liquid radioactive waste into the Sea of Japan near Hokkaido, the sale for scrap iron to a South Korean firm of two comparatively new Russian aircraft carriers and forty-four other ships of the Pacific Fleet using the aid of some murky consortium of retired and evidently very greedy Russian admirals acting as middlemen, the shocking statement by Vladimir Zhirinovsky—the leader of the Russian Liberal Democratic party—reclaiming Alaska from the United States and his threat (if he became Russian foreign minister) to use the Russian navy to blockade the Japanese islands if Japan refuses to sign a peace treaty with Russia, conflicting statements by Russian officials regarding the validity of the Soviet Union's 1961 treaty with the Democratic People's Republic of Korea, the clumsy attempt by the governor of the Russian Maritime Province to publicly force Moscow to revise the treaty on the border delineation signed by Moscow and Beijing in 1991, the strong "Russian trace" of the infamous Japanese Aum Shinrikiyo religious sect turned terrorist group, the rude rejection by President Yeltsin of the compassionate offer by the government of Japan to help in rescue work and to provide humanitarian aid to the victims of a devastating earthquake in Sakhalin in May 1995—to mention just the most disgraceful.

Furthermore, while selling its aircraft carriers dirt cheap ($80.00 per ton),[2] the best means for "showing the flag" overseas because Moscow could not afford to maintain the vessels in seaworthy condition, the Russian leadership has brazenly tried to revive the imperialist naval doctrine of Soviet Admiral Gorshkov. "Our presence in the world's oceans must be expanded," declared Russian foreign minister Andrei Kozyrev, speaking in March 1994 before sailors on board a Russian navy vessel. "Our partners will only respect us more," he added, mentioning Latin America as a possible destination.[3]

All such "happenings," combined with the constant and deliberate dodging by Moscow on the "Northern Territories" issue with Japan, did not add to the regional appreciation of Russian foreign policy in the Far East. However, there are a few bright spots of Russian diplomacy in Asia that stand out against such a woeful background.

The most significant success is Russia's steady, positive development of relations with its great southern neighbor, China, relations that already border on partnership. Another achievement is the inclusion of Russia in the Asian Regional Forum that was established by the ASEAN postministerial meeting in 1993. In 1995, Kozyrev participated in that forum in Brunei, peddling the slightly refurbished set of Russia's usual confidence-building and security-enhancing proposals.[4] Another development having some significance was the setting up of the Trilateral Forum on North Pacific Security, which allows government officials, top military officers, and scholars from Russia, the United States, and Japan to discuss relevant security issues in the North Pacific and to organize some joint naval maneuvers as part of the efforts to enhance trust between the participants. In 1994, a joint U.S.-Russian naval exercise took place near Vladivostok, and, in 1995, another joint naval exercise in peacekeeping operations took place near Hawaii.

In the sphere of economic relations, the three biggest regional achievements of recent times were the more or less successful development of the Nakhodka free economic zone around that Russian Pacific port, where close to five hundred enterprises with foreign investments are now operating, the completion of a fiberglass cable link between Russia and Japan that soon will be connected across Siberia to the European communications network, and the signing of the production-sharing agreement by the Russian government and the Sakhalin administration with a consortium of four oil companies—two Russian companies, the U.S. firm Exxon, and the Japanese Sakhalin Oil and Gas Development Company (SODECO) for the development of the offshore oil fields near Sakhalin.[5] This deal covers a forty-year period and involves an initial investment in the project of $15.2 billion, an investment estimated to generate $67 billion in income. The two non-Russian companies each have a 30 percent interest in the deal.

However, all those events, positive and negative, are just sideshows in the process of fundamental military-political change that is gradually evolving in the region and that will heavily influence the global geopolitical balance in the twenty-first century. Those developments are not easy to grasp because they are influenced by a multitude of factors and events. Moreover, the process unfolds almost imperceptibly, driven by some inner logic of the multifarious geopolitical interactions of the major players in the region with a minimum of their actual or deliberate direction of the process. This process stems from the imperative of political maneuvering by the leading and lesser states in the classic multipolar balance of power that reemerged in the region in place of the inflexible bipolar confrontation of the cold war period and instead of some regional new order.

It is well known that the global bipolar confrontation between the Soviet and the U.S. blocs was critically undermined at the end of the 1960s when China deserted the "socialist camp" and became the third force in the Asia-Pacific region, if not on the global stage. That was the main cause of the détente that soon developed between China and the United States as well as that between the Soviet Union and the United States, which allowed each of the three players to maneuver between the other two to enhance its own power and influence.

The collapse of the Soviet Union in 1991 undermined Moscow's power over its allies and clients in the region and lessened the importance of the U.S. containment strategy, with its "umbrella of protection" that was widely advertised in Asia. The "tripolar" balance of power was replaced by a complex multipolar power equation in East and Southeast Asia in which there are four main players—the United States, Japan, China, and Russia—and very many lesser players, such as Canada, both Koreas, Taiwan, Mongolia, members of ASEAN (which from the summer of 1995 includes Vietnam), and some others.

Four specifics of the present balance can be discerned. First, not military but political, communication, economic, demographic, and cultural factors essentially determine the chances of participants in the game of nations. Second, simultaneously with rising nationalism, and, in a way, as phenomena antithetical to it, "economic imperatives are creating borderless economies and open regionalism."[6] Third, moves by lesser players and their coalitions are now becoming meaningful factors in shaping a general geopolitical picture in the region in contrast to the cold war days, when the actions of Moscow and Washington essentially determined everything. Fourth, formal treaties and agreements between the states of the region dating back to the cold war are much less relevant now when a basic realignment of forces is taking place. As an afterthought, one could add to this list the vagueness of forthcoming political developments in China, North Korea, Russia, Indonesia, and even Japan and United States (after the 1996 elections).

Each country in the region is vigorously pursuing its national goals, with far fewer constraints than before. The interplay of those goals in the region creates an intricate military-political-economic environment whose direction and speed of evolution is difficult to predict. One thing, however, is certain: fifteen to twenty years from now, the balance of power and the geopolitical picture in the region will be drastically different from the present situation.

In order to orient oneself in the changing strategic environment, one must understand the national interests of at least the main regional powers.

The National Interests of Russia in Asia

The Russian national interest in the region can be described as follows: to prevent the Russian Far East and Siberia (or parts thereof) from seceding from the Russian Federation and to attract foreign investment in the region;[7] to involve those territories more actively in international economic activity in the Asia-Pacific region; to maintain the balance of power in the North Pacific in whatever way it can; to develop cooperative ventures, including military ventures, in the region with the United States and Canada; to maintain and strengthen friendly relations with the People's Republic of China; to improve relations and develop economic ties with Japan; to develop economic ties with South Korea while restoring and improving political, economic, and military ties with North Korea; and, generally, to promote friendly relations with the countries of Southeast Asia (e.g., through participation in the region's political and economic affairs).

These are the goals that any intelligent observer, following the foreign policy of Russia, would currently deduce as the main ones. In some way, they might be inferred from such official documents such as President Yeltsin's State of the Union messages to the Russian parliament, the Concept of the Foreign Policy of the Russian Federation, adopted by the Russian Foreign Ministry in 1993, and former Foreign Minister Kozyrev's address to the Chinese People's Diplomacy Association in Beijing in January 1994.[8]

Regrettably, if one tried to find some up-to-date official statement of Russian goals in the North Pacific or Asia in general or an account of the achievements of Russian diplomacy in Asia for the past three years in the latest pronouncements or writings of Kozyrev or his successor, Yevgeny Primakov, one would be deeply disappointed. For instance, Kozyrev's book, published in 1995, is stuffed with the stale clichés and worn-out proposals of the Soviet era. Against such a background, even Gorbachev's initiatives of the 1980s regarding the region look fresh and imaginative.

At the same time, however, Kozyrev admits that

regions of Siberia and of the Far East, tremendously rich in resources, turned into an economic backyard of the Asia-Pacific region. While visiting the region, talking to sailors of the Pacific Fleet, business managers of the Maritime Province, fishermen and builders, one can clearly see what our country incurred on itself because of the fact that our relations with Japan have not been settled for many years, because of our ideological squabbles with China, and our economic inaccessibility and self-imposed isolation. I saw with my own eyes the effects of such a policy on the Russian-Chinese border in the region of Blagoveshchensk and Aihui. On our side behind military pillboxes and underground shelters along the Amur River—a zone of desolation, where for a quarter of a century nothing was built in expectation of a military clash with China. On the Chinese side—a center of international trade and a forest of lifting cranes.[9]

Kozyrev's fumbling as well as the incoherent pronouncements of other high government officials on the problems of Russian policy in Asia once again demonstrate the lack of consensus in those quarters on the state interests of Russia.

The other handicap for Russian foreign policy—and not only in Asia—is the lack of effective leverage to support its diplomatic actions. Strategic nuclear force does not work nowadays as leverage in day-to-day diplomacy. The conventional forces that, according to Kozyrev, have been recently cut in half in the Russian Far East do not work very well either.[10] This weakness is due not only to the demilitarization of great power politics in the area but also to the exceedingly pathetic state of the Russian Pacific Fleet and Russia's land-based forces in the Far East.[11]

Russia's only economic asset that would attract foreign investors is its abundant natural resources of Siberia. Despite all the government's declarations over the past quarter century about the necessity of accelerating the development of Siberia and the Far East and the region's economic cooperation with the countries of Asia, the region's infrastructure is still terribly underdeveloped, with the exception of mining and smelting and military industries that are hard to convert to peaceful uses. Currently, thousands of economic refugees are fleeing northeast Russia. These are often the people who settled there in the old days because of the lure of good pay but whose life savings (like those of all Russians) have been wiped out by the 2,000–3,000 percent devaluation of the ruble from pre-*perestroika* days.[12]

Presently, the only trump card that Russia holds in its Asian foreign policy is its geostrategic location. Russia continues to straddle the heartland of Eurasia. It is also the premiere nuclear power in the region, which gives it clout in international relations in spite of its present handicaps. The Russian leaders do try to use the country's advantageous geostrategic position as leverage in international bargaining.

To boost Russia's Eurasian role, in the spring of 1994, Pavel Grachev, the Russian defense minister, tried to sell to NATO Moscow's own idea of "pragmatic partnership for peace," as he called it. He proposed creating a collective security system in Europe based on the Organization for Security and Cooperation in Europe and at the same time creating a similar system in Asia, with Russia the connecting link between the two. But none of Russia's partners were enthusiastic about the proposal. Later on, in May 1995, Grachev aired the same idea "at the other end"—in China—by resurrecting the proposed Asian collective security system. But Chinese officials gave his idea the cold shoulder. Beijing does not want to enter any blocs. It prefers to play balance-of-power politics in the region. At the same time, it is not clear why, with a zeal that might be put to better use, Moscow continues to peddle its Asian collective security program when it is a notion originally meant to contain China. It is clear that the recently established Asian Regional Forum ensures constructive dialogue on key security issues in the region and has the potential for further development.

Some American scholars assert that playing balance-of-power politics is a matter of choice.[13] This is a flawed view. Living in a community of nations is like living in a neighborhood: you must mingle with your neighbors and in the process develop preferences; you make friends with some people and occasionally help them, are indifferent to some others, purposely distance yourself from still others (or from everyone—total isolationism), and deliberately undercut the bad guys when opportunity arises. The perennial game of nations goes on, of which even the cold war was just one manifestation of the balance, there appearing on the global scene a temporary bipolar opposition between superpowers.[14]

Presently, the world has returned to classic balance-of-power politics on the regional and global levels, with a multitude of individual participants mapping their own foreign policy courses. As just one country among many, Russia is involved in the game of nations in the Pacific, despite its poor hand.

The National Goals in Asia of the Other Powers

The national goals (relevant to the problem under discussion) of the other big players seem to be the following.[15]

After the end of the cold war, the United States did not relinquish the role that it had played in Asian security, although the possibility of such a move was hotly debated in the U.S. media and scholarly journals in the early 1990s. It continues to be the predominant power in the North Pacific, adapting to the changing geopolitical environment by placing greater stress on the nonmilitary aspects of diplomacy while still maintaining a significant military presence in the region.

The United States aspires to friendly relations with all the countries of the region. It is not averse to moderating local conflicts or crises—if mediation does not cost much. It actively plays balance-of-power politics, skillfully maneuvering among sworn allies, neutral states, and unfriendly parties.

It wants to keep Japan as a loyal and politically dutiful ally and blunt the sharpness of economic competition with Japan without yielding much of its own ground. It is against any attempt by Japan to move politically closer to either China or Russia. It welcomes free economic competition in the area and will facilitate the development of appropriate institutions for promoting regional trade like the Organization for Asian-Pacific Economic Cooperation (APEC).

It values and nurtures its business relations with China. For Washington, China is still the main counterbalance to Russia, but it is at the same time a potential global rival. Since, realistically speaking, the United States cannot make a strategic partner of China, it is eager to help China play the role of a natural counterbalance to Russia for as long as possible.

As to Russia, the United States wants it to develop along democratic lines and to entrench private property as the economic basis of the new regime. It wants maximum demilitarization of Russia, especially in the sphere of strategic nuclear weapons, and will continue to aid the process of Russian nuclear disarmament (despite some rash resolutions adopted in 1995 by the Republican majorities in the U.S. Congress). It does not seek the breakup of the Russian Federation, realizing full well that the satellite states thus set free would fall under the influence of neighbor states, not the United States. It works to create in Russia and other CIS countries a strong segment of the population with an American-style education and pro-American proclivities. It does not want any further consolidation of the Commonwealth of Independent States under Moscow's aegis.

The strong support that the United States has given the "new Russia" thus far is undoubtedly a hedge against the possible revival of Communism, militarism, and imperialism in Russia. That such a revival is possible is also undoubtedly one of the reasons why the United States still has not drastically reduced its defense budget and continues—globally and regionally—to guard against such an unwanted development.

Officially, U.S. policy in Asia is based on the "three pillars": "stronger efforts to combat the proliferation of weapons of mass destruction on the Korean peninsula and in South Asia," "multiple new arrangements to meet multiple threats and opportunities," and support for "the wave of democratic reform" allegedly sweeping the "new Pacific community." As President Clinton summed up U.S. strategy in Asia: "To deter regional aggression and secure our own interests, we will maintain an active presence and we will continue to lead."[16] The new American strategy is officially one of *engagement and enlargement*. By *enlargement* is evidently meant the further expansion of the American sphere of influence, by *engagement* involving potential adversaries in cooperative ventures or at least a constructive dialogue. *Engagement and enlargement* seems intended as an improvement on *negotiations*, a term coined when President Nixon was initiating détente with China.

A quarter century later, Washington feels that "engagement" is necessary, but with the traditional reliance on a "forward military presence." Such a presence, according to Joseph Nye, former U.S. assistant secretary of defense for international security affairs, is the "oxygen" supporting both political and economic life in Asia.[17]

Evidently for the purpose of engagement and enlargement, the new East Asia Strategic Report, made public by the Pentagon in February 1995, defines the necessary strength of the American forces in Asia at ostensibly the usual level of 100,000 troops. Meanwhile, the former commander-in-chief of the U.S. forces in the Pacific, Admiral Richard Macke, gave the real present strength of those forces as at 300,000.[18] This figure is no different from that of U.S. forces stationed in the Pacific at the end of the cold war.

Japan's main goal is to put its huge economic potential to better use—for political and security purposes. The alliance with the United States suits the Japanese ruling class so far, but it feels that the free pursuit of its national interests in Asia and elsewhere is constrained by too close ties with the United States.[19] It will gradually try to loosen the shackles of the security treaty with the United States and generally the latter's friendly but tight grip on Japan. At one point after the beginning of *perestroika* and reform in Russia, the Japanese elite strongly desired closer ties to the Soviet Union/Russia. Those ties were to be developed after what was expected to be the quick resolution of the problem of the "Northern Territories," a "problem" important not only because it meant territorial expansion (and especially the expansion of its territorial waters) but also as a matter of principle, of seeing justice done.

However, after witnessing all the incomprehensible zigs and zags of the "new Russian foreign policy" vis-à-vis Japan for the last ten years, the Japanese leadership evidently lost all hope of any speedy solution of the territorial dispute. The matter was put on hold, awaiting what it hopes will be more auspicious circumstances in the future. In the meantime, Japan is—cautiously yet profitably—pursuing cooperative ventures with Russia, for example, developing the vast natural resources of the Russian Far East and Siberia. The negative experience with Russia has also prompted Japan to try to develop closer ties with China, economic and otherwise, although wisely not investing too much in the relationship until the problem of succession and the resulting prevailing political order is resolved.

The Peoples' Republic of China's main national interest is to sustain for as long as possible the present international situation and the balance of power in the Asia-Pacific region, both of which are favorable to China's rapid economic development. It will continue to play balance-of-power politics and will try to remain on friendly terms with all the major and minor players, with of course some exceptions.

China's present leadership is satisfied with the developing partnership with Russia because, while Russia is too weak to threaten China, it is not too weak to serve as an effective counterbalance to the United States. Beijing might even allow the present cooperation to develop into a real strategic partnership between the two countries if it feels pressured or threatened by any of the powers that wield influence in the region. The Chinese leadership is also eager to build up relations with other countries of the Commonwealth of Independent States, such as Kazakhstan and Kyrgyzstan, with due caution not to infringe on the legitimate strategic interests of Russia in the region.

As was discussed earlier, although relations among countries in the region are formally bilateral, for all practical purposes they are increasingly moving toward multilateralism. The result is that an ever-increasing number of factors are entering the equations that determine the relations between states. In fact, it is often the case that diplomatic maneuvering is more strongly influenced, not by the interests of the parties involved, but by the effect on some third party or the general political environment. For this reason, I will not deal further with relations between individual countries (which are well covered in the international press) but will instead focus on the interrelations among groups of states in order to clarify the dynamics of geopolitical developments in the region. Such an approach is especially advisable in view of the fact that, as noted above, direct U.S.-Russian relations are essentially nonexistent (barring a few joint ventures and the almost moribund exchange of goods and services between Alaska and the Far East). Indirect relations between the two states (via third parties) are, however, thriving.

Interactions in the region that urgently need monitoring can be broken down into three main configurations: those between the United States, China, and Russia; those between Russia, Japan, and the United States; and those between the United States, North and South Korea, and Russia. It should of course be taken as given that, in actual fact, such configurations are part of more complex regional networks.

The United States, China, and Russia

The United States–China–Russia triangle that emerged as an intensive power relationship toward the end of the cold war is still very important in regional and global politics. At one point in the 1970s, the main architects of this particular balance, Richard Nixon and Henry Kissinger, attempted to turn China into a strategic U.S. ally and even to assign China the responsibility of handling a big war in Asia (evidently against the Soviet Union), while cutting back on U.S. preparedness from the alleged ability to wage two and a half global wars to only one and a half. However, even though he was involved in a bitter dispute with Moscow at the time, Mao Zedong was wise enough to refuse Washington's "generous gift." Finally, under Deng Xiaoping, China concentrated on playing the United States against the Soviet Union, as far as it could. For its part, Washington continued to refine its balance-of-power game in Northeast Asia.

Much U.S. diplomatic action—or inaction—with respect to China in recent years has been informed and indeed often dictated, not by some liberal/conservative, moral/immoral agenda (the framework within which public debate on U.S. foreign policy is usually held), but by sheer balance-of-power politics. Beginning with the circumspect official reaction to the June 1989 Tiananmen Square massacre, one can also cite Washington's muted reaction to Chinese shows of force in the South China Sea (especially in connection with the Spratly archipelago, to which a number of states lay claim), the decoupling by President Clinton in 1994 of China's trade status and its record on human rights, Washington's comparatively mild reaction to the sale by China of M-11 missiles to Pakistan (in violation of the Missile Technology Control Regime [MTCR], to which China supposedly adheres) as well as to China's supplying Iran with atomic reactors (in comparison to the enraged global reaction to similar deals made by Russia), the quiet acceptance of the U.S. trade deficit with China ($29.5 billion in 1994),[20] and the weak U.S. protests against China's exporting of goods produced by prison inmates.

In other words, the U.S. government is being careful not to irritate one of the most influential countries in Asia and not to hinder China as it strengthens its relations with its northern neighbor. Of course, in taking such a line, Washington is also considering the importance of China's vote in the UN Security Council and its influence with the unpredictable Pyongyang. For the same reason, it is also patently clear that, whatever lure of increased cooperation with and potential membership in NATO

Washington might dangle before Moscow, no U.S. government would ever commit so egregious an error as to extend NATO's sphere of action to the borders of China.

As for China itself, Beijing seems to have been satisfied until recently with the way U.S.-Chinese relations developed, although not allowing the United States to interfere in other aspects of Chinese foreign policy, not to mention domestic politics. With a weakened Russia in the north and plenty of opportunities for Chinese businesses in the underdeveloped Russian Far East, China started to cultivate what might be called a close political, economic, and, to some extent, military partnership with Russia.

Russia reciprocates to a great extent, even selling modern military hardware to China to the tune of $1–$2 billion a year.[21] Russian specialists in military technologies are actually employed by China. And, in recent years, an active exchange of visits between high-ranking officials has resulted in the conclusion of a number of important agreements dealing with border problems, industrial cooperation, and bilateral trade (including arms sales).

When, in September 1994, Chinese president Jiang Zemin visited Russia, he and President Yeltsin signed an agreement delineating the western sector of the Russian-Chinese border and a joint statement agreeing not to target strategic missiles at each other (an agreement similar to those Moscow has with the United States and the United Kingdom). Each also reaffirmed the pledge not to be the first to use nuclear weapons against the other and agreed to slash still further the number of troops stationed on his side of the Russian-Chinese border.

Several years ago, I wondered whether the Russian course of close military cooperation with China was a manifestation of strategic cretinism or the result of Moscow's belief that it would fare better as Beijing's junior partner than as Washington's errand boy in the emerging new geopolitical alignment (the United States vs. China).[22] It is clear now that, in choosing to develop its relations with China, Russia chose wisely. Not only is such a course a viable alternative to its hitherto unsuccessful attempts at integration with Europe; it also shores up Russia's position in the Far East, ensuring — for the time being at least — that Washington's attempts to play Moscow off of Beijing and thereby make political capital will come to nothing.[23]

In the summer of 1995, tensions between the United States and China were exacerbated by the unofficial visit of Taiwanese president Li Teng-hui to the United States. Majorities in both houses of Congress voted to grant him an entry visa despite the fact that the United States does not officially recognize Taiwan, which the People's Republic considers just a renegade province. Beijing was infuriated, and a Chinese government spokesman declared that, by allowing the visit, the United States thereby renounced the one-China policy established in 1972 in the famous Shanghai communiqué issued after Nixon's first visit to China.[24]

There have been other negative developments in U.S.-Chinese relations: for example, the arrest in China of the U.S. citizen (and former Chinese dissident) Harry Wu, who entered China on a valid Chinese visa; the recall of the Chinese ambassador to Washington and Beijing's foot dragging in approving the newly appointed U.S. ambassador to China, Jim Sasser; and the launching of Chinese missiles toward Taiwan. Fuel was added to China's fire by a Republican-sponsored rider to a resolution pending in the U.S. Senate that demands that the United States institute the post of U.S. ambassador to Tibet.

The policy of maintaining a delicate balance seemed to many to have been smashed to smithereens. The architect of this trilateral balancing act, Henry Kissinger, fresh from his latest trip to China, produced a panicky *Washington Post* article in which he accused the authorities of grossly mismanaging U.S. Chinese policy: "The United States and China are on a collision course. Twenty-five years of U.S. bipartisan policy pursued by six administrations is coming unglued. . . . Choices are narrowing, and Sino-American relations are becoming vulnerable to accidents beyond the control of either side. It is dangerous to base policy on the frequently heard proposition that good relations with China were important during the Cold War but have lost their significance with the collapse of the Soviet Union. The opposite is true."[25] Observing that, during 1995, the United States had confrontations with both Japan and China, Kissinger suggested a return to moderation and the abandonment of the American habit of dictating to another sovereign country what it ought to do at home and how it ought to behave in the international arena.

Evidently, Kissinger's reasoning had its effect, as did the pressure exerted on the administration by big business, which immediately started to lose some very lucrative deals with China to its European competitors. On 28 July 1995, in a major speech on U.S. strategy in the Asia-Pacific region, U.S. secretary of state Warren Christopher in effect apologized to the Chinese: "Few nations are able to play as large a role in shaping Asia's future as is China. . . . With its vast population, its geographic reach, its rich history of cultural influence across Asia, its growing military power and its new economic dynamism, China is unique." Calling China's concern over Li Teng-hui's "private visit" unwarranted, Christopher stated, "It did not constitute a shift in our policy toward China and Taiwan. The United States has not and does not intend to change its longstanding one China policy. . . . The policy of engagement reflects the fundamental understanding that our ability to pursue significant common interests and to manage significant disinterest, would not be served by any attempt to isolate or contain China. We do not intend to try to do so."[26]

Of course even to think about isolating China nowadays is ridiculous. As to its containment, it is unlikely that Washington has that option either, given that there are 1.3 billion Chinese in Asia and that the United States and its fifteen NATO allies have for over two years failed to contain a mere two million Serbs waging a war of ethnic cleansing in the former Yugoslavia.

Despite such limitations, and contrary to disclaimers by official U.S. spokesmen, it looks like the United States does entertain some notions of containment, which, to use Michael Howard's expression, is, effectively, "an update on the traditional balance of power." In other words, Washington has started preparing for future potential adversarial encounters with China as a direct reaction to, to put it delicately, China's misbehavior in Asia and such other developments as the forthcoming deployment by China of modern mobile intercontinental ballistic missiles capable of reaching the United States. Such diplomatic moves by Washington as the restoration of diplomatic relations with Vietnam, continued attempts to improve relations with India, widening ties with ASEAN, activating U.S. dealings with Taiwan, and the maintenance of a strong naval presence in the Pacific and substantial numbers of land-based forces in the area are telltale signs of Washington's expectations. Another, similar development is the increased U.S. pressure on Japan "to recognize China as a potential threat" in the framework of the U.S.-

Japan security alliance that Washington has again put at the top of the bilateral political agenda.[27]

No doubt the current "misunderstandings" between Washington and Beijing will somehow be smoothed over because both sides are reluctant to cause an irrevocable break in relations. But the basic geopolitical tension between the United States and the People's Republic—an emerging giant not only on the Asian but on the world scene, one that will inevitably challenge U.S. predominance, at least in Asia—will increase, in no small part because of unsolicited and often rude U.S. meddling in the affairs of Asian nations. It will require much more wisdom and tact than are currently available in official Washington to keep things quiet for long.[28]

Meanwhile, Russia's options in this situation are also clear: to continue to cultivate a partnership with its great neighbor, to further demilitarize the existing border with China, and to use the accumulating "disinterest" that characterizes U.S.-Chinese relations to its advantage. The 1995 squabble between Washington and Beijing once again gave Russia the opportunity to demonstrate its unswerving loyalty to Beijing by publicly reconfirming its support of a one-China policy during Chinese prime minister Li Peng's June visit to Russia.[29]

Russia, Japan, and the United States

In Russia's current relations with Japan, there is more talk than substance. High Russian officials are very fond of visiting Japan (because of the excellent reception they get there) to advertise "great opportunities" for Japanese businessmen in Russia etc. But, in fact, relations between the two countries are frozen and sometimes become sour, as when, for instance, Russian coastal guards start shooting the Japanese fishermen who earn their living by fishing the waters around the southern Kurils, which Russia considers to be its exclusive maritime zone.

There is no end in sight to the political friction between Russia and Japan stemming from the failure to resolve the territorial problem. The upsurge of Russian nationalism would not allow even the most benevolent ruler of Russia, who would voluntarily relinquish that vast empire, to part with the several tiny islands that never belonged to Russia in the first place. But the Japanese can now afford to play it cool and wait for what from their point of view will be a truly just solution. Russia is the clear loser here because it thus denies itself the full measure of assistance that the second mightiest economy in the world could give to the process of the economic rejuvenation of Russia—particularly, the Russian Far East, which is totally neglected by Moscow. Furthermore, not only is Japan an economic power, but it is also the country that is spiritually closer to Russia than many other Western nations since its model of development and experience with a government-directed private economy offer useful parallels to the current Russian situation.

Some harebrained Russian "experts" occasionally air the view that Moscow should appeal to Washington to moderate the protracted Russian dispute with Japan. But why should the United States help Russia out? Washington surely welcomes the tense nature of Russian-Japanese relations, which denies Japan the opportunity to play balance-of-power politics in the Russia–Japan–United States equation, in other words, to use its Russian connection to ease out from under U.S. political domination. The only alternative partner to whom Japan can turn is China, but its memories of Japanese aggression are still fresh, and it is also naturally apprehensive about Japanese commercial expansion in the region. Nevertheless, economic ties between Japan and China are developing rapidly. In fact, the United States and Japan are involved in an intense competition for the enormous Chinese market, while Russia with its traditional merchandise of military hardware is no match in this game.

The possibility of China's collusion with Japan no doubt worries American leaders in theory, but they do not believe that it is likely to occur in the near future. First, they well understand the vast differences keeping Japan and China apart. Second, they know that, if it does deal with China, Japan will always look to the United States for security guarantees. Third, they understand that both China and Japan are actively competing for the economic and political lead in Asia, which limits cooperative ventures to Japanese investment in the Chinese economy. Finally, Washington is pretty sure that it does not have to worry about a sudden rapprochement between Russia and Japan. Moscow can assuredly be relied on to choose the worst possible course of action for itself. It is simply a miracle that, under recent Chinese direction, Moscow is acting quite atypically. Its twenty-year break with China incurred tremendous costs — first the colossal militarization of the Russian Far East, then the no less costly demilitarization of the area — and evidently taught the Russians a useful lesson.

The freeze in Russian relations with Japan is tremendously beneficial to U.S. strategic planners. They can continue to use Japan as an American military base in the North Pacific — the base that pays for itself[30] — with little fear that current economic frictions will escalate to the point that Japan will initiate a drastic change in its relations with the United States. Japan has nowhere to go, except along the pathways overseen by the United States, such as APEC, the Asian Forum, etc.

However, hedging against the unexpected eventuality of Russian-Japanese rapprochement, the United States is trying to get Japan to join NATO, thus "disciplining" Tokyo with the privileges of membership in the exclusive "Atlantic club" and at the same time involving NATO in the problem of Russo-Japanese relations — an attack from the east instead of the west, as it were.[31] So, while constantly warning (to put it mildly) Russia about the inevitable forthcoming expansion of the NATO alliance ever closer to Russia's western borders, American politicians still entertain what might be called two-front strategic ideas or, to put it less delicately, "squeezing Russia from both ends." Such a strategy cannot pass unnoticed by the Russian military leadership, despite Russia's participation in NATO's "Partnership for Peace."

The United States, North and South Korea, and Russia

Once the cold war had ended, the resolution of tensions in the relations between the United States, Russia, and North and South Korea should have been simple. Both Russia and the United States — the dominant influences in the North and South, respectively — should have pushed for normalization on the Korean peninsula, undoing the damage caused when they split Korea in two in 1945. The Soviet Union should have recognized South Korea and established normal relations with it, the United States reciprocating with North Korea, and from there "the process would have initiated itself," to use Mikhail Gorbachev's favorite phrase.

In June 1990, Gorbachev met informally with South Korean president Roh Tae Woo in California; later that same year, Moscow established full diplomatic relations with the Republic of Korea. In 1992, President Yeltsin of the new Russia paid an official visit to Seoul. Russia had big plans with regard to South Korea, seeing in it a source of massive capital investment and technology.

Unfortunately, the United States was in no hurry to reciprocate by normalizing its relations with Kim Il-sung's regime. (Washington did not even take North Korea off its "red countries" list.) Nor was South Korea anxious to become the driving force behind Russia's economic reconstruction. By 1995, Russia was heavily in debt to the Republic of Korea (which had delivered on $1.47 billion of a promised loan of $3 billion), while few of the countries' businesses have invested in Russian projects.

Meanwhile, North Korea felt terribly betrayed by Russia, especially after the Russian authorities announced that the mutual assistance clause in the 1961 friendship treaty was no longer effective and began curtailing its military cooperation with North Korea.[32] Reacting to his country's resulting isolation, and needing to counteract the consequences of his ruinous socioeconomic policies, Kim Il-sung decided to attract world attention and make direct contact with the United States[33] by breaking with the International Atomic Energy Agency (IAEA), which monitors nuclear power facilities in nuclear nonproliferation treaty (NPT) signatory countries.[34] It turned out that Pyongyang withdrew from the NPT just when the United States and the IAEA began to suspect it of diverting the plutonium contained in the spent fuel rods of its Russian-built nuclear reactors to the manufacture of nuclear weapons.

That North Korea might become a nuclear power by clandestinely making a few nuclear bombs is, realistically speaking, not seen as a serious threat by Russia. In 1992–94, Russian relations with North Korea visibly cooled, and, as President Yeltsin revealed at the 1994 G-7 meeting in Naples, Russia has even stopped delivering spare parts for arms to North Korea.[35] In October 1992, the Russian security ministry took the well-publicized step of removing more than sixty Russian scientists, mostly nuclear missile specialists, from a plane bound for Pyongyang from Moscow's Sheremetyevo-2 airport.[36]

Moscow's only real concern with Korean nuclear armament is that Pyongyang's demonstrative withdrawal from the NPT and break with the IAEA could set a very bad precedent for nuclear wanna-bes and those states not yet party to the NPT.[37] Such a precedent might doom the nonproliferation regime and is definitely not in Russia's best interests. Only with great difficulty, and U.S. support, did Moscow manage to persuade the republics of the former Soviet Union to renounce their nuclear status. It is therefore willing to give the UN Security Council a relatively free hand in punishing North Korea, barring military action or sanctions, which neither Moscow nor Beijing will allow.[38]

At the same time, playing around the issue as a "highly involved party" provided Moscow some status in Far Eastern diplomacy. It is not for nothing that, the moment the issue heated up a bit in March 1994, Deputy Foreign Minister Aleksandr Panov, who is supervising Russia's policy in the Far East, declared that Moscow was intent on observing the 1961 treaty between the Soviet Union and North Korea and "would provide assistance to North Korea in the event of unprovoked aggression against that country."[39] Although the next day Panov declared that "there was no change in the Russian policy with regard to the Korean crisis,"[40] the diplomatic fog was deployed, obscuring Russia's intentions in the crisis and thus enhancing its role.

Commenting on this episode, *Izvestia* opined that Russia is not eager to quarrel with Washington and Seoul because of the nuclear ambitions of Pyongyang. However, the paper recognized that Russia tried "to utilize the situation on the Korean peninsula to strengthen its positions in Asia."[41] Foreign Minister Kozyrev's proposal to convene an international conference to discuss the problem of the denuclearization of the Korean peninsula, later repeated by President Yeltsin, was a move of the same order: to stay abreast of events.[42]

The Clinton administration and the U.S. media blew the "nuclear crisis" up out of all proportion. And, in its zeal to pacify North Korea, Washington actually admitted that Pyongyang probably possessed one or two nuclear warheads. Its strategy boiled down to buying off the North Korean government with various sops (including building free of charge two modern light-water nuclear reactors in North Korea—at the U.S. allies' expense) in exchange for the latter's promise not to build more nuclear weapons and to continue to be a party to the nonproliferation treaty.[43] The U.S.–North Korean framework agreement that for the moment at least settled the crisis was concluded in October 1994.[44]

Although the agreement is flawed in that it postpones for at least five years the inspection by independent experts of the suspect nuclear-waste dumps in North Korea (which would have allowed the IAEA to discover the extent to which plutonium was diverted to weapons construction), such an outcome greatly devalued Russia's North Korean trump card.[45]

Frantic attempts by Russia to participate in the deal by offering to supply the light-water reactors failed because of the opposition of South Korea and Japan. In a Kuala Lumpur agreement supplementing the Geneva framework agreement, North Korea and the United States agreed that the reactors would be supplied by South Korea, with Japan's help, but that they would carry no indication that they were made in South Korea.

So Russia has been effectively shouldered out of the deal. To compensate, Moscow stepped up its diplomatic overtures to Pyongyang. Some Japanese sources assert that Russia restored military ties with North Korea. According to those sources, in September 1994, Panov offered to sign a secret protocol authorizing the joint production of MiG fighters in North Korea. It is claimed that he also delivered a personal message from Yeltsin to "the Commander in Chief Kim Jong-Il," in which Yeltsin expressed Russia's readiness to develop and improve its relations with North Korea across the board.[46]

But Pyongyang had still more tricks up its sleeve. In June 1995, evidently eager to obtain even more concessions from the pliant United States, Pyongyang told the U.S.-led UN Command in Korea that it was pulling out of the armistice agreement that ended the 1950–53 Korean War, although it stopped short of declaring the pact void. In August 1995, in the port of Chongjin, North Korean authorities impounded a South Korean dry cargo ship carrying 5,000 tons of a promised humanitarian aid package of 150,000 tons of rice, grudgingly requested by North Korea only when faced with impending famine.[47] The crew was arrested and accused of spying!

These events show that, despite all its promises to engage in dialogue with the South, North Korea has no intentions of holding up its end of any bargain—at least not yet. This creates a window of opportunity for Moscow to resume an active diplomatic role on the Korean peninsula, for surely the United States and its partners will now realize that Russia should have been involved all along. As far as Korean unification is concerned, evidently no one besides South Korea and the United States is anxious for it to occur.

The Inevitability of Common Work

While many difficult problems remain to be solved in the region, real cooperation between Russia and the United States is lacking. Occasional meetings of both countries' Asia experts in the Russian Foreign Office or the U.S. State Department do not lead to significant cooperation toward solving the region's problems. And those presently are not so much the problems of security in Northeast Asia as they are the problems of economic and human well-being.

All the countries of the region suffer from the deteriorating ecological situation in Northeast Asia, which first affects the aboriginal populations there. Rising crime and terrorist activity affect all the countries, as does trafficking in narcotics. Piracy, the scourge of the eighteenth century, is again on the rise, especially in the South China Sea. Deadly diseases that were thought to have been eradicated have resurfaced and again affect thousands of people. These are some of the problems that ought to be energetically tackled by all the countries of the Pacific community if we want to leave our grandchildren the legacy of a livable world.

That is why such initiatives as the international conference on land use in the Usury River basin held in Harbin in February 1995, the international discussion of the deteriorating ecological conditions in the Arctic that took place in Norilsk in August 1995, or generous Japanese help to Russia in building facilities to process the liquid radioactive waste produced by the Russian Far Eastern navy can mean much more for tranquillity and stability in the region than the occasional diplomatic get-together.

Notes

1 Sergei Agafonov, "Andrei Kozyrev Not Invited to Asian Political Games," *Izvestia,* 26 March 1994, in *Current Digest of the Post-Soviet Press* (hereafter CDPP), 20 April 1994, 26.

2 *Izvestia,* 8 August 1995, 1.
3 *Nezavisimaya gazeta,* 16 March 1994, 1.
4 This time, Kozyrev offered to adopt a "code of interstate intercourse in the Asia-Pacific." As a starting point for such a code, Kozyrev passed on to his colleagues the Russian draft of a "declaration on principles of security and stability in the Asia-Pacific." He suggested convening a special international meeting of experts in Moscow in the spring of 1996 to discuss the draft (*Segodnya,* 2 August 1995, 2).
5 However, the wild outburst of criminal activities in the zone (the most notorious being the war between the Chechen and Russian gangs there) scares many potential foreign investors away. (See, e.g., an interesting investigative article by the *Izvestia* correspondent Igor Korolkov, "The Hunt in the Free Zone: How the Militia Created a Criminal Structure That Broke Out of Its Control," *Izvestia,* 24 July 1995, 3.)
6 Byung-Joon Ahn, "Politics and Economics in the Asia-Pacific Region: Beyond the Cold War," in *Nuclear Policies in Northeast Asia,* ed. Andrew Mack (New York and Geneva: United Nations Institute for Disarmament Research, 1995), 63.
7 By colossally increasing the fares for air and rail transportation, the Russian authorities unwittingly created a powerful stimulus for the Far Eastern provinces to limit economic relations with European Russia and to seek partners abroad in the East and South. The businesses of the Far East simply cannot afford to pay for deliveries from European Russia, while their own produce sent West becomes uncompetitive. Hence, separatist trends in the region were enhanced.
8 See *Rossiyskaya gazeta,* 25 February 1994, 7; *Rossiyskie vesti,* 17 February 1995, 5; and *Kontseptsiya vneshnei politiki Rossiiskoi Federatsii* (The concept of foreign policy of the Russian Federation), in *Segodnya,* 4 February 1994, 3. None of those documents mentions the problem of U.S.-Russian relations in Asia.
9 Andrei Kozyrev, *Preobrazhenie* (The transfiguration) (Moscow: Mezhdunarodnie Otnosheniya, 1995), 238. Kozyrev's book might well be recommended as a good source for researchers interested in the details of the constant row going on in the high echelons of the Russian government with regard to the policy taken toward Japan. It is incomprehensible how a foreign minister of a big country, one overwhelmed with difficult foreign policy problems, finds time to write books and innumerable articles for the press!
10 Ibid., 244.
11 In the middle of the summer of 1995, the commander of the troops of the Far Eastern military district, Colonel-General V. Chechevatov, sent the following telegram to the Russian Ministry of Defense: "The indebtedness of the Far Eastern military district for communal services, electricity, fuel comes to 200 million rubles. Many garrisons are being disconnected from the sources of water and energy supply, the deliveries of fuel are discontinued, the expeditionary delivery of materials and fuel, including the resupply of the Arctic districts, has not begun. Without immediate resolution of the financing problem I shall be

compelled to begin the evacuation of personnel of formations and units from the Arctic North, from Kamchatka, Sakhalin and Kuril Islands" (*Komsomolskaya Pravda,* 26 July 1995, 2).

12 Roughly 40 percent of the population has left the Magadan region and Chukotka peninsula (*Izvestia,* 2 August 1995, 5). Tens of thousands more cannot leave simply because they lack the money to do so.

13 See, e.g., Zalmay Khalizad, "Loosing the Moment? The United States and the World after the Cold War," *Washington Quarterly* 18, no. 2 (Spring 1995): 84–103. As do many other contemporary American political scientists, Khalizad supports, not balance-of-power politics, but the unquestionable global dominance and leadership of the United States. Such a position is understandable, but the extreme of national egocentrism that pervades so much political science writing in the United States today is not. It is as if the entire world now depends exclusively on the vision of the United States—a new world creator!

14 At the time, John Foster Dulles rightly remarked that a third group of states—the so-called nonaligned nations—was actually "neutral against the United States," that in other words they in fact sided against the United States.

15 This is my interpretation, not the official Russian government position. As was mentioned above, it is very difficult nowadays to understand the practical foreign policy goals of the Russian government, whether global or regional. The only subject to which all branches of government give their undivided attention is dividing up former state property and padding their own bank accounts. Of course the occasional "problem" forces itself on their attention: the war in Chechnya and the opposition to it in the West; the war in Bosnia and support for the Serb forces; miners and other workers in the still-state-owned industries striking over unpaid wages; earthquakes; terrorist attacks; the approaching elections. Under these conditions, foreign policy is the last thing that would attract the attention of the powers that be. As the renowned political analyst Stanislav Kondrashov commented sadly, "There is no elite [in Russia] worthy of the name, that is of an upper strata, which, granted all the disagreements in it, affordable and useful for the forward movement, would act within the framework of a state interest, without rocking the boat, but just correcting its course" (*Izvestia,* 29 July 1995, 4).

16 President William J. Clinton, *A National Security Strategy of Engagement and Enlargement* (Washington, D.C.: White House, July 1994), 23–24.

17 Speaking at a hearing before the House International Relations Committee's Subcommittee on Asia and the Pacific, Nye said: "Among the most important reasons for East Asia's economic successes are American alliances in the region and the continued presence of substantial U.S. forces. Critics who ignore the importance of security in the region are like people who forget the importance of the oxygen they breathe" (*Federal News Service,* 27 June 1995). Nye developed similar notions of the dependence of the political order and prosperity on military force or a forward U.S. military presence in his "East Asian Security: The

Case for Deep Engagement," *Foreign Affairs* 78, no. 4 (July–August 1995): 90–105. It seems that Nye is confusing political order with a police state. When, e.g., armored vehicles are stationed at many Moscow intersections, the order thereby obtained is that of a police state, not true political order. When American children must pass through X-ray machines and metal detectors and under the strict eye of a guard in order to go to school and listen to a teacher lecture about, say, law and order in America, they will inevitably take *order* to mean living in a police state since, on entering their school, they have been presented with irrefutable evidence leading to such a conclusion. The same conclusion must be drawn about the "order" that is established with a forward or a backyard deployment of military forces.

18 Admiral Richard Macke, speaking before the House International Relations Committee's Subcommittee on Asia and the Pacific (*Federal News Service,* 27 June 1995).

19 Henry Kissinger is absolutely right when he says: "Japan is transforming its political institutions and probably the orientation of its postwar foreign policy. . . . The shock of defeat has worn off; the end of the Cold War has destroyed the conviction that American and Japanese perceptions of the national interest are inevitably parallel. The size of the Japanese defense budget—already the third largest in the world reflects this shift toward a more national orientation" ("Heading for a Collision in Asia," *Washington Post,* 26 July 1995, A23).

20 *U.S. News and World Report,* 17 July 1995, 34.

21 China and India are presently the two biggest buyers of Russian arms. Russia sells China such advanced weapons systems as SU-27 jet fighters, S-300 surface-to-air missile systems, "Varshavyanka" attack submarines (Kilo-class in NATO's designation), and T-80 supermodern tanks.

22 See Henry Trofimenko, "International Politics and U.S.-Russian Relations," in *Russia and America: From Rivalry to Reconciliation,* ed. George Ginsburgs, Alvin Z. Rubinstein, and Oles M. Smolansky (Armonk, N.Y.: M. E. Sharpe, 1993), 325–42.

23 One such "project" was publicly aired by Zbigniew Brzezinski in 1994 in an influential U.S. foreign policy journal. Brzezinski suggested that the United States join with China for "some quiet American-Chinese political consultations" on the subject, evidently, of how to further tear away from Russia the Central Asian states of the former Soviet Union, taking into consideration "China's growing economic impact on the region and its natural interest in the future of the adjoining Central Asian states" ("The Premature Partnership," *Foreign Affairs* 73, no. 2 [March–April 1995]: 81). However, Beijing has evidently not been enthusiastic about this and similar U.S. projects.

24 The joint U.S.-Chinese communiqué of 28 February 1972, summing up the results of the first official visit of a U.S. president to the People's Republic of China, stated: "The United States acknowledges that all Chinese on either side of the Taiwan Strait maintain there is but one China and that Taiwan is a part of

China. The United States Government does not challenge that position" (the full text of the communiqué can be found in Henry Kissinger's *White House Years* [Boston: Little, Brown, 1979], 1490–92). Kissinger remarks, "I do not think anything I did or said impressed Chou [Chou En-lai, then prime minister of China, Zhou Enlai in the current transcription] as much as this ambiguous formula" (p. 783).

25 Kissinger, "Heading for a Collision in Asia," A23.

26 "Christopher: U.S. Pursues Four-Part Strategy for Asia-Pacific" (transcript of the secretary of state's address to the National Press Club, 28 July 1995, USIA Wireless File," 29 July 1995, 19–20). As is absolutely typical of recent U.S. government pronouncements on the Asia-Pacific region, Russia's role in Asia was totally ignored in this policy-making speech!

27 "America, Japan and the Unmentionable" *Economist,* 25 February 1995, 33.

28 "We are dealing with a very uncooperative regime which can't stand the United States and everything it stands for," says David Shambaugh, editor of the *China Quarterly* and professor of politics at the University of London. "This is a systemic struggle — not just over visas, dissidents and arms sales. The stronger and more assertively nationalistic China becomes, the sharper the tensions will become" (*Washington Post,* 21 June 1995, A17).

29 There are of course problems in Russian-Chinese relations as well, the main one being the massive influx of illegal Chinese immigrants across the border into Russia. There are by some estimates already more than 2.5 million Chinese on the Russian side of the border in the Far East, among the 7 million indigenous inhabitants. Experts of the Far Eastern branch of the Russian Academy of Sciences assert that it is already possible to speak about the formation of a new Chinese national minority in the Russian Far East. Some suspect that in this way a new "natural economic territory" is being created for China. Responding to the concerns of the local Russian population, in 1994 Moscow severely tightened its control over border crossings and terminated the liberal visa system for incoming Chinese.

30 Speaking before a House subcommittee (see n. 17 above), Joseph Nye remarked, "Japan's host nation support is very generous — over $4.5 billion in the Japanese fiscal year '95, which makes it cheaper for us to have troops in Japan than to have them at home."

31 Writing in an official NATO publication, Hiroshi Fukuda, deputy foreign minister of Japan, underscored that "there are many common problems which Japan and NATO can tackle together with respect to world stability, through close dialogue and cooperation. One of the most important common concerns between Japan and NATO is the question of Russia" ("Regional Security Initiatives and NATO-Japan relations," *NATO Review,* no. 4 [July 1995]: 25).

32 Article 1 of the treaty, signed in Moscow on 6 July 1961, states: "In case one of the contracting parties becomes an object of an armed attack from a state or a coalition of states and thus will find itself in a state of war, the other contracting

party will immediately provide military and other aid with all the means in its disposal" (*Otnosheniya Sovetskogo Soyuza s Narodnoi Korejey, 1945–1980: Dokumenty i Materialy* [Relations of the Soviet Union with the Democratic People's Republic of Korea, 1945–1980: Documents and materials] [Moscow: Nauka, 1981], 196).

33 Since 1952, the year the armistice was negotiated in Korea, the overwhelming obsession of the North Korean leadership has been obtaining official U.S. recognition and establishing direct relations with Washington, without the interference of Seoul. For the past forty years, Pyongyang used dozens of tricks, many of them dirty, to get into direct contact with the U.S. government.

34 At U.S. urging, Moscow pressured North Korea to sign a nuclear-safeguard agreement with the IAEA, which it finally did in January 1992.

35 *Washington Times,* 12 July 1994, A10.

36 This action did not stop North Korean spies from attempting to obtain Russian nuclear secrets by taking advantage of the present chaotic situation in Russia. Some of these agents worked from the North Korean embassy in Moscow. Speaking in Russia's Far East, Sergei Stepashin, then head of the Russian counterintelligence agency, revealed that three North Koreans were detained in the Maritime Province, not far from the Russian border with North Korea, on suspicion of trying to obtain nuclear-weapons components (*Washington Post,* 5 July 1994, A1). In the U.S. Congress, Senator De Concini stated that, according to press reports, "a number of former Soviet scientists are now on the North Korean payroll" (*Congressional Record,* 1 July 1994, 58257).

37 Actually, as early as 1990, the Russian KGB had discovered that North Korea manufactured an atomic explosive device. In June 1994, *Izvestia* published a complete text of the secret memo of then KGB chairman Vladimir Kryuchkov to the Soviet leadership dated 22 February 1990 detailing the agency's findings: "According to the information received, said the memorandum, the development of the first atomic explosive device has been completed at the DPRK's nuclear research center, located in the city of Yongbyon, in Pukdo Province. At present, no tests of the device are planned, in the interests of concealing from the world public and international monitoring organizations the very fact that the DPRK has produced an atomic weapon" (*Izvestia,* 24 June 1994, 4).

38 "If, after much American huffing and puffing, North Korea emerges with a nuclear weapons capability—or a capability it can rapidly activate—stability in Asia, America's role in Asia and nonproliferation will all be gravely jeopardized," writes Henry Kissinger (*Washington Post,* 6 July 1994, A19).

39 *Izvestia,* 31 March 1994, 3.

40 *Izvestia,* 1 April 1994, 3. Panov's initial statement was even more puzzling because in February 1993 Moscow officially served notice on Pyongyang that it would no longer honor the 1961 military alliance (*Wall Street Journal,* 12 February 1993, A10). At a press conference on 2 June 1994 reviewing the outcome of the Russian–South Korean summit in Moscow, President Yeltsin reminded jour-

nalists that article 1 of the 1961 friendship and mutual assistance treaty with North Korea, which Russia inherited from the Soviet Union, was amended in 1990. The document no longer contains strict wording obliging Moscow to provide comprehensive assistance to Pyongyang in the event of armed conflict (*Segodnya,* 3 June 1994, 1).

41 *Izvestia,* 1 April 1994, 3.

42 "Useful idiots" from the Russian extreme Left (or Right?—it is now very confusing!), who expressed in a statement in the main North Korean newspaper their "deep concern" in connection with the exacerbation of the situation on the peninsula and denounced "vain attempts of U.S. imperialists and their puppets in the south of Korea," inadvertently contributed to the image of Russia as deeply involved in the crisis and thus deserving to be one of the main architects of its solution.

43 Speaking before a House subcommittee (see n. 17 above), Representative Ki said: "Looking back, my understanding is that North Korea was clearly violating the NPT agreement. . . . And it seems kind of ironic that we have to pay them some $40 billion to make sure that they comply with the NPT, which is—they've got to comply anyway, in the first place. And then after that, we have to cancel our annual joint military exercise [with South Korea]—so-called Team spirit. And then we agreed to give them our oil—$22 million of oil a month. Then I understand they've been diverting this oil to military use" (*Federal News Service,* 27 June 1995).

44 The full text of the agreement, signed in Geneva on 21 October 1994 by Kang Sok Ju and Robert L. Gallucci, heads of the North Korean and U.S. delegations, respectively, can be found in *Nuclear Policies in Northeast Asia,* app. A, pp. 251–54.

45 The U.S.–North Korean agreement was severely criticized in the American press. "Pyongyang has set a dangerous precedent," wrote B. J. Cutler. "By flagrantly violating the nonproliferation treaty, it has blackmailed the West into accepting it as a foreign aid client" (*Washington Times,* 23 October 1994, B-4). "The negative side here is that others may decide to start bargaining rather than complying with special inspection requests," said Leonard Spector, a nuclear proliferation expert at the Carnegie Endowment for International Peace (*Washington Post,* 20 October 1994, A32).

46 *Izvestia,* 23 December 1994, 1.

47 "That action ran contrary to decades of North Korean commitment to an ideology of Juche, or self-reliance. And it showed, even more than the nuclear deal, that North Korea's economy is reaching the point of desperation" (Jim Mann, *Los Angeles Times,* 10 July 1995, 5).

Conclusion

When Dostoyevsky envisaged Russia's future in Asia more than one hundred years ago in his essay "Geok-Tepe: What Is Asia to Us?" the implicit civilizing mission resonated with high expectations: expansion would be the handmaiden of prosperity and prestige. Russia had but to "build two railroads," one to Siberia, the other to Central Asia, "and at once you will see the consequences." But, as a new century approaches, Russia's prospects in Asia are bleak beyond what could have been imagined in the most pessimistic of worst-case scenarios. It is no longer what Russia thinks of Asia that matters but rather that Asia now gives hardly any thought to Russia.

Past discussions of great powers in Asia—especially of Russia—centered on assessments of military capability or ideological affinity. Paradoxically, Moscow's preoccupation with military power is part of the reason that the former Soviet Union had and Russia now has so little influence in the region. More than ever before in this century, economic considerations, state capacity, and industrial-technological momentum are the decisive determinants of regional power relationships. What Mohammad Noordin Sopiee, director of the Malaysian Institute of International Studies, told a Moscow conference in 1987 remains no less true today: "The central game in the Pacific is not a military one. The power that has comprehensive capability, that is able to participate in every area of activity, is the power that is likely to play the biggest role in the Pacific."[1] Measured by these criteria, Russia falls abysmally short of being a true competitor in Asia now and is not likely to become one in the foreseeable future. By any criterion, Russia's weakness is undeniable, its influence diminishing, and its prospects narrowing.

All the essays in this book confirm Russia's decline in Asia, the confusion in Moscow about what to do, and the limited leverage it possesses. Russian policy lacks institutional and intellectual coherence or consistency. This parlous state of affairs is compounded by the tension between the Ministry of Foreign Affairs and the Ministry of Defense and by the diminished role of the military, which had been the backbone of eastern Siberia's economy to, if anything, an even greater extent than it had been of the overall Soviet economy. Gorbachev's concessionary policy promoted the normalization and improvement of relations with China, Japan, and South Korea and increased Soviet participation in the burgeoning Asian economy. Unfortunately for Moscow, the Soviet regime did not institute the reforms that might have attracted substantial Asian investment, complete the negotiations for a return of the "Northern Territories" to Japan and normalize relations between Moscow and Tokyo, or gain large-scale South Korean engagement in Siberia's economic development.

Under Yeltsin, the always evident ambivalence about Asia continues. Russian foreign policy remains the object of a fierce but unresolved ideological debate. Moscow's propensity is still to look mainly to the West for trade, investment, and ideas for reforming society. As a result, Asian governments consider Moscow the odd capital out in their ongoing efforts to advance regional integration and expand trade. As John Stephan observed over a decade ago, while Russia is *in* Asia, it is still not yet *of* Asia: "Essentially, Soviet images of Asia are inextricably bound up with self-images. Asia is simultaneously part of the USSR and an alien entity. Feelings of propinquity and distance, familiarity, and exoticism, affinity and repulsion all appear to be widespread, and may even coexist within the same individual."[2] Russia's economic marginalization is nowhere more evident than in its continued exclusion from the eighteen-nation Organization for Asian-Pacific Economic Cooperation (APEC), which was established in 1989 by the United States and Asian states to promote free trade and economic cooperation.

Domestic uncertainties and political myopia also hamper the efforts of "Eurasianists" who would shift Russia's foreign policy orientation to Asia, which accounts for more than 50 percent of the global gross domestic product (GDP) and available investment capital and is the fastest-growing region in the world. Although their thinking seemingly enjoys ascendancy today in Moscow, as Smolansky suggested, the invocation of such a policy must contend with real structural factors on which policy must also be based. And here neither the Eurasianists nor their rivals, the

"Atlanticists," have shown an ability to grapple successfully with those problems. More of Russia's land mass is situated in Asia than in Europe, but only 8 million of the country's 147 million inhabitants are settled in Siberia. Thus far, efforts to encourage Russians emigrating from the "Near Abroad"—the non-Russian republics that became independent with the collapse of the Soviet Union—to settle in the Asian part of Russia have been a failure. Instead, somewhere between 500,000 and 5 million Chinese migrants—workers and shuttle merchants—are said to be in Russia's Far East, and no one knows how to count them.[3] The inability to track this migration hints at the state's fundamental incapacity at both the regional and the central levels that inhibits Russia's engagement with Asia.

Moscow's ineptness in confronting the challenges of its Asian hinterland also turns up in its handling of three other major policy problems. Nothing is more crucial to Siberia's links to European Russia than the Trans-Siberian Railroad. For decades, the Great Transsib, as it is called, was "the sole 'thread' connecting the center with the Pacific coast": "Its significance grew even more when through traffic between Europe and the countries of the Asian Pacific region was opened up in 1970. Suffice it to quote numbers such as these: about three thousand 'international' containers 'traveled' the Transsib in 1971, and fifty thousand in 1976. It is twice as much today."[4]

But the Transsib is falling into disrepair and neglect: bridges and tunnels are not being maintained; there is a bottleneck at the Amur because the bridge there is still single track; and, without modernization, which requires enormous investment, the ties, equipment, railcars, and locomotives have deteriorated. As a consequence, competitiveness with alternative transit routes is diminishing. In brief, Russian Siberia is becoming ever more remote from European Russia and less capable of servicing the needs of the expanding Asian market.

Furthermore, today, Moscow's economic policy has greatly increased tariffs and transportation costs, to the point where Russia's Asian products are severely discriminated against in their terms of trade with Russia, on whom they depend for virtually all finished goods. This policy, which local leaders claim is ruining them, has greatly stimulated efforts at regional independence in Khabarovsk and Primorskii Krai. The confluence of these factors means that, as Siberia and the Maritime Province become less able to optimize their participation in Asian economics, the terms of trade at home are also turning against them and the state inhibits their ability to participate freely in the Asian economic revolution. This breakdown of central-regional relationships has been a substantial impediment to any rational Asian policy in Russia and to the coherence of the state in general.

Second, although Russia's border extends to the Amur and Ussuri Rivers, there are signs that what was acquired by conquest could be lost in the future by default and demographic shifts. Few Russians are moving into Siberia; far greater numbers are leaving. And over the border lies a Chinese population of 1.2 billion people that is still growing despite the Chinese government's best efforts at birth control. Chinese and Korean illegal immigrant populations are considerable and on the increase. Although the actual figures are debatable, the demographic movement that is slowly changing the composition of Russia's Far Eastern population is not. Moscow's inability to cope with this influx threatens a further diminution of its effective ability to control the area at a time when the unreported and uncontrollable cross-border trade is an increasingly important factor in the region's economic life.

Finally, whereas previously Moscow's Far Eastern regions depended heavily on European Russia for trade and investment, the Soviet Union's collapse "has shattered these links, leaving the eastern provinces to fend for themselves": "The market economy cannot, overnight, substitute for the subsidized shipment of crucial supplies over thousands of kilometers of territory. The eastern provinces find themselves in the paradoxical situation of facing poverty amid plenty and suffer from shortages of food, energy, and financial resources."[5]

Moscow's unwillingness and inability to launch a historic devolution of authority that would allow provinces and autonomous regions maximum latitude in restructuring their economies perpetuates bureaucratic, inefficient leadership that is antithetical to reform and democratization. This tension between the centralizing tendencies that predominate among governmental elites in Moscow and the proponents of decentralization must be resolved. Otherwise, the eastern provinces will have to tolerate "criminality" and "regional warlordism" at all levels of society and function with an ethos that places a premium on survival rather than stability and that emphasizes short-term gain rather than long-term investment and growth. As John J. Stephan has observed, Russia must overcome stubborn obstacles before it can develop its Far Eastern provinces: "infrastructural weaknesses, inflation, regulatory and legal confusion, political uncertainty, and — to put it delicately — a different business etiquette. Firsthand acquaintance with local conditions has sobered many a foreign entrepreneur. Most joint ventures have failed. Yeltsin's placebos for the Northern Territories dispute (inaugurating confidence-building measures postponing a final disposition of the islands) neither satisfied irredentists at home nor reassured creditors in Japan."[6]

As long as Moscow cannot overcome its internal crises and establish a feeling of confidence in its Far East, it will also not be able to overcome local hostility to the center or to the Chinese inflow, nor will it be able to control its own state apparatus and make coherent and effective Asian policy. In an era when economic instruments are essential for political influence, the weaknesses of the state make Russia a pauper.

Inevitably, therefore, its strategic importance has been localized. Changing security relationships involving China, Japan, the two Koreas, and the United States are conceptualized and negotiated with little regard for Russia's interests or wishes. And, increasingly, Asian states are taking scant notice of Russia as a factor in their security policies. Certainly, this is true for Japan and the United States even if Japan's Defense Agency ritually invokes the Russian threat for political purposes. But even China and both Koreas, not to mention Southeast Asia, see little reason to help Russia back into the ring and are satisfied to have Russia as a weak, somewhat dependent, albeit relatively stable partner in Asia.[7]

Although still a nuclear superpower, in the post–cold war and post-Soviet period, Russia is not considered a military threat. Not only do the regional actors possess significant military capabilities of their own that insulate them from incipient neoimperial ambitions of their neighbors, but Russia's conventional military structure is also rapidly deteriorating. The once mighty Pacific Fleet is rusting, and large numbers of ships are being sold for scrap metal, while the army is demoralized, underfunded, and alienated — witness its appalling performance in Chechnya.

Given these diminished assets, Russia seeks the best arrangements it can negotiate with individual countries. Its policy is driven primarily by domestic pressures and factional intriguing; strategic and security concerns are difficult to discern. Only the confirmed optimist could find the essentials of a coherent and well-defined Russian national interest other than domination of the Commonwealth of Independent States in the erratic course followed by Yeltsin. Instead, we find only a collection of disparate and uncoordinated themes that seem to shape policy.

First and foremost, Russia's emphasis is on improving relations with China. Advanced weaponry is the main coin of the Russian realm. Eager to sell in hard-currency markets and largely outmaneuvered and outfinanced by Western competitors in lucrative Middle East markets, Russia has opened its arsenal of high-tech conventional weapons and nuclear technology to China. Its military-industrial establishment and parts of the armed forces (but *only* parts, not the entire military establishment, as Stephen Blank has shown) have been major advocates of arms sales, relishing the red-carpet treatment and generous "gifts" of Chinese counterparts.

Lost, or deliberately ignored, in the wheeling and dealing are the strategic dilemmas inherent in helping accelerate the modernization of neighboring China's military capability. Indeed, by purchasing lavishly, China's leadership is giving Russia's military-industrial complex a strong stake in continuing close ties to China and avoiding strategic rivalry in East Asia. These commercial ties might also bind Russia to China's approach to Taiwan. Alternatively, Russian weapons may ultimately be used directly against Russia itself. But, for the time being, arguments against such sales abound—like the letter published by a retired army colonel in *Nezavisimaya gazeta,* which is only one of the many caveats warning against training Chinese officers in Russian military academies and selling them the most modern Russian weapons that are lost in the rush to the China market.[8] Trafficking in arms remains the heart of government-to-government trade.

Various border disputes have been amicably settled, but regional administrators have raised objections to the point where the chief agreement, dealing with the long segment of the river-based frontier from Mongolia to the sea, has yet to be submitted for ratification by the state Duma. The reason may well be that the proposal would run into trouble in that venue and that failure would mark a major international embarrassment for the Yeltsin government.[9] As Deputy Foreign Minister Aleksandr Panov has noted, failure to uphold the border treaty with China would cause an "explosion." On the complex and difficult issues of illegal cross-border trade, smuggling, illegal Chinese immigrants in Siberia, and rising criminal activity, Moscow seems incapable of action. Its relative impotence is a boon for China, which, by comparison, is unified, growing militarily stronger, economically booming, and spreading its influence in the region. China's close ties to Russia serve Beijing's diplomatic interests by signaling Washington that it has other alternatives, should the U.S.-Chinese relationship sour.

So intent is Russia on strengthening its ties to China that it has virtually dropped out of the erstwhile intensely waged Sino-Soviet rivalry for influence on the Korean peninsula. With the exception of a brief period in the 1960s, Moscow exercised preeminent control over North Korea for almost forty-five years after the de facto division of Korea that was intended as a temporary demarcation line between Soviet and U.S. forces. By the late 1980s, Soviet influence had lessened significantly, as Gorbachev extended his "New Thinking" to improved relations with South Korea, in the process alienating North Korea. Although continuing to supply Pyongyang with weapons and assistance in developing its nuclear capability, Moscow viewed South Korea, too optimistically as it turned out, as a major source of economic assistance and normalized relations with South Korea in September 1990. Moscow preferred that South Korea be Russia's main partner on the Korean peninsula, but thus far its hopes have remained unrequited.

Meanwhile, China had preceded Moscow in Seoul, expanding economic ties after Mao Zedong's death in September 1976 and participating (as did the Soviet Union) in the Olympic games in South Korea in 1988, despite Pyongyang's opposition. Far more successfully than Moscow, Beijing has bettered relations with South Korea while retaining its influence in Pyongyang. Thus, even as it expands economic ties with South Korea, China has become North Korea's principal trading partner. The contrast with Moscow's declining or stagnating economic relationship with both Koreas is startling. In the all-important military-security sphere, too, Moscow is losing out to China. In September 1995, Moscow officially gave Pyongyang the required one-year notice of its intention to terminate the 1961 Soviet–North Korean defense treaty. On the other hand, Chinese President Jiang Zemin stated two months later that Beijing does not plan to abrogate the defense treaty between China and

North Korea. In the short term, this may not change much in Russia's relations with the two Koreas, but these developments are indicative that the center of political leverage is shifting even further away from Moscow. In the struggle between Moscow and Beijing for the position of "honest broker" on the Korean peninsula, China is clearly in the ascendancy.

However, Moscow's most troublesome relationship in East Asia is with Japan. After tentative overtures to Tokyo to settle the territorial issue of the disputed islands, Moscow backed away. Neither Gorbachev nor Yeltsin was willing or strong enough domestically to strike a bargain with Japan in the face of determined and influential ultranationalist opposition. This inability to solve the territorial issue prevents any rapprochement, to say nothing of comprehensive cooperation, between the two countries. The issue continues to simmer. For example, on 8 December 1995, the Russian embassy in Japan protested the "removal of 18th–19th century maps designating [the] South Kurile Islands as Russia's" from a joint exhibition organized by the Russian State Library and the Japanese Parliamentary Library in Tokyo at the end of November, and it reaffirmed Russia's ownership of the islands.[10] In January 1996, the new Russian foreign minister, Yevgeny Primakov, publicly suggested shelving the debate on the issue, further indicating Russia's refusal to normalize its relationship with Tokyo and intention to pursue an exclusively China-oriented policy in the Asia-Pacific region.[11]

Given that Moscow's grip on the loyalty of regional political leaders in the provinces of Sakhalin, Primorskii Krai, Magadan, and Kamchatka is tenuous, prudent policy is to do nothing. In the parliamentary elections held in December 1995, the strong showing in the Russian Far East for ultranationalist candidates like Vladimir Zhirinovsky's Liberal Democratic party (LDP) put Moscow on notice that it dare not ride roughshod over those who, out of expedience or conviction, resist extensive concessions to Japan. Disregarding the views of these regional oligarchs could well exacerbate separatist tendencies that could lead to the fragmentation of the federation along regional lines, thus leaving Moscow in charge of a rump state.

Conventional wisdom held that, when checked in Europe, Russian/Soviet diplomatic strategy was to push in Asia—and vice versa. In retrospect, however, this postulate has little to commend it. As archival material becomes available, shedding new light on the determinants of key decisions, Russian policy seems more akin to a loose sail than a pendulum; it often reflected miscalculation, not missed strategic opportunity. Witness Russia's role in triggering the Crimean War in 1853, the Russo-Japanese War of 1904–5, and the Korean War in 1950 and its simultaneous estrangement of China, Japan, and the United States in the 1970s. Moreover, the belt of perennially weak and vulnerable states that prevailed along Russia's Central Asian and Asian borders for more than two hundred years until the end of the twentieth century is a thing of the past.

As Russia's ability to control itself weakens, so too will its ability to control Central Asia. Nonetheless, Moscow's policy, as laid down in a 14 September 1995 Yeltsin decree, is to reintegrate Central Asia (and the Commonwealth of Independent States) with Russia in economic, political, and military affairs, along lines that serve Russian interests and clearly undermine the real sovereignty of these states.[12] Yet, even as Moscow pursues this policy and seeks Chinese cooperation against a rise of any form of nationalism in the region — a nationalism that it invariably calls *fundamentalism* out of combined crass political opportunism and atavistic Russian feelings of hostility to Islam — Central Asia is expanding its ability to deal independently with both Asian states and the broader world around it. Its trade (and not just in oil) is slowly moving from a dependence mainly on Russia to reliance on a broader pattern of integration with the world economy. Thus, Moscow's ability to impose economic coercion is steadily eroding.

Today, Russia is "the sick man of Asia" — militarily weak, systematically in turmoil, and economically in decline. Whatever the options, and they are limited for the foreseeable future, Russia is more dependent on the behavior of others than on its own wishes. Its diminished position gives it little room to maneuver in Asia or in Europe.

Still, old patterns are hard to shed. In Russian policy-making circles (as well as in American ones), there is an ongoing tug-of-war between those favoring reconciliation and cooperation and those viewing the former adversary as an incipient strategic rival. Russians who push integration into the Western-dominated international economy and the establishment of a market-oriented socioeconomic system at home confront those who see continued strategic humiliation by the United States, minimal diplomatic cooperation, and endless roadblocks to political partnership. This latter group includes many of the Eurasianist persuasion who believe in greater attention to Siberia's development and engagement in the Asia-Pacific region. Members of this group also think that the appropriate counter to U.S. policy is close cooperation with China.

Russian nationalists do not see the United States showing due regard for Russia's interests anywhere in Northeast Asia — neither on the Korean peninsula nor vis-à-vis Japan. Indeed, they note that, far from trying to broker a settlement of the Russo-Japanese territorial dispute, U.S. partisanship in upholding Japanese claims is undisguised, as was evident in early December 1995, on the very eve of Russia's parliamentary elections. On that occasion, U.S. ambassador Thomas R. Pickering infuriated Russian officials when, during an interview in Yuzhno-Sakhalinsk on the island of Sakhalin, he said that the United States supported Japan in the dispute over the islands off northern Hokkaido — Etorofu, Kunashiri, Shikotan, and Habomais.[13] On the other hand, those skeptical of Russia's commitment to democracy and acceptance of the territorial status quo along its Far Eastern and Central Asian borders point out that its key aim in Northeast Asia remains severing the security relationship between the United States and Japan, an outcome that would unhinge the current stable structure of power in Asia.

Addressing himself to the confusion pervading Russia's Asian policy, Konstantin Sarkisov, director of the Center for Japanese Studies of the Russian Academy of Sciences, warned that, should a new Russian doctrine for Asia, if and when it emerges, turn out to be "nothing more than irritation and disappointment with respect to the West, and a desire to set in opposition to it a new alliance," that would signify a hopeless situation indeed: "There are no very brilliant prospects in the East for Russia if it goes there as a country that has been ill-used or rejected, and without some real trumps and ideas, They [Asian countries] will not believe in its sincerity and, what is the main thing, they are hardly likely to want to play along with it in opposition to the West, although the Asian countries have their own bones to pick with the West, especially the United States." Sarkisov also cautioned against relying too much on

China because, in the final analysis, it is the United States that "plays a pivotal role in the Asia-Pacific region, being guarantor of the security and stability of the majority of countries in the region."[14]

Perhaps it is too soon to write Russia off as a "has-been" in Asia. Location, resources, nuclear capability, and an imperial tradition warrant careful attention. A recovering, engaged Russia can contribute much to the emerging reconfiguration of power relationships in Asia. How Russia develops will depend primarily on its own behavior, but it will also depend on what the United States does, or does not do, in encouraging Russia to move into the mainstream of developments in Asia. None of this will happen quickly, but, unless it does, Russia's role in Asia will continue to decline, with profoundly negative consequences for its people and state.

Notes

1 As quoted in Henry Trofimenko, "Long-Term Trends in the Asia-Pacific Region: A Soviet Evaluation," *Asian Survey* 29, no. 3 (March 1989): 244.
2 John J. Stephan, "Asia in the Soviet Conception," in *Soviet Policy in East Asia,* ed. Donald Zagoria (New Haven, Conn.: Yale University Press, 1982), 37.
3 Viktor Larin, "'Yellow Peril' Again? The Chinese and the Russian Far East," in *Rediscovering Russia in Asia: Siberia and the Russian Far East,* ed. Stephen Kotkin and David Wolff (Armonk, N.Y.: M. E. Sharpe, 1995), 290–301; James Clay Moltz, "Regional Tensions in the Russo-Chinese Rapprochement," *Asian Survey* 35, no. 6 (June 1995): 519–26.
4 *Rossiyskaya gazeta* (Moscow), 20 October 1995, in *Foreign Broadcast Information Service, Central Eurasia* (hereafter *FBIS/SOV,* 6 November 1995), 34–35.
5 Peter Rutland and Ustina Markus, "Russia as a Pacific Power," *Transition* 1, no. 17 (22 September 1995): 68.
6 John J. Stephan, "The Russian Far East," *Current History* 37 (October 1993): 336.
7 On Southeast Asia, see Pushpa Thambipillai, "Southeast Asia, Russia, and the Ex-Soviet Republics: Expanding the Links," *Contemporary Southeast Asia* 16, no. 1 (June 1994): 93–107.
8 Ivan Terekhov in *Nezavisimaya gazeta,* 17 November 1995, A8.
9 For this insight, we are indebted to George Ginsburgs, Rutgers University School of Law.
10 ITAR-TASS (Moscow), 8 December 1995, reprinted in *FBIS/SOV,* 11 December 1995, 20–25.

11 Interfax (Moscow), 18 January 1996, and *Izvestia,* 18 January 1996, both in *FBIS/SOV,* 19 January 1996, 24–25.

12 *Rossiyskaya gazeta,* 23 September 1995, translated in *FBIS/SOV,* 28 September 1995, 19–22.

13 Alessandra Stanley, "U.S. Envoy's Comment on Disputed Islands Outrages Moscow," *New York Times,* 10 December 1995, 10.

14 Konstantin Sarkisov in *Moskovskie novosti,* no. 67, 18 October 1995, 5, in *FBIS/SOV,* 9 November 1995, 19.

Index

Contributors

Stephen J. Blank is MacArthur Professor of National Security Affairs, Strategic Studies Institute, U.S. Army War College, and author of *Mikhoian, Stalin, and the Struggle for Power in the Transcaucases 1919–1922,* and *SDI and Defensive Doctrine: The Evolving Soviet Debate.*

Alvin Z. Rubinstein is Professor of Political Science, University of Pennsylvania. Among his publications are *The Soviets in International Organizations: Changing Policy Toward Developing Countries, 1953–1963; Yugoslavia and the Non-Aligned World: Soviet Foreign Policy Toward Turkey, Iran, and Afghanistan; The Dynamics of Influence: Moscow's Third World Strategy; Perestroika at the Crossroads: The Soviet Military and the Future;* and *Regional Power Rivalries in the New Eurasia: Russia, Turkey and Iran.*

Hongchan Chun is Professor of Russian Politics at Pusan National University in the Republic of Korea. His recent publications include "The Russian Federation and A New Security Order in the Asia-Pacific Region"; "The Russian Far East, East Asia, and the Asia-Pacific: Security and Strategic Dimensions"; and "Russia and the Korean Peninsula: Historical Continuities and Changes."

Bruce Elleman is Assistant Professor of Russian and Chinese History at Texas Christian University, and specializes in the history of Russia, China, and their relationships with other Asian states. He has published several articles on Russia, China, and Mongolia.

Harry Gelman recently retired as a senior analyst at the Rand Corporation. Among his most well-known works are *The Brezhnev Politburo and the Decline of Detente; The Rise and Fall of Soviet National Security Decisionmaking; Russo-Japanese Relations and the Future of the U.S.-Japanese Alliance;* and *Northeast Asia in an Age of Upheaval.*

Rajan Menon is Professor of Political Science and International Relations at Lehigh University. Among his publications are *Soviet Power and the Third World,* (edited); *The Limits to Soviet Power;* and *Central Asia's Foreign Policy and Security Challenges.*

Oles M. Smolansky is Professor of International Relations at Lehigh University, and is the author of *The Soviet Union and the Arab East Under Khrushchev; The*

USSR and Iraq; Russia and America: From Rivalry to Reconciliation (with George Ginsburgs and Alvin Rubinstein), and *Regional Power Rivalries in the new Eurasia* (with Alvin Rubinstein).

Henry Trofimenko is Professor at the Russian Diplomatic Academy of the Russian Academy of Sciences, a Senior Analyst at Moscow's Institute for the Study of the U.S.A. and Canada, and the author of *The U.S. Military Doctrine* and *USSR–US: A Half-Century of Peaceful Coexistence.*

Charles E. Ziegler is Professor of Political Science at the University of Louisville and Executive Director of the Louisville Committee on Foreign Relations. He is the author of *Foreign Policy and East Asia* and *Environmental Policy in the USSR.*

Library of Congress Cataloging-in-Publication Data

Imperial decline : Russia's changing role in Asia / Stephen J. Blank and Alvin Z. Rubinstein, editors.

p. cm.

Includes index.

ISBN 0-8223-1905-5 (cloth : alk. paper). — ISBN 0-8223-1897-0 (paper : alk. paper)

1. Russia (Federation) — Foreign economic relations — Asia. 2. Asia — Foreign economic relations — Russia (Federation) 3. Russia (Federation) — Economic conditions — 1991– I. Blank, Stephen J., 1950– . II. Rubinstein, Alvin Z.

HF3630.2.Z7A785 1997

337.4705 — DC20 96-30130 CIP